CORPORATE
WASTELAND

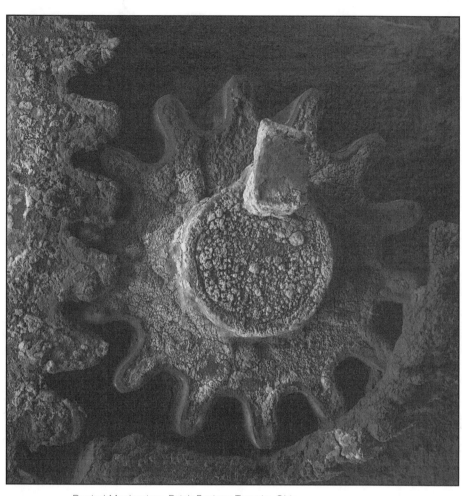

Rusted Mechanism, Brick Factory, Toronto, Ohio

CORPORATE WASTELAND

The Landscape and Memory of Deindustrialization

STEVEN HIGH & DAVID W. LEWIS

ILR PRESS

An imprint of
CORNELL UNIVERSITY PRESS
Ithaca and London

Corporate Wasteland

LIBRARY OF CONGRESS CATALOGING-IN-PUBLICATION DATA

    High, Steven C.
        Corporate wasteland : the landscape and memory of deindustrialization / by Steven High and David W. Lewis.
        p. cm.
    Includes bibliographical references.
    ISBN 978-0-8014-7401-9 (pbk. : alk. paper)
    1. Deindustrialization – United States. 2. Deindustrialization – Canada. 3. Plant shutdowns – United States. 4. Plant shutdowns – Canada. 5. Industrial sites – United States. 6. Industrial sites – Canada. 7. Industrial buildings – United States. 8. Industrial buildings – Canada. I. Lewis, David W., 1946– II. Title.
    HD5708.55.U6H54 2007
    338.6′042 – dc22

2007031120

Table of Contents

Acknowledgements

THIS BOOK WAS INSPIRED BY THE PLANT SHUTDOWN STORIES told to us by working people on both sides of the Canada-United States border. Displaced workers spoke eloquently about what job loss meant to them, their families, and the places they called home. So I would like to begin by thanking the dozens of men and women who agreed to be interviewed between 1998 and 2006. This book could not have been written without them. *Corporate Wasteland* is our attempt to communicate and interpret the landscape and memory of deindustrialization. While only a few stories could be included, all of the interviews have shaped our understanding of the issues surrounding plant closings and job loss. We would especially like to thank Gabriel Solano for guiding us around Detroit, Michigan; Hubert Gervais and Bruce Colquhoun for all their assistance in Sturgeon Falls, Ontario; and Wayne LeBelle, also from Sturgeon, who generously read and provided insightful feedback on two chapters. Thank you!

A number of other people have assisted in the research process. I would especially like to thank Kristen O'Hare, who conducted most of the first round of interviews in Sturgeon Falls. Rob Shields, Amy Brandon, Nina di Sabatino, and Kayla Bilton were employed as research assistants at various points in time. They did a superb job. I also benefited from the volunteer work of Dave Hunter and Louise Bidal, both of Sturgeon Falls. A note of appreciation also goes out to Henri Labelle, Larry Patriquin, Dana Murphy, Petra Dolata-Kreutzkamp, John Walsh, Stan Lawlor Jr., James Murton, Jarrett Rudy, Francoise Noel, Carolyn and Gerald High, Harold Bérubé, Graham Carr, Ron Rudin, Dimitry Anastakis, Garth Williams, Nancy Rebelo, and Joyce Pillarella. I also benefited from the feedback of audiences in Canada, Germany, and the United States. The students in my 2006 "Working Class Public History" seminar at Concordia University provided me with particularly useful feedback. An earlier version of chapter 3 appeared in *History Workshop Journal* 54 (2002), and other parts of that same chapter were previously published in *Labour/le Travail*. Financial support came from Nipissing

University, Concordia University, the Canada Research Chairs Program, and from the Social Sciences and Humanities Research Council. Most of all I would like to thank David Lewis for agreeing to work with me. It has been a privilege collaborating with someone of David's calibre. Over the past four years, I have learned a great deal while watching him do what he loves.

We very much appreciate the advice (and patience) of our editor, Paul Eprile, who worked with us every step of the way. He pushed us to make this a much better book. We would also like to thank David Vereschagin for his wonderful design and layout.

I dedicate my part of the book to Barbara Lorenzkowski, to our son Sebastian, and to the new member of our family, Leanna.

– Steven High

A PHOTOGRAPHER INCURS MANY DEBTS ALONG THE WAY. I would like to acknowledge the many people in the United States and Canada who helped me identify abandoned mines, mills, and factories to photograph. This project would not have been possible without the help of M.A. (Billi) Onley, RN, Doug Chadwick, Jurgen Lorenzen, Jim Riegel, Claudia Aubertin, Jill and Ted Schwitzer, Michael Gilbert, Rev. John Lockyer, Elsie Vokes, and the late Dale Holtzman. Especial thanks to my wife Billi for her support.

– David Lewis

Brick Factory, Toronto, Ohio

INTRODUCTION

THE LANDSCAPE
AND MEMORY OF
DEINDUSTRIALIZATION

I heard about the closure on television on the six o'clock news. Then a couple of weeks later they phoned me up and said, "You got a thirty-five year pin that we have here. We'd like to give it to you." I said OK. He said, "Meet us at the front gate." You know, everything was closed, so the fellow, our superintendent at the time, he gave me the thirty-five year pin. You can picture a chain-link fence; he handed it to me through the fence. "Here is your thirty-five year pin."
　　– steelworker, Lackawanna, New York, 1998

From the earliest days of documentary work, photographers have observed the making and unmaking of American landscapes and have found ruins.
　　– Elizabeth Blackmar

THE TEN-STOREY, 440,000 SQUARE FOOT, ARMSTRONG CORK factory (pictured on the front cover) stands alongside the Allegheny River in Pittsburgh, Pennsylvania. Built in 1901, the three-building complex operated for more than seventy years before it was abandoned in 1974. Thirty years later, David Lewis saw the monumental structure from across the river. He asked several passersby if they knew whose factory it was, but nobody seemed to know. It turns out the Armstrong Cork building is semifamous in the Pittsburgh area; the graffiti that cover every square inch of the interior are even the subject of a recent book of photography.[1] At its height, the factory employed 1,300 people making cork stoppers for bottles. Though long abandoned, the building continues to dominate the surrounding Strip District. There is no denying its allure, but it is disconcerting to know that a company could simply walk away from an operation of this size. At the very least, the mill is a testament to the inability of working people to control the destructive forces at work in Pittsburgh and across North America.

It was not always this way. Industrial landscapes were once the proud symbols of human progress and modernity. With the advent of the mass production factory, engineers envisioned a place that could run like a machine. Historian Lindy Biggs points to the seminal importance of Henry Ford's River Rouge complex as the first full-scale "rational factory."[2] Its modern exterior was celebrated in the interwar period by the photography and art of Charles Sheeler, who identified mills and factories as the ultimate "American Landscape."[3] Landscape, Sharon Zukin reminds us, "imposes and represents a visual order" – a moral landscape.[4] With its multi-storey red brick buildings, blast furnaces, great chimneys, water towers, and conveyors, the industrial landscape evoked a way of life and its rhythm, as well as a specific economic and cultural order.

How things have changed. Sheeler's iconic images, like "Criss-crossing Conveyors," have been reduced to ruins. The overhead conveyors, smokestack, and romanesque architecture recorded in David Lewis's photograph of Armstrong Cork now represent something altogether different. If landscapes are "storehouses" of meaning, as Delores Hayden has suggested, then the Armstrong Cork building – like tens of thousands of other modernist ruins – signals the birth of a new American Landscape, a deindustrialized one.[5]

The recent cultural turn in the scholarship on factory closings has generated a great deal of insight into the meaning of economic change. Deindustrialization – once defined by Barry Bluestone and Bennett Harrison as "a widespread, systematic disinvestment in the nation's productive capacity"[6] – is not simply an economic process, but a cultural one as well. In their introduction to the 2003 anthology *Beyond the Ruins: The Meaning of Deindustrialization*, historians Jefferson Cowie and Joseph Heathcott sought to shift the scholarly focus from the "body counts" associated with mill and factory closings, to the cultural meaning of deindustrialization in the aftermath. To that end, they urged us to "rethink the chronology, memory, spatial relations, culture, and politics of what we have come to call deindustrialization."[7] In *Corporate Wasteland*, we take up the challenge to widen the scope of the discussion, not by moving it "beyond the ruins," as Cowie and Heathcott suggest, but by interrogating the cultural meaning of industrial ruins themselves. We aim to do so without moving the discussion beyond the workers as well.[8] *Corporate Wasteland* delves into the landscape and memory of deindustrialization in North America through a combination of interpretative chapters, transcribed plant shutdown stories, and photographic images.

The book's unique focus is made explicit in its two-part structure. In Part I, "The Deindustrial Sublime," chapters 1 through 3 explore the rituals, representations, and explorations of millennial, abandoned industrial landscapes. The iconography of industrial ruins and their demolition constitutes a new aesthetics of deindustrialization. In Part II, "Oral History and Photography," the book situates oral history in active, explicit relation to the photographic images of David Lewis. Chapters 4 through 9 offer a counterpoint – the tension between evocative people-less landscapes of dereliction, and vivid life stories. These strategies force us to move beyond either nostalgia or populist criticism, and lead into the heart of a dilemma which is, in so many ways, an imaginative as much as an historical challenge: how to think about, and respond to, and understand, these profound changes. The book considers this problem in new ways, grounded in, yet moving beyond, case studies.

THE POLITICAL AND ECONOMIC CONTEXT

The various versions of the American dream and its Canadian equivalent have had a powerful hold on people. James Guimond helpfully defined this dream as the conception of North America as a "magic environment or society that has the power to transform people's lives."[9] By the 1970s, many blue-collar people had come to see themselves as part of the middle class. The higher wages won by unionized workers offered millions of families a home in the suburbs and a broad range of consumer goods. However, this higher standard of material wealth did not change the fact that industrial workers remained vulnerable to economic change. The job losses of the past three decades have undermined people's faith in this urban and industrial version of the American Dream. Surveying the catastrophic effects that plant closings have had on his hometown of Flint, Michigan, Michael Moore commented: "It's not the American dream anymore, it's the American nightmare."[10]

In recent decades, tens of millions of blue-collar workers have lost their livelihoods to plant closings. Between 1969 and 1976, the United States lost 22.3 million jobs.[11] Another two million manufacturing jobs were lost between 1995 and 2002.[12] Several dozen steel mills, auto assembly plants, and rubber factories closed across the United States. In 1985, there were five million unionized factory workers in the United States. By 2002, there were only three million left.[13] Industrial unions have accordingly suffered heavy membership losses, and thousands of union locals have been dissolved. The United Steelworkers lost 105,000 members between 1979 and 1983, and disbanded an astonishing 1,097 local unions in that short time span.[14] Until recently, Canadian unions have fared better despite massive job losses. Whereas the rates of unionization in the two countries were comparable in the early 1960s, they have since diverged dramatically. By 1986, 41 percent of Canada's non-agricultural workers belonged to a union; more than double that of the United States.[15] Since then, though, the American situation has deteriorated further.

Why the divergent trajectories? The most compelling explanation comes from the differing economic conditions prevailing in each country. Even though Canada has had a higher unemployment rate than the United States since the late 1980s, this is not due to job losses in manufacturing. In fact, unemployment has been consistently lower in Southern Ontario than in virtually all other regions of the country. According to a recent economic study by Alliance Capital Management, Canada is one of only two industrial countries in the world to maintain manufacturing job levels between 1995 and 2002.[16] The bout of recent mill closings in Canada's forestry, textile, and auto parts sectors is, however, chipping away at this achievement.

How has Canada been able to retain industry? No doubt, the low exchange value of the Canadian dollar has historically provided some protection to Canadian exporters. There is also the matter of socialized medicine. Canada's universal medicare program has reduced the financial burden on employers who, elsewhere, pay significant sums of money on health benefits. But there are other reasons. In *Industrial Sunset: the Making of North America's Rust Belt* (2003), I suggested that Canadian nationalism legitimated government intervention in the plant closing process. Trade unionists vocalized their struggle as one that pitted "Canadian workers" against "American bosses." During the 1970s and early 1980s, federal and provincial politicians in Canada were compelled by trade unionists to legislate mandatory advance notice of mass layoffs, severance pay, preferential hiring rights, pension reinsurance, and job placement. Because the United States has been slow to follow suit, American unions have been placed in the untenable position of trying to negotiate these same provisions at the bargaining table. The results have been disastrous. American workers who resented the resulting wage and benefit concessions also reacted angrily to unions that failed to win new job

Lumber Mill, West Virginia

security provisions. Either way, trade union leaders faced fierce criticism from their American members. Canada's legislative actions, by contrast, softened the blow of displacement and enabled many unions to withstand concession bargaining during the 1980s and 1990s. The diverging trade union fortunes in Canada and the United States no doubt contributed to the breaking away of several Canadian unions from their American-based internationals. The Canadian Auto Workers was one of the first.[17]

Canadian nationalism also bolstered public demands to save jobs. The federal and provincial governments prevented major plants from closing in several key instances, running them as publicly owned Crown Corporations. Faced with a troubled aerospace industry in the 1970s, for example, the Canadian government owned and operated De Havilland in Toronto and Canadair in Montreal for years, before selling the factories to Bombardier. Today, Bombardier is a world leader in the production of regional jets. There are other, more recent, examples. During the recession of the early 1990s, the Ontario New Democratic Party government worked closely with its trade union allies. It prevented Algoma Steel in Sault Ste. Marie and several pulp and paper mills from closing. Most of these mills continue to operate profitably to this day.[18] There is likewise a long history of state intervention in Quebec's economy.[19]

There were failures to be sure. A corrugated paper mill in Sturgeon Falls, Ontario, owned by MacMillan Bloedel (see chapter 4) received government financial aid to convert the mill to recycled paper in the early 1990s. It closed anyway, ten years later, once American-owned Weyerhaeuser purchased the company. The mill did not close because it was unprofitable, but because the multinational company had other, more modern, corrugated paper mills south of the border. Despite such failures, tens of thousands of industrial jobs have been preserved in Canada.

There is no similar tradition of public enterprise in the United States. The closest equivalent, the Employee Stock Ownership Plan (ESOP), has had a decidedly mixed record. Two of the largest efforts – at Wierton Steel in West Virginia, and at McLouth Steel in Trenton, Michigan – have ended in closure.[20] The ideological commitment to an unfettered "free market" has always been greater in the United States.

The contrasting cross-border thinking was evident during the famous Chrysler bailout of 1979–1980. The Canadian and American governments both agreed to extend loan guarantees and other assistance to the troubled company, but they attached different conditions. Whereas the U.S. Congress only agreed to intervene if workers accepted major wage and benefit concessions, the Canadian government tied its assistance to job guarantees.[21] Dimitry Anastakis argues in an article which appeared in a special issue of *Urban History Review* on "The Politics and Memory of Deindustrialization in Canada," that the Chrysler bailout resulted in massive new investments in Windsor and other Southern Ontario auto towns.[22] New auto plants were being built in Canada at a time when they were being closed in record numbers in the United States. The Canada-United States border mattered in the pre-free trade era. To what degree this has remained true since January 1st, 1989, is an open question.

While deindustrialization has attracted considerable public interest south of the border, abandoned industrial landscapes in Canada continue to be associated with the troubled resource sector. Mining, forestry, fishing, and farming have traditionally provided most of the employment in Canada's hinterland regions. Whereas primary resource industries employed 1.1 million Canadians in 1951, that number had declined to just 868,000 in 1991.[23] In terms of overall employment, the percentage of Canadians making their living in the primary sector fell from 21.3 percent to 6.1 percent during this forty-year period.[24] Single-industry towns in hinterland areas have been especially vulnerable to abandonment. The closing of anything as large as a pulp and paper mill is a disaster, the Canadian Pulp and Paper Association advised in 1972. Since then, numerous mills have closed across Canada. The faded towns scattered across Canada's provincial northlands attest to the extreme dependence of resource towns on a single enterprise, and on nearby natural resources.[25]

Notwithstanding these national differences, there is a widespread belief in Canada and the United States that plant closings are inevitable – a natural by-product of corporate capitalism. This supposition sometimes results in the claim that the people living in hard-hit areas are themselves to blame for this decline. The devaluation of mill or factory work in today's society has contributed to this blame game. In the so-called postindustrial era in which we live, "individuals still employed in basic manufacturing industries look like global benchwarmers in the competitive markets of the modern world."[26] Historian Judith Stein has suggested that the "green sensibilities" of Americans have "anesthetized the middle class to industrial decline."[27] The great reform movements of the 1960s therefore "had very little to say" about deindustrialization. In effect, North America's manufacturing and resource towns have grown old since their heyday during the 1940s and 1950s. Industries that once symbolized modernity and progress have come to represent an antiquated and polluted past that should be put behind us.

There are a variety of reasons for plant closings, but two of the most important are plant relocation and factory obsolescence. Companies wishing to reduce labour costs and rid themselves of expensive, high-seniority, or unionized workers, move work to low-wage areas. This once meant moving production to low-wage areas within Canada and the United States, but has increasingly meant exporting the work altogether. Free trade and falling trade barriers have allowed companies to move production virtually anywhere in the world. It is not as if the world is becoming any less industrialized. Rather, capital continues to move from one location to the next in search of competitive advantage through cheaper labour costs and reduced environmental obligations.[28] New mills and factories were built elsewhere with owners knowing full well that older plants would eventually close. The pace may have picked up in recent years, but the underlying impulse has remained the same. Some fifty years ago, economist Joseph Schumpeter characterized capitalism as a "gale of creative destruction" that sweeps the globe, devouring the old in order to create the new.[29] Simultaneous growth and decline produce spatially uneven development. In effect, people and places have become disposable.

THE DEINDUSTRIAL SUBLIME

Few towns or cities escaped major mine, mill, or factory closings in recent decades. This economic upheaval has caused the Industrial Midwest of the United States to be re-envisioned as a no man's land between fading smokestack industries and the ascendant post-industrial economy. These rusting monoliths, however, are not restricted to the "Rust Belt." They are found from Canada's far north to Louisiana, from the Pacific Northwest to Newfoundland's fishing outports – and all points in between. In Homestead, Pennsylvania for example, twelve "disembodied smokestacks" and the pump house (now a museum) are all that remain of the once mighty Homestead Steel Works.[30] Likewise, a 585 foot smelter smokestack stands over post-industrial Anaconda, Montana, as a "proud symbol of the city's heritage."[31] These physical remains serve as reminders that workers who once stood at the centre of local life are now relegated to the periphery. As anthropologist Kathryn Marie Dudley has convincingly shown in Kenosha, Wisconsin, which lost its auto assembly plant in 1988, the economic transformation underway was a social and a cultural process: "Many of the cultural symbols, beliefs, and values that once fortified a sense of moral order in our capitalist economy have been cast into doubt."[32] Mills and factories have been converted to condominiums and art galleries, demolished, or left to the elements.

There has been a rush to photograph these transitional places before they fall victim to the wrecker's ball. While most of the books have been produced by commercial publishers, and include very little historical context or analysis, several outstanding studies have combined photographic images with ethnographic or historical fieldwork. Many of these books examine the lives of workers undergoing a plant closing. The results are often striking. Bill Bamberger, for example, records the human tragedy that unfolded in the dying days of White Furniture in Mebane, North Carolina.[33] A similar story revealed itself in black and white at the Inglis factory in Toronto, Ontario.[34] Other collaborators have meanwhile focused on a local industry. Milton

Rogovin and Michael Frisch combined portraiture and oral history to tell a profoundly moving story of displaced steelworkers in Buffalo, New York.[35]

In recent years, a flurry of coffee table books has also appeared, celebrating everything from the vanishing "Wheat Kings" (country grain elevators) to the "Industrial Cathedrals of the North" (mine headframes).[36] Alternatively, one's local library is sure to have a helpful guide to the "ghost town" nearest you. This nostalgia for vanishing landmarks, and the transformation of some derelict landscapes into popular tourist sites, extends to abandoned mills and factories. The "museumification" of industrial landscapes is one response to economic change.[37] Abandoned industrial sites also appeal as "ruins." British geographer Tim Edensor has called the aesthetics of industrial dereliction "modern gothic."[38] He notes that abandoned mills and factories provide space for leisure, adventure, cultivation, acquisition, shelter, and art.[39] Closed mines and factories, for example, regularly act as movie sets when something needs to be blown up.[40] The Internet is rich with websites dedicated to the industrial ruins of North America.[41] The most famous of these digital elegies is Lowell Boileau's "The Fabulous Ruins of Detroit" – Yahoo's "Pick of the Year" for 1998. Like Edensor, Boileau finds beauty in his ruined city.

Industrial ruins are memory places, for they make us pause, reflect, and remember. But remember what, and to what end? To answer this question we must go beyond a vague, melancholy regret, or "smokestack nostalgia."[42] French historian Pierre Nora has observed that memory "fastens on sites" and is by nature multiple and subjective.[43] If memory places bind people and communities together, and are symbolic in nature, then these abandoned mills and factories unite displaced workers in a memory community of "anger and sorrow."[44] These physical vestiges even become symbolic sites of identity for those workers who have come to identify *with* their displacement.

The popular belief that the industrial era is ending is reinforced by the orderly demolition of former economic landmarks which once loomed large over local landscapes: grain elevators, mine headframes, industrial smokestacks, and blast furnaces have fallen to the ground. There is no mistaking the ritualistic nature of these public demolitions. In Thunder Bay, Ontario, a port city at the head of Lake Superior (and my hometown), the demolition of the huge concrete Saskatchewan Wheat Pool elevator in December 2000 sent a stark message to the thousands of spectators. In the seconds

Nipissing High Grade Mine, Cobalt, Ontario

that it took this giant structure to crumble and fall to the ground, residents could not help but conclude that Thunder Bay's standing as an important grain port was coming to an end.[45] The repetition of this secular ritual across North America – and the diffusion of these dramatic images in the media – reinforces the sense of inevitability surrounding industrial decline. Older industries are literally vanishing before our eyes.

The first part of this book explores the emerging aesthetics of deindustrialization, from various vantage points. In chapter 1, "Industrial Demolition and the Meaning of Economic Change," we follow the thread of an unspoken conversation about the meaning of economic change. The demolition of landmark industrial structures, highly ritualized and widely represented, dramatized the changes underway. At a local level, the ceremony and ritual surrounding industrial demolition lent authority and legitimacy to the idea that specific towns and cities were making the transition to a post-industrial era. The message seemed to be that there was no going back. If industrial demolition served to confirm this transformation at a local level, its message was communicated far and wide by the media and the Internet. The cultural meaning of deindustrialization is embedded in these universalized images of falling smokestacks and imploding factories.

The next chapter interrogates the "abandonment stories" told by so-called "urban explorers." The transnational Urban Exploration (UE) movement that emerged around Toronto's Jeff Chapman, code-named "Ninjalicious," in the mid-1990s, will be our entry point. His "Infiltration" zine and website inspired thousands of young people from across North America and around the world to go "places you're not supposed to go." On this website and on others like it, there are hundreds of heavily illustrated stories that recount what urban explorers saw and felt while investigating former industrial sites. These are fundamentally stories of discovery and possession. To enter an abandoned site is, in some small way, to cross an imaginative divide separating the post-industrial present from the industrial past. With its focus on youth encounters and the blogosphere, this chapter explores the drawing power of industrial ruins. What do they tell us? The aesthetic of deindustrialization that emerges from this specialized genre of travel writing can best be described as the "deindustrial sublime": a sense of being swept away by the beauty and terror of economic change.

These two transnational chapters are followed by a case study. In chapter 3, "From Cradle to Grave: The Politics of Memory in Youngstown, Ohio," we explore the local and trans-local efforts to remember one town's steelmaking past. In their thought-provoking book, *Steeltown, USA*, Sherry Lee Linkon and John Russo interrogated the memories of work and job loss in Youngstown, one of the most famous deindustrialized places on the planet.[46] The "Youngstown story" will be familiar to some readers. Situated along the Mahoning River in northeastern Ohio, Youngstown had long viewed itself as one of America's great steelmaking centres. The beginning of the end came with the closing of the giant Campbell Works on September 19, 1977, "Black Monday." This mill closure was followed by four others in quick succession. The valiant efforts of Steel Valley residents to keep the plants open were widely acclaimed at the time, but to no avail. Youngstown has experienced another kind of struggle since the mill closings: a struggle over memory. How should the steel era be remembered or commemorated? Should closed mills be demolished or preserved? Whose past is to be represented? Once a shout, the story of community defiance and resistance has become little more than a whisper. Instead, a dominant narrative has taken hold, that foregrounds victimization and loss.

Building on the work of Linkon and Russo, this chapter investigates the politics of memory in Youngstown from another angle.[47] Whereas *Steeltown USA* is a study of "local culture," we look at the interplay between local and trans-local remembering. Our close attention to the dialogue between local and non-local cultural producers represents a significant reframing of the struggle over memory. Linkon and Russo tell us a great deal about how work is remembered in Youngstown and how the town's "constitutive narrative,"or creation myth, was shattered. But their study is premised on a locally-bounded notion of community. For them, a "real" or "genuine" community is local. We reject this claim. Community is too narrowly equated with locality in their work.[48] As Craig Calhoun and others have argued, communities are lived-in social networks, created in places, and imagined at a distance. They therefore exist at varying scales: local, regional, national, transnational, even global.[49]

How Youngstown remembered its industrial past was thus influenced as much by non-local artists, journalists, and activists, as by locally-based ones. "Every participant and bystander in a plant closing drama," observed Kathryn Marie Dudley, "is drawn into a national 'conversation' about cultural values."[50] In widening our frame, we find that American writers and artists have used John Steinbeck's fictional Dust Bowl-era story of the Joad family as a familiar template to communicate the meaning and magnitude of deindustrialization. In this story, Youngstown stands for Oklahoma. Youngstown residents, by contrast, have opted to tell a less universal story. Even so, both versions of the Youngstown story are premised on a political strategy that emphasizes hardship and hurt rather than resistance, in order to elicit an emotional response from their mainly middle class audiences. The irony, here, is that in an effort to inspire collective action in the future, they have effectively silenced collective action in the past.

ORAL HISTORY AND PHOTOGRAPHY

To explore these ideas further, the second part of *Corporate Wasteland* draws on the plant shutdown stories told by Canadian and American workers, and the photographs of abandoned industrial sites taken by David Lewis. In *Let Us Now Praise Famous Men* (1939), James Agee wrote that the photographs taken by Walker Evans "are not illustrative. They, and the text, are co-equal, mutually independent and fully collaborative."[51] The same holds true here. Over the next five chapters, through his photography, David Lewis raises some disturbing questions about corporate behaviour. These are the same questions that are posed by displaced workers themselves. The question on everyone's lips was "why?" Why did the company pick up and leave? Why did it depart the way it did? Why didn't the government or the union do more? The interviewees wrestled to find the words to communicate their deep-seated emotions as well as their attachment to former co-workers and workplaces. David struggled to visualize the same.

Plant shutdown stories tell of the special bond that united long-service industrial workers before the closures, the shock and demoralization that accompanied the news, the efforts to save their jobs, and the uncertain aftermaths. What did economic change mean to those most directly affected? The stories included in this part are selected from forty-three interviews that I conducted with displaced workers in Detroit, Windsor, Hamilton, and Buffalo in 1998; and another seventy-nine interviews conducted since 2003 by our research assistant, Kristen O'Hare, and myself, with displaced pulp and paper workers in Sturgeon Falls, Ontario. The oral history interviews act as a crucial counterpoint to the nostalgia that the photographs may produce. By telling us how mills and factories came to be abandoned, these plant shutdown stories remind us that this was no natural disaster. In the words of Hamilton worker John Livingstone, "You were a number then, and now you are a computer number, which makes it worse because you're out on the streets faster."[52]

The oral narratives strike a balance between stories of hardship and hurt on the one hand, and those of anger and resistance on the other. These were no passive victims. Interviews generally followed the life course of the person, but the interview style was kept open-ended to allow for the unexpected. The resulting plant shutdown stories tell of the special bond that long-service workers had with their mill or factory. When asked what these jobs meant to them, these men and women used home and family metaphors to express their attachment. Almost to a person, they insisted that their old co-workers were "like a family." In doing so, they remind us that job loss was about more than wages. It was about identity and belonging, too.

Life-story interviews are an especially rich source for understanding the multiple layers of significance in people's lives. Life stories are living things, always changing. As a result, oral sources tell us "not just what people did, but what they intended to do, what they believed they were doing, and what they now think they did."[53] Oral historians must therefore work on both factual and narrative planes, as well as on the past and on the present. Memory is "not a passive depository of facts, but an active process of creation of meanings."[54] The question of memory should not be seen as a "problem" that needs to be "overcome," but rather as a "unique resource, a collective and individual expression of the past in the present."[55] It is the subjective quality of these oral narratives that makes them so meaningful. In the memorable words of Studs Terkel, these are *"their* truths."[56]

Like the oral narrators recorded, every individual photographer presents a viewpoint, or interpretation of the world.[57] David Lewis is not a documentary photographer in the traditional sense. John Grierson, the great Canadian filmmaker of the 1930s and 1940s, once defined "documentary" as a "basic force" that is "social, not aesthetic."[58] David, by contrast, is primarily interested in the aesthetic. He sees himself as a photographic artist, and his work has been put on display in art galleries across Canada, the United States, Europe, and Asia. At least superficially, his commercial work for Kodak and other corporations earlier in his career, and his more recent photo exhibitions, have more in common with the modernist art photography of the 1940s and 1950s than they do with the "hard times" photography of the 1930s. Yet a "bitter edge," or quiet anger, is evident throughout his work.

As part of this project, I conducted an oral history interview with David to better understand his motivations, as well as his interpretation of the meaning of his work. When asked about the origins of his interest in dereliction and abandonment, David pointed to his childhood feelings of ostracism and rootlessness. Bouncing from one house to another throughout his youth, David saw his father six times in eighteen years. He had no home to speak of. He was always the oldest kid in grade school because he kept flunking out; it was only later that he was diagnosed with dyslexia. Because of this learning disability, David finds expression through his photography. "There is a story to be told everywhere," David says. "What I am doing is recording history in a meaningful way." His earliest photographs included the weathered barns and old houses of the countryside around him north of Toronto. Looking back, he notes that these places were as "lonely and desolate" as he felt himself.

David Lewis has been drawn to derelict industrial landscapes for twenty-five years, but the photographs included in this volume were all taken within the past six years. He sees beauty in these old, abandoned sites. David is fascinated by the inventions of the human mind, especially the clever machines found inside former industrial buildings. He is equally impressed by the design, construction, and layout of mills and factories. "Man created something beautiful," he told me.

His use of infrared film and the bromoil process sets his photographs apart. Infrared film creates an ethereal effect – an eerie quality that can't be recorded with conventional film. Black skies and silver vegetation are two of the results. Some of David's photographs were developed using the lengthy, "one time," bromoil process. The etching-like bromoil images are hauntingly beautiful. As David explained in his first book, the bromoil print is simply a "silver bromide or chlorobromide photograph from which the silver image is removed and a greasy pigment substituted."[59] Having learned his craft in Europe, David has developed an international reputation for this broadly expressive visual art form. "I can put my soul into the photographs," he told me. The bromoil process allows David "complete artistic interpretation and control over the subject matter."[60] In effect, these bromoil and infrared photographs create an atmosphere, an added dimension that is missing in conventional documentary photographs. The photographs are beautiful, but they need to be kept in context.

There is drama and social commentary in David's photographic images of abandoned mills and factories. In dramatizing a viewpoint, David shares Grierson's desire to "make a drama from the ordinary."[61] In fact, David was profoundly influenced by some of the greatest names in twentieth century documentary photography: Lewis Hine's searing images of child labour; Walker Evans's southern sharecroppers; and Dorothea Lange's dust bowl migrants.[62] All three sought to use their photographic images to advance social or political reform. For Hine, staff photographer for the National Child Labor Committee, social photography represented a "lever" for "social uplift."[63] It was similar for Lange, who used her photographs, most memorably "Migrant Mother," the classic icon of the Great Depression, as catalysts for political debate in the United States. David Lewis was perhaps influenced most by Evans, who bridged the divide between art and document. Among his contemporaries, Evans's photography had the clearest emphasis on aesthetic qualities.[64]

Readers will note the absence of people in the photographs in this book. In fact, the only people appearing are our two guides: Gabriel Solano of Detroit, and Henry Labelle of Sturgeon Falls. In part, the camera lens is focused on abandoned places rather than on displaced workers for the purely practical reason that many of those interviewed in 1998 have moved or are no longer with us. Time has made a complete visual portrait of our interviewees impossible. But there may be more at work here. David's previous book, *The Passion Pit: A Tribute to the Drive-in* (2001), was also devoid of people. The abandoned snack bar at an old drive-in reminded me of the underwater photographs of sunken vessels that you sometimes see on television. These are places where time seems to stand still; where once bustling places now lie emptied and silent.

In one important respect, *Corporate Wasteland* represents a departure for David: the images are arranged into a series of photo essays. According to Karin Becker Ohrn, the photo essay sometimes shows different aspects of the same scene to "enhance the audience's understanding of the subject," or combines photographs at different times and places to "illustrate relationships among diverse people, places, or events."[65] Ours do both. Each chapter in this section approaches its subject in a unique way – allowing us to interrogate the meanings of deindustrialization from multiple angles.

Chapter 4, "Out of Place: The Plant Shutdown Stories of Sturgeon Falls (Ontario) Paperworkers," investigates place attachment and identity in the wake of a mill closing in a single-industry town located in Ontario's northland. For more than a century, the mainly French-speaking residents of Sturgeon Falls – located in northeastern Ontario between Sudbury and North Bay – made their living from the woods. The corrugated paper mill was the town's major employer until the day it closed in 2002. Oral history interviewing began while attempts to reopen the plant persisted, and ended after these attempts had failed and the mill was being demolished. The life-story interviews with mill workers, their families, civic officials, and economic development agents record the raw emotions released during displacement. They also reveal a deep disconnect between the "mill families" on the one hand, and town officials on the other. Mill towns like Sturgeon Falls are not homogenous places: deep-seated social cleavages widened at the time of the mill's closing. This chapter shows that the town's economic and cultural shift from industrialism to post-industrialism began years before the mill closed. Yet nobody told the workers. They continued to believe that Sturgeon Falls was a "mill town" until that wintry day in December 2002 when Weyerhaeuser ended production and walked away.

The next chapter, "Gabriel's Detroit," takes readers on a personal journey into the heart of the Rust Belt. Gabriel Solano's story is bound up in the decline of post-war Detroit.[66] Between 1978 and 1984, Detroit lost 180,000 manufacturing jobs.[67] The photographs are arranged in the sequence of the daylong tour that Gabriel generously gave us in 2004. Juxtaposed against these images of industrial dereliction and abandonment are oral history passages from Gabriel's 1998 interview. When we crossed the Detroit River into Canada (chapter 6), we found a very different urban landscape. There are few abandoned mills or factories in Windsor or in many other southern Ontario cities; just lone plants, deindustrialized fragments. There are exceptions to be sure. As we have seen, abandoned mills loom large on the resource frontier in northern Ontario. The former silver-mining town of Cobalt, for example, has invested heavily in industrial heritage tourism. While Cobalt sells the romance of its century-old mine headframes, nobody visits the decidedly unromantic buildings of the former Nipissing refinery pictured on page 10. Amidst the photographs of abandoned industrial buildings in Windsor, Wallaceburg, Hamilton, and Cobalt, readers will find fragments of the oral history interviews conducted with Ontario workers.

The two remaining chapters are short photo essays. In chapter 7 we focus on the coal towns of West Virginia. The mine companies owned everything. When the mines closed, entire towns were emptied. The past is everywhere: in the abandoned mine frames, the derelict buildings, and in the stories told of the struggles or prosperity of former times. The book ends with the former Allied Paper mill in Kalamazoo, Michigan. Closed in

1998, the mill was mostly torn down shortly after David Lewis photographed it. A short introduction at the outset of each photo essay provides historical context.

By broadening our focus to include interpretive essays, photographic images, and workers' voices from either side of the Canada-United States border, we hope to break out of the localism that has defined much of the scholarship on deindustrialization. The economic forces at work are transnational. So are the politics and aesthetics. It is our hope that *Corporate Wasteland* will be seen as something more than a lament for a bygone industrial age. In framing the book as we have, we are proposing a method, and an approach to an argument on the tension between industrial "ruins" and all they imply, and the vitality and complexity that unfold via the recorded oral histories and the photographed landscapes. One of the anonymous readers of the draft manuscript commented that, "There is a sense of walking around and around an elusive primary focus of interrogation, an exploration via indirection of some crucial core, difficult to appreciate directly." The text-based chapters of the first part, and the photographic essays and oral histories in the second, are therefore complementary approaches – another dimension of meditation on the politics and meaning of economic change. For historian Elizabeth Blackmar, abandoned mills represent nothing short of "smoking guns of criminal neglect."[68] At a minimum, working people deserve more than a locked factory gate and a thirty-five-year company pin passed through a chain-link fence.

PART I
THE DEINDUSTRIAL
SUBLIME

CHAPTER 1

INDUSTRIAL DEMOLITION AND THE MEANING OF ECONOMIC CHANGE IN NORTH AMERICA

The cars that stop along Joseph Campeau Street ignore the "no standing" signs and sit there, their motors sighing idly, their drivers watching silently as wrecking balls chew away on a piece of the past. The old Dodge Main car plant is going down, and its destruction is a jumbled symbol of distress and progress in the city of Detroit, which surrounds this little urban village, as well as an emblem of a lost era when the automobile industry was still a golden magnet for workers around the country and the world.

– Iver Peterson

ROOSEVELT JOHNSON SAT IN HIS 1976 DODGE CORONET ONE wintry day in January 1981, watching the destruction of Detroit's Dodge Main auto plant, his former workplace. It was his third visit to see the dying plant. Johnson had moved to Detroit from a Mississippi farm, at age eighteen. When he walked through the factory gates for the first time, he thought he had it made. Johnson's hold onto middle class status, however, was a tenuous one. Autoworkers enjoyed middle class wages in good times, but risked layoffs and plant closures in bad times, and these were the worst of times in the "Motor City." Johnson had not worked since Dodge Main closed two years earlier in January 1979. The sight of machinery tearing apart the multistorey factory hurt; it was "his family in there, good times and bad, and you see, it's like a piece of my life going down."[1]

Henry Rembecki, a Polish immigrant, had also come to say goodbye to his factory. He sat nearby in his Dodge van, silently watching. Like Johnson, Henry Rembecki had forged a personal connection to the auto plant: "That place has been a homestead to me. I know every hole in the place, I've worked from one end of it to another. I put three kids through school on it."[2] He agreed that "progress is progress," but he would still like to see cars being produced at Dodge Main. In stating his views this way, Rambecki was clearly acknowledging another viewpoint – one that he believed to be the prevailing one – that the plant's demolition constituted progress. The planned reindustrialization of the Dodge Main site was small consolation to the unemployed men lined up outside the gates.

We know what was running through the minds of these two men only because Iver Peterson, a *New York Times* journalist, went up to their idling vehicles, and asked them. As Peterson made his way from one American-made vehicle to the next, he heard starkly similar stories of hardship and hurt from the occupants. It was, he said, as though there was a "thread of an unspoken conversation between the silent watchers and rememberers dotting the curb."

In search of another vantage point, Peterson walked through the factory gates and into the demolition contractor's trailer. There he found the white-helmeted Jim Saunders. Peterson asked him what he thought about the silent vigil occurring outside the fence. Saunders replied that: "There are people who walked in and out of these gates for thirty-five years. They come by and point and say, 'I worked at that window up there,' then they pick up [a] brick or a piece of stone and go away."[3] These autoworkers had spent their lives working in the assembly plant and in the process had forged strong attachments to people and place. Workplace communities were remembered warmly that frigid day.

The story unfolding outside the gate at Dodge Main has been repeated in towns and cities across North America. We live in a "post-industrial" age, or so we are told. Mill and factory work no longer defines North American society and it is fast losing its saliency at the regional and local levels as well. Manufacturing and other blue-collar sectors are in a forty-year decline. In the United States, manufacturing represented 21 percent of overall employment in 1985, but only 16 percent in 2000.[4] The decline of manufacturing in Canada has not been as sharp, but a spate of recent mill closings in the forestry, auto, rubber, and manufacturing sectors is erasing this national difference. Millions of North Americans have lost their blue-collar jobs, and towns that once defined themselves as industrial are being forced to reinvent themselves as something other.

Plant closings and their subsequent demolition are secular rituals that dramatize North America's transition from industrialism to post-industrialism. Just as the plague was met by order (quarantine and body pick-up) in seventeenth-century Europe, deindustrialization was met by order in late twentieth-century North America.[5] The demolition of industrial buildings, of all shapes and sizes, but especially landmark structures that dominated their surroundings, was widely represented in the electronic and print media. When images of the demolition were recorded and represented, the same event also served to reinforce the sense of inevitability surrounding industrial decline, a sense that prevails nationally and internationally. The "thread" of the "unspoken conversation" that the reporter heard outside the fence of the dying Dodge Main plant in Detroit thus extended far and wide, becoming part of a far larger unspoken conversation about the economic changes underway.

By analyzing the rituals and representations of industrial demolition, we can ascertain the prevailing meaning of economic change in North America since the 1970s. Deindustrialization is, clearly, much more than an economic process involving job loss. It involves the displacement of industry and industrial workers to the cultural periphery. Industrial demolitions serve as the "ritual context within which a symbolic transformation can occur."[6] As anthropologist Kathryn Marie Dudley notes,

> I think the symbolism of a plant closing is about the meaning
> of change itself. The abandonment, gentrification, and outright
> destruction of old factory buildings signifies not just social
> change, but a particular kind of social change. When chrome
> and glass skyscrapers rise out of the rubble of an industrial plant,
> when bombed-out factories are left to crumble in urban waste-
> lands where vibrant communities once thrived, the message is
> not just about the inevitability of change, but about the obsoles-
> cence of the past.[7]

We will explore this cultural shift in two important ways. First, we will re-examine the landscapes of exclusion and abandonment that spatialized economic rise and decline in North America. Second, we will examine industrial demolitions as secular ritual. Industrialism has lost its cultural centrality in North America. Industrial workers who once inhabited a central place have been displaced to the periphery: they have become outsiders looking in. Job loss has meant far more than losing a pay cheque for these blue-collar workers; it has meant losing a fundamental part of themselves, part of their inner being.

LANDSCAPES OF ECONOMIC EXCLUSION

The perceived shift from industrialism to post-industrialism frames our understanding of the meaning of economic change. It infuses our language – "old" versus "new" economy, "sunset" versus "sunrise" industries – and our sense of what the future will hold. It also shapes our sense of geography. The economic geography of North America reflects its changing place in international political economy and in the international division of labour. The impermanence of industrial landscapes is apparent to anyone; capitalism creates and destroys built landscapes.[8] More to the point, corporate capital's command of spatial relations, through investment and disinvestment, becomes a crucial weapon in management's arsenal in its fight with organized labour.[9] This process of creative destruction, and its accompanying geography of rise and decline, is the essential fact of capitalism.[10]

Michel Foucault has shown that human societies contain their problems: imprisoning criminals, institutionalizing the insane, hospitalizing the sick, and imaginatively localizing racial "others" in "Chinatowns," "Indian Reservations," and "Black Ghettos." Economic problems are similarly spatialized and categorized into a hierarchy of "have" and "have-not" regions of the mind. These "have-not" places can span vast geographic distances ("Appalachia"), or small ones (the "Lower East Side" in Vancouver).

The Rust Belt is a case in point. Many of the industrial cities of the northern tier of the United States were overwhelmed by racial strife and deindustrialization.[11] The "Rust Belt" label thus emerged in the 1980s as a northern counterpoint to the ascendant "Sun Belt." It was imaginatively tied to the Great Lakes states of Wisconsin, Illinois, Indiana, Michigan, and Ohio, as well as western Pennsylvania and western New York. The abandoned industrial areas of the northeastern United States are sometimes included, as are declining industrial districts in other regions.[12] The discourse of industrial decline and the emergence of the Rust Belt label provided a spatial fix for Americans' generalized insecurities and complaints about economic change in the late twentieth century.[13]

The Rust Belt label, however, did not spill over into Canada. Ontario's "Golden Horseshoe" did not rust.[14] In *Industrial Sunset: The Making of North America's Rust Belt*, I argued that Canadian trade unionists wrapped themselves in the maple leaf flag in order to politicize the plant closing issue. In sharp contrast to their counterparts in the United States, Canadian politicians passed a variety of laws designed to soften the blow of job loss. To what degree this politically-charged atmosphere influenced corporate decision-making as well, is impossible to know for certain, but there was no mistaking the fact that companies (especially foreign multinationals) that closed plants in Canada could pay a political price in the 1970s and early 1980s. Before Free Trade, the politics of Canadian nationalism acted to constrain managerial prerogative to close mills and factories at will. In some instances, political pressure in Canada even resulted in the reopening of closed plants under public or employee ownership.[15]

Author Carlo Rotella nevertheless reminds us that "there's still plenty of manufacturing, but it's not what it used to be. It's not at the center of city life any more."[16] Working in a factory to provide a middle class life for your family is, according to Kathryn Marie Dudley, "no longer considered a legitimate goal." Industrial workers are increasingly subjected to ridicule, censure, and even blame. They were, Dudley concludes, the new "American primitive" – they belonged to the past, not to the present: "In America's new image of itself as a postindustrial society, individuals still employed in basic manufacturing industries look like global benchwarmers in the competitive markets of the modern world."[17] It appears that vanishing auto and forestry workers have dislodged the "vanishing Indian" from the North American imagination.

INDUSTRIAL DEMOLITION AS SECULAR RITUAL

If the imagined geographies of "Rust Belt" and "hinterland" have served to quarantine the blue-collar flu in North America, the transition to a new post-industrial era was made visible in the ritualized act of industrial demolition. Ceremony and ritual are often used to lend authority and legitimacy to particular persons, interests, world views, and moral orders.[18] Secular rituals, like sacred ones, are traditionalizing instruments mounted with the intention to establish a sense of stability and continuity through repetition and order. In this case, the repetitive images of falling smokestacks and imploding mills and factories lead to predictability and, ironically, the promise of continuity in a time of transformation. Secular rituals are declarations against indeterminacy and serve to hide troubles, conflicts, and uncertainties.[19] By discouraging enquiry, the ritualized and routinized demolition of industrial sites naturalizes these changes, even as they are used to interpret things which are very much in doubt. According to Sally F. Moore and

Barbara G. Myerhoff, "ceremony can make it appear that there is no conflict, only harmony, no disorder, only order, that if danger threatens, safe solutions are at hand, that political unity is immediate and real because it is celebrated, and so on."[20] The post-industrial ethos is graphically represented by the "wrecking ball," the falling smokestack, the pulverized grain elevator, and the shattering implosion.

THE "WRECKING BALL" AND "HISTORIC BUILDINGS" IN PUBLIC DISCOURSE

Since 1945, the wrecking ball (or "wrecker's ball") has loomed large in public debates about urban change in North America. A keyword search of the indexes of the Toronto *Globe and Mail* and the *New York Times* revealed hundreds of articles that discussed and debated urban renewal, slum clearances, development, and historic preservation. By the 1970s the wrecker's ball was being employed regularly by preservationists as a rhetorical weapon in their campaign to save "historic buildings." In 1977, for example, the *Globe* editorialized that "nothing stood up to the wrecker's ball" in post-war Toronto: "We were in a frame of mind that associated newness with improvement and progress; antiquity with decay and inertia."[21] The wrecking ball was a useful image to draw upon in these large debates about urban change.

In 1972, at least one Canadian journalist took a closer look at the wrecking ball as an actual tool of demolition. Crane operator Don Morton, thirty-nine, who had been swinging the ball on unwanted buildings for seventeen years, stated that he found demolition work more creative than construction work. "When you're doing construction," he said, "there is a plan to follow, and things go in an orderly way. With this type of work you're always coming into new situations. You play a lot by ear. Now you take that corner that's sagging over there: if you hit it the wrong way it'll buckle."[22] It was a skill to "hit a wall to make it fall inward or outward. You can chip down a building brick by brick. You can swing the ball, especially the smaller three thousand pound ball – in graceful S-arcs, destroying as much coming back as you do going out."[23] When asked if it was frustrating not to be able to see the results of his work later on, Morton replied that this was not the case. He explained that he would sometimes take his boy to "flat stretches" of the city, or to a new building, and tell him what used to stand there. Morton clearly believed that his demolition work contributed to the nation's progress.

The movement to preserve North America's built environment from the wrecker's ball was in large part a reaction to this orgy of destruction. But whose history was worth preserving? The discourse of "historic building" preservation that emerged in the 1970s focused on the aesthetic value of certain building types. Toronto's preservation battles, for example, involved the homes and businesses of the wealthy, as well as civic buildings such as Toronto's Old City Hall, and Union Station. Newspapers were full of stories lamenting the loss of historic landmarks: "Tacky pizza parlors are built on the graves of heroes, historic mansions torn down to make room for parking lots."[24] Yet mills and factories and other working class or ethnic institutions were rarely seen as being worthy of preservation. This elitism came under fire in 1975 when sociologist Herbert Gans criticized the preservation movement for its focus on elite buildings. He argued in the pages of the *New York Times* that when preservation is paid for by taxpayers, it must attend to everyone's past and not just that of a wealthy few.[25]

Despite these entreaties, closed mills and factories rarely avoided the wrecker's ball. Most derelict buildings were demolished for tax reasons or (in the United States) simply abandoned. Multi-storey, light-industrial buildings located in the urban core appear to be the most likely candidates for conversion into condominiums, nightclubs, and loft studios for artists.[26] Montreal's Lachine Canal, for example, is now lined with condominiums. The transformation of the area is explored in *Condoville* (2005), a play by David Fennario. It is a sequel to the playwright's celebrated *Balconville* (1979) which explored the daily lives of the area's English and French-speaking working class. In the sequel, Fennario's working class characters now had to contend with condo owners in their midst.

Only a handful of former mills and factories, by contrast, have found new life as industrial museums in Canada and the United States.[27] These "historic factories" are typically picturesque stone mills located in small towns and rural areas. Their aesthetic value is not in doubt. The same, however, could not be said of the more functional industrial structures built in the twentieth century. Attempts to preserve closed steel mills and grain terminal elevators have met with considerable difficulty, in terms both of finding public support, and of overcoming the very real economic and environmental obstacles in the way. Efforts to preserve the Jeannette Blast Furnace in Youngstown, Ohio, for example, came to naught in the 1990s, as did similar efforts in towns and cities on either side of the Canada-United States border.[28] My father, a railway worker in Thunder Bay, Ontario, tried unsuccessfully to save the old roundhouse from demolition. Coming, as they do, in the wake of deindustrialization, proposals to preserve industrial structures are usually judged on their tourism potential as part of a town's efforts to retool for the post-industrial era.

No industry was more closely associated with the industrial age than steel, and no region of North America was more closely identified with the steel industry than Pennsylvania. Pittsburgh was the home of U.S. Steel, "Iron City" beer, and the Steelers in the National Football League. Several steel mills were located within city limits and many more were situated in the valleys nearby. In the wake of mill closings, industrial heritage organizations appeared in Pittsburgh, Bethlehem, Johnstown, and Homestead.[29] The campaign to preserve the Bethlehem Steel Works, the home plant of Bethlehem Steel, once the second-largest U.S. steel producer, is one of the more successful efforts. At its peak, the Bethlehem steel works employed thirty thousand and sprawled over 1,800 acres along four and a half miles of the Lehigh River.[30] When the mill closed in 1998, the area became the biggest "brownfield" site in the United States.

What to do with this massive site? Inspired by the preservation of a steel mill in Duisburg, Germany, Bethlehem Steel proposed to reuse part of the site. Because the former mill lands and buildings were highly contaminated, making the site unsuitable for housing or schooling, the company proposed a mixed-usage plan that consisted of an industrial and office park, a high technology district, an entertainment complex, retail stores, and a new Smithsonian-affiliated museum dedicated to America's industrial history. The blast furnaces and other signature mill structures would be preserved in an effort to draw tourists to the complex. Bethlehem's industrial past would be celebrated and preserved, but the plan promised to take the town into the post-industrial future. The aim was to create a unique "historic industrial district" of consumption.[31]

This ambitious redevelopment plan was thrown into uncertainty in 2003 when Bethlehem Steel slipped into bankruptcy, but the new landlord has since moved forward with the planned developments, as well as a massive casino complex equipped with three thousand slot machines.[32] The National Museum of Industrial History will be housed in a giant machine shop, built in 1889, located in the former Lehigh Division at the western end of the complex. This part of the Bethlehem steel works was chosen because of its long history of steelmaking: the division had rolled steel for the Golden Gate Bridge, the battleship Mississippi, and many of New York's great skyscrapers.

Not surprisingly, the sudden move away from steelmaking to entertaining has resulted in a seismic shift in local culture in Bethlehem. Mayor Don Cunningham Jr. told PBS television that:

> There were no restaurants in this city. It was a blue-collar city, working class. It was extravagant if you went out to eat. In the last three years the biggest development we've had has been restaurants and bars in both downtowns, on the south side and on the north side. What that's a reflection of is the economic transition. There are more high-tech businesses, there are more, younger, wired workers here, and that's what they're looking for.

The PBS program, "A Rebirth in Bethlehem," then cited the example of Orasure Technologies, a biotech startup, founded by three young men who grew up in blue-collar America. "All of us share the same value system," said founder Bill Hinchey. He strongly identified with Bethelehem's steelmaking past. In this instance, at least, there was no animosity expressed towards the vanishing working class culture in Bethlehem. As we will see, this was not always the case.

The preservation movement, at its core, valued industrial buildings for their architectural beauty and for their potential for reuse as post-industrial spaces. This orientation goes some way in accounting for the oft-mentioned ambivalence of working people to industrial preservation. The factory-scape might be retained, but the jobs were gone, as were the workplace cultures on which industrial workers depended for status and solidarity. Through all of this, the wrecking ball lost some of its symbolic force. Buildings were increasingly being brought down with excavators and explosives. Even though Ontario demolition tycoon Ira Greenspoon still eschewed the "fancy stuff" in 1987, he admitted that the days of the ball and chain were coming to an end. The main tool was now a backhoe – a "breaker" – with a demolition hammer on it. The wrecking ball only came out on "ceremonial occasions."[33] If the wrecking ball was becoming anachronistic, rolled out for ceremonial occasions, this was not the case of the explosive demolition of mill and factory smokestacks.

FALLING SMOKESTACKS

Industrial smokestacks loomed large in working class districts throughout the twentieth century. They physically dominated their surroundings
and stood tall in people's minds. The cultural significance of mill and factory
smokestacks surfaces in the plant shutdown stories told by industrial workers. Marcel Boudreau, a former paperworker in Sturgeon Falls, Ontario,
whose plant closed in 2002, expressed the stacks' significance this way: "I
guess Sturgeon will always be Sturgeon. But this has been known as a paper
mill town. It was always a situation when you pulled into town – didn't matter
where you were coming from – you always saw steam coming out of those
stacks there. When you saw steam coming out of those stacks, you knew
you were making money."[34] To Boudreau, the mill's smokestack confirmed
the industrial and working class identity of Sturgeon. Its destruction in 2004
demolished his sense of place.

Place attachment is a complex phenomenon that involves affect, emotion, feeling, and memory. Irwin Altman and Setha M. Low note that rituals,
and the linguistic act of narrating, either through storytelling or naming,
are important in establishing and maintaining place attachment (symbolic
bond), and in communicating identity.[35] Places are constructed out of a particular constellation of social relations that meet and weave together at a
particular locus. When people invoke "place" and its attendant meanings,
they are imagining geography and creating identities.[36] Anthropologist Tom
Dunk has suggested that smokestacks and other massive structures defined
a place as industrial and as working class.[37] The forty-five-metre-tall smokestack at the Canadian Vickers shipyards in Montreal's east end, for example, had long been an "east end landmark." The *Montreal Gazette* called its
1999 demolition "an end of era," noting that the now closed shipyard once
employed thirty thousand people.[38] North American newspapers are littered
with such references. Accordingly, many of the cultural symbols, beliefs,
and values that once fortified a sense of industrial order were cast into doubt
by the demolition of industrial landmarks.[39]

The demolition of an industrial smokestack is a public spectacle. A crowd
estimated at twenty-eight thousand, for example, gathered one April morning in 1988 to watch the twin smokestacks at Montreal's Miron quarry come
down. The throng, according to one journalist, wanted the stacks "blasted
to rubble – nothing less."[40] Big band music blared from loudspeakers, and
people ate ice cream and drank beer, while others lounged in lawn chairs. A

freelance photographer was there hoping to take some "saleable pictures of the tall stacks tumbling down."[41] Another entrepreneur sold memento T-shirts depicting the smokestacks. There was even a master of ceremonies.

The crowd's mood was festive. One of those in attendance was Guy Lafrance, who brought his wife and daughters to watch the spectacle. They arrived three hours early to get a good seat right up against the quarry's fence. "There aren't that many smokestacks left in Montreal so it's like watching history," he said. Not everyone, however, felt like celebrating. Nathalie Labelle, twenty-one, regretted the loss of the stacks. She told the *Gazette* that they had always given her a sense of comfort as she drove down Metropolitan Boulevard. "As soon as I would see them," she said, "I'd know I was back in Montreal."[42] If the stacks were like old friends for some, they represented much more to longtime quarry worker Paul Frechette, fifty-five, who protested the demolition. "You work at a place for thirty-seven years, you want it to stay there," he said. "They should leave them standing."

Once the sirens called out their warning, the voice on a walkie-talkie counted down the final five seconds to the blast. It took thirty minutes to bring the first smokestack down, but the second refused to budge. When the second one failed to fall, the crowd left. "The party was over. But it was fun for a while," wrote the journalist from the *Gazette*. An embarrassed Paul Cloutier, the president of the demolition company, blamed the initial failure on a stack more heavily reinforced than the blueprints indicated. The stubborn stack finally came down a month later, but there were no huge crowds in attendance.

Yet the significance of falling smokestacks was not limited to the surrounding localities. Since mills and factories began to close in large numbers in the 1970s, and when talk of "post-industrialism" emerged in North America, falling industrial smokestacks have become a regular feature in newspapers and on the evening news. I can still vividly remember seeing on Canadian television, over a decade ago, the dramatic demolition of the seven, one-hundred-metre smokestacks – or the "Seven Sisters" – that once dominated the Detroit waterfront.[43] Part of the appeal of these events is of course the visual drama – first an explosion, and then the stacks falling to the ground with a thud. But this innate appeal does not fully explain the continued fascination. For anthropologist Kathryn Marie Dudley, industrial demolitions "provide the occasion for an important kind of ritual communication."[44]

Falling smokestacks, like plant shutdowns themselves, therefore constitute a ritualized marker of economic change.

The end of Cape Breton Island's industrial age was marked by the toppling of the steel mill's blast furnaces and stacks. Industrial Cape Breton, Nova Scotia, has experienced the ravages of deindustrialization, and the poisoned environmental legacy left behind in the tar ponds. After being saved in 1967, the island's steel mill closed in the 1990s. So have its coal mines.[45] For Halifax journalist Pat Connolly, the demolition ended any uncertainty surrounding the future of the province's steel industry. It had no future:

> Five smokestacks bit the dust in Sydney on Thursday to a mixed
> reaction from politicians, retired steelworkers, environmentalists
> and the public: resentment and resignation. From those who held
> hope for a last-minute miracle that would breathe yet another
> life into Sysco, the demolition of the smokestacks spelled game,
> set and match for the century-old steel plant. After 35 years of
> uncertainty about the future of Sydney Steel, this was the final
> judgment. There will be no appeal and no tomorrow.[46]

To those Cape Bretoners who criticized the government for felling the stacks without providing the public with advance warning, Connolly said that the "right or wrong" of the decision was "irrelevant" now that the stacks were down. Unencumbered by the past, Cape Breton was now free – in her words – to follow Pittsburgh and other cities into a golden post-industrial future.

This line of argument provides a good example of how industrial demolition foreclosed possibilities (the reopening of the mill) and served to depoliticize economic change. For Connolly, as for much of the North American media in recent years, the demise of steel was inevitable. It was therefore best to "avoid public demonstrations that would have served no useful purpose, other than to embarrass a government that had clearly run out of options for Sysco."[47]

Pat Connolly, however, went further when she hailed these changes as progress. For her, the stacks that once dominated the surrounding area symbolized air pollution and the oppression of women. In making these linkages, Connolly claimed that she spoke on behalf of the "silent majority" of homemakers on the island who had, for generations, washed dirty clothing by hand with a scrubbing board, only to have the drying clothes dirtied by pollution from the stacks, and who presumably supported the end of the steelmaking era. These women never protested the pollution problem when the mill was alive – "honouring the company line that the uncovered stacks were the price of their husbands' and sons' employment. Shut up and wash: the company code that died by dynamite on Thursday." However much one might question Connolly's ability to speak on behalf of the "silent majority," she was not alone in viewing industrial demolition as a sign of social progress.[48] Falling smokestacks, like other ritualized moments marking the economic transformation underway, are thus contested symbols.

GRAIN TERMINAL ELEVATORS

If falling smokestacks have marked the triumph of the post-industrial era, the destruction of massive concrete terminal elevators has signalled the decline of many port cities on the Great Lakes. Canada's terminal elevators were once world-famous. European architects such as Le Corbusier praised their geometric form and called them symbols of the modern age. The expansion of the St. Lawrence Seaway in 1959, and changing world markets, however, have resulted in the obsolescence of many of these massive concrete structures. Grain elevators have an "almost Egyptian monumentality," according to the Kingston *Whig Standard*. Even in their abandonment they still evoked "the majesties of a departed civilization."[49] Yet, unlike the pyramids of Egypt, which were apparently timeless "not only in the masterful structural soundness but also in the values and ideologies they represent," the concrete silos of the terminal elevator proved to be vulnerable to change. The "rhythmic pendulum swing of the wrecker's ball," the journalist reported, was like a "slow-motion metronome urging the building to keep pace with the times."

For Kingston, Ontario, the "end of an era" came in July 1988 when the Canada Steamship Line's grain elevator on Cataraqui Bay was levelled. The expansion of the Seaway enabled big ocean going vessels, or "salties," to travel all the way to Thunder Bay and Duluth at the head of Lake Superior. There was no longer any need to transship grain at Kingston. The elevator continued to eke out an existence until 1986 when it closed permanently.[50] Two years later its demolition was front page news in Kingston.

A similar story unfolded in other port cities on the Great Lakes. Dozens of terminal elevators have fallen in the past twenty years and many more stand abandoned. Toronto's waterfront has undergone a similar transformation, with the demolition of several grain elevators, including Maple Leaf Mills in 1983 and Victory Mills in 1995. Their erasure provided yet another occasion for public reflection on the economic changes underway. Journalist Frank Redican, for example, began by reminding his readers that when it opened in 1928, Maple Leaf Mills embodied Toronto's prosperity and progress. Victory Mills, built in 1944, was similarly described as a "monumental structure" that dates back to "an age when Toronto was a railroad city and a functioning port." The demolition of both terminal elevators signified "another chapter in the decline of Toronto as a commercial port, and the opening of the waterfront to the public."[51] If buildings "can be said to die," wrote the *Toronto Star*'s Christopher Hume, "the Victory Soya Mills are now being killed."[52] Since the building of these "waterfront landmarks," the structures had become an "anachronism."[53] Toronto's industrial lands were giving way to a landscape of consumption.

Not every closed terminal elevator has been erased from North American waterfronts. Montreal's Grain Elevator No. 5 is still standing, even though its fate has been a source of heated public debate since it closed in 1994. The *Montreal Gazette*'s Ingrid Peritz defended the terminal elevator: "To stand before the elevators today is to sense something of Montreal's former glory as an international trading city. Massive, surrounded by silence except for the sound of water lapping in the adjoining Windmill Point Basin, the elevators rise like pale ghosts on the city's edge."[54] Others, by contrast, looked on the massive concrete silos of the terminal elevator as "towers of urban blight."[55] Residents of nearby condos, for example, wanted Grain Elevator No. 5 demolished so they could get a view of the water. "It's old cement. It's ugly. It's crazy to talk about it as heritage," said Huguette Huard. The chief editorial writer for *La Presse*, Alain Dubuc, agreed. For him, "living cities" are characterized by a constantly changing environment: "A city isn't a cemetery, a frozen gallery of mummies that bear witness to the moments of its past."

It has been some time since grain elevators instilled a sense of the technological sublime. Yet, as we have seen, they have continued to serve as a "classic symbol of an age of heroic industrial architecture and boundless hope."[56] For Rosemary Horne – chairperson of the Toronto Historical Board – who tried, unsuccessfully, to have Victory Mills placed on the city's inventory of Heritage Properties, these buildings were "an integral part of who we were and what we are."[57] Grain elevators, like other landmark industrial structures that are disappearing from our cities, have become landmarks of the past, rather than of the future.

INDUSTRIAL IMPLOSIONS AND OTHER DEMOLITIONS

Industrial implosions have become a familiar part of evening television. The October 1994 demolition of the Sears Merchandise Warehouse in Philadelphia, for example, drew fifty thousand spectators: "Crowds cheered, bands played, protesters protested and street vendors hawked commemorative 'implosion' memorabilia."[58] In response to growing public interest in explosive demolition, the industry launched the Internet site <IMPLOSIONWORLD.COM> in 1999 by with a real-time webcast of another explosive demolition in Philadelphia. The site includes photographs of every conceivable building type falling in clouds of dust: hospitals, stadiums, bridges, apartment towers, Las Vegas casinos, commercial buildings, military complexes, and yes, industrial buildings. There are literally thousands of images available on this website. It also contains a listing of the "world records" in explosive demolition. The largest explosively demolished building (Sears Merchandise in Philadelphia), the tallest building (Hudson's Department store in Detroit), most structures demolished at once (the 1997 blast at the Hamilton Stelco steel mill that destroyed twenty structures at once), and so on. For Brent Blanchard, chief writer for the site, photographic images of imploding buildings were "visual testaments to man's mastery of engineering," seen on "countless evening newscasts and documentary programs."

Explosive demolition men, or "blasters," were the glamour boys of the post-industrial era. They found themselves besieged for autographs and TV interviews and soon came to see themselves as celebrities: "For as long as most of us in the demolition industry can remember, the visual allure and chest thumping power of explosive charges dramatically bringing down a giant structure have captivated young and old, male and female, veteran and novice. For many spectators and supporting participants, it is a once-in-a-lifetime experience that is recounted in dramatic detail for years to follow." The machismo of the work was often on display. Eric Kelly, who brought down the Sears Warehouse in twelve seconds, told reporters that explosive demolition was "better than sex" because it "lasts longer"![59]

One of the exceptions to this problem-free world of implosion was an online essay written about the demolition of the Sydney Steel mill in Cape Breton. The Protec demolition team first brought down five smokestacks and then, several months later, tackled the mill's blast furnace and seven stoves. Here is the blaster's account:

> It was during the previous trip that structural inspectors discovered local residents harbored deep resentment towards the steel mill and the perceived health problems that accompanied its operation. It quickly became obvious that no activity – including the destruction of some of the offending structures – would be received well, and that the pre-blast inspection of nearby homes would meet with considerable resistance.

As Gardner [the blaster] later observed, "In my experience, working near contaminated sites poses one of the most difficult types of public relations challenges our team can face … right up there alongside interacting with historical preservationists before a deteriorating local landmark is imploded. In many cases, these folks are pretty wound up long before we arrive.… I once had people throwing D-cell batteries at me and my vehicle before I could even step out and introduce myself."

The demolition men nevertheless worked to win the trust of local residents, because they needed access to their properties in order to do multi-angle blast photography. When the blaster, Eric Kelly, set off the explosive charges, the blast furnace "slowly listed to the west and steadily gained momentum until it impacted the ground with a 'smash.' Seconds later, four of the stoves also toppled harmlessly into receiving pits as planned." However, the two remaining stoves, though leaning precariously, remained upright. To finish the job, the team inelegantly used a long-reach excavator to nudge the two stubborn burners until they came crashing down. A video of the blast furnace and ovens coming down was posted online at <www.sysco.ns.ca>, as were animated "before" and "after" photographs of the blast furnace and open-hearth furnaces.[60]

The demolition business clearly operates on an international scale, and these specialists are in hot demand. An online article, for example, told readers how one demolition company destroyed fifteen structures in four countries on a single weekend. No wonder, then, that all this globe-trotting shaped how these men looked upon "local people." In some instances, local people were portrayed as obstacles to progress, and at other times they were depicted as fawning fans of these post-industrial superheroes: "For local residents and community officials in these towns, the events would provide more unprecedented thrills and topics of conversation for years to come. However, for the demolition contractors involved, and the team at Protec, it was just another weekend at the office." Just how irrelevant locality has become in their minds is made evident in Implosionworld's photograph galleries that identify the imploded building, the name of the blaster, the company he worked for, but not the city in which the building was once located. This oversight provides yet another indication of the universalism of industrial demolition imagery on the one hand, and the disembeddeness of the demolition industry on the other.

CONCLUSION

The study of the rituals and representations surrounding industrial demolition enables us to inquire into the meaning of economic change itself. This meaning is contested and framed by the secular rituals, media representations, and imagined geographies that accompany this transformation. They make North America's transition from industrialism to post-industrialism appear natural and inevitable. As sociologist Pierre Bourdieu has argued elsewhere, an established order must make its world view appear taken for granted.[61] The toppling of large industrial structures – the "visual signatures" of industrialism – signals the transformation underway.[62] Plant closings and their demolition put workers in their place: that "place" now being on the margins of local, regional, national, and global culture. In one town after another, on either side of the Canada-United States border, mill workers have struggled to understand their changing place in their local and national communities. What they saw frightened them.

CHAPTER 2

"TAKE ONLY PICTURES AND LEAVE ONLY FOOTPRINTS"

Urban Exploration and the Aesthetics of Deindustrialization

urban exploration n. the investigation of manmade structures not designed for public consumption, from mechanical rooms to stormwater drains to rooftops; usually such areas are off-limits

*– Infiltration: The zine about going places
you're not supposed to go*

We are all spatial story-tellers, explorers, navigators, and discoverers, exchanging narratives of, and in, the city.

– Jane Rendall

NOSTALGIA, DEFINED BY HISTORIAN PETER FRITZSCHE AS A "melancholy feeling of dispossession," entered our collective vocabulary in the nineteenth century during the upheaval that accompanied urbanization, industrialization, and political revolution.[1] This deep rupture in people's sense of time produced a "vague collective longing for a bygone era."[2] If some people cherished the past, and lamented the changes underway, they also believed that there was no going back.[3] This paradox is the source of nostalgia's melancholy. Narratives of loss and victimization, embodied in the figure of the "exile," surfaced repeatedly in songs, stories, and autobiographies of the time. This melancholy was also expressed in art where archaic or medieval ruins evoked a sense of the picturesque or the sublime. These artful ruins were "symbolic of the inevitability of life passing,"[4] ruins "being at the end of things," as Kathleen Stewart has noted.[5]

The massive dislocation of deindustrialization in the late twentieth century has produced similar sentiments of nostalgia and loss. In some respects, the figure of the "displaced worker" is not unlike the nineteenth-century exile. Their life-story narratives share the same sense of disconnection with the past, and a deepening dread of the future. If recent decades have been full of workers who mourn the past, these workers are not alone. Industrial heritage tourism has expanded rapidly – an indication of its perceived value as a tool of economic development in hard-hit areas, and of a popular desire to learn more about a "vanishing" way of life. Industrial heritage trails, for example, have sprouted up across Europe and North America.[6] The desire to preserve or commemorate the passing of the industrial age is also behind the proliferation of industrial museums, national parks, historic sites, and *ecomusées*.[7] Many of these efforts represent a "last resort" for former blue-collar places.[8]

Industrial heritage tourism is part of the larger phenomenon of "dark tourism" – defined by historian Carolyn Strange as the "preservation, marketing and organized visitation of sites associated with suffering and death."[9] Historic sites of death, disaster, and depravity have drawn the interest of growing numbers of tourists around the globe.[10] Much of this interest has focused on Nazi concentration camps, former battlegrounds, or sites of natural catastrophe. Dark tourism, however, is not restricted to officially designated and interpreted sites of memory. Nor is it restricted to sites of death and disease. The post-modern tourist, traveller, or explorer in search of authentic experience is also drawn to industrial ruins and other abandoned urban landscapes as sites of loss and nostalgia. Abandonment is a powerful cultural motif in the modern world.[11]

We can interrogate the aesthetics of deindustrialization through the travel narratives, or adventure stories, told by so-called "urban explorers" – mainly white, middle class youth between the ages of fifteen and thirty. Urban explorers are drawn to parts of the city that are deemed off-limits to the public – abandoned buildings of all kinds, rooftops, tunnels, and drains, and to the infiltration of active sites. The North American urban exploration (UE) movement emerged in the mid-1990s around Toronto-based Jeff Chapman. Chapman, whose *nom de plume* was "Ninjalicious," created the extraordinarily popular magazine *Infiltration* in 1996 – "*the zine about places you're not supposed to go.*"[12] In each issue (there were twenty-five in all), Chapman picked a "target" to infiltrate, and then wrote about his mission. His targets ranged from active sites such as the innards of the Royal York Hotel, to abandoned factories and disused military facilities. Ninjalicious was proficient in this highly specialized kind of travel writing. For one reader, it was like "some postmodern version of Fodor's [travel guide]."[13]

The Infiltration website <http://infiltration.org>, launched in 1997, brought together thousands of enthusiasts from around the world. The site offers a heady mix of practice, theory, and resources. New York-based *Jinx*

Magazine, a journal of "worldwide urban adventure," had the following to say about the *Infiltration* zine and website:

> It is a revolutionary pamphlet, a front-line journal, a manifesto on usufruct. The philosophy, boiled down, to essence, is "Trespass for adventure's sake." The simplicity of the idea has burned it into the culture, and now there are tens of thousands following it across the world, many publishing magazines and Web sites of their own.[14]

Chapman was not only the catalyst in the formation of a transnational UE "community" or "movement." He is also widely credited with having coined the term "urban exploration."[15] Ninjalicious "told them they were urban explorers and started a worldwide dialogue." In 2001, Carolyn Hughes, a journalist with the *Washington Post*, called urban exploration a "growing and global network."[16] Two years later, Ninjalicious estimated that there were three hundred to three hundred and fifty identifiable urban explorer groups worldwide.[17]

Yet the adoption of the term "explorer" is freighted with historical and ideological baggage. It is associated with European voyages of discovery and the possession of the "Orient," "Darkest Africa," and the "New World."[18] There is, of course, a vast scholarship on the cultural construction of the racial "other" in the era of European expansion and colonialism. These imperial travel narratives feature the "taming" of distant lands and peoples.[19] The "wilderness," for example, has served for millennia as the counterpoint to civilization and has reinforced white people's sense of their own superiority.[20] The history and rhetoric of exploration is thus imbued with the language of race and class.

The imaginative geography of urban exploration, like the colonial encounters of earlier times, is premised on being on the outside looking in.[21] The missions of urban explorers cross into undiscovered lands, "partitioned space" that was set apart from society and outside the usual dictates of time. For many urban explorers, it is like travelling back in time, or, like tourists, crossing great distances. Tourism and the tourist aesthetic transform the meaning and representation of space. For sociologist James Overton, "tourism produces not only new arrangements of space but new subjects with new gazes."[22] To photograph and catalogue places is in some measure to appropriate them.

Anyone studying the landscape and memory of deindustrialization will find value in UEers' determination to document their adventures and post them online. There are thousands of accounts in archived UE fora. Most of the stories uncovered are from North America, but there is a scattering of other postings from Europe and Australia. Three of the main websites are particularly revealing: Ninjalicious' Infiltration, Avatar X's Urban Exploration Resource <www.uer.ca>, and the Urban Explorers Network <www.urbanexplorers.net>. So are the sites of New York's *Jinx Magazine* <www.jinxmagazine.com>, Andrew Henderson's "Forgotten Ohio" <www. forgottenoh.com>, and the online "journals" of local UE clubs in Montreal <http://uem.minimanga.com>, Vancouver <www.wraiths.org>, and London, Ontario <http://uel.minimanga.com >, amongst others.[23] In all, there are several hundred "abandonment stories" that tell of industrial ruination, available on these websites.

Urban explorers will be our chief guides through this abandoned industrial landscape. Through their narratives we will attempt to answer several nagging questions. What is the drawing power of industrial ruins? Why do these enthusiasts represent their hobby as "exploration"? Is urban exploration a way of seeing, feeling, and experiencing these modern ruins differently? Do UEers challenge norms about how deindustrialization is framed and represented, or do they reify them? What do these ruins tell us?

First, we will tackle the movement itself, situating it within the context of youth culture. Then will examine the online narratives for meaning and motivation. This will lead to some thoughts on the politics of urban exploration. We will find that these urban explorer stories turn former sites of production into sites of consumption, transforming them into deindustrial playgrounds. As Ninjalicious wrote on his website, "I've always seen abandoned factories as being among the most authentic and exciting playgrounds on earth."[24] The aesthetic of deindustrialization that emerges from these stories provides us with yet another perspective on the meaning of economic change.

THE EMERGENCE OF URBAN EXPLORATION

Youth culture in recent decades has been profoundly shaped by urban crisis and industrial collapse. Punk music, raves, graffiti, zines, and even urban exploration emerged as underground movements of mainly white, middle class youth. In his book *Lipstick Traces: A Secret History of the 20th*

Century (1990), Greil Marcus made a direct link between the American and British punk scenes of the 1970s and 1980s, and the German Dadaists and French Situationists of the immediate post-war era who sought to explore the city through the senses.[25] Since then, urban thinkers like Jane Jacobs and Michel de Certeau have urged city dwellers to step out of everyday routine to reclaim our cities.[26] Certain aspects of youth culture have influenced and, in turn been influenced by, these intellectual developments.

All-night rave parties originated in Great Britain during the Thatcher years in the 1980s. They swept North America the following decade, in the wake of industrial dislocation and the rise of the "new economy." Dancing to computer-generated music known as "techno," young ravers consumed water, non-alcoholic "power drinks," and amphetamines (ecstasy). In the early years, ravers shifted from one location to the next, favouring abandoned warehouses, secluded fields, and former dance clubs. Like punk rock, the rave scene was supposed to be about more than the party – "peace, love, unity and respect," the PLUR ideal.[27] In recent years, promoters and corporate sponsors have taken the all-night party "out of the industrial zone and into legitimate venues," according to one Canadian journalist.[28] Nightclubs, hockey arenas, and even Montreal's mammoth Olympic Stadium have largely replaced abandoned warehouses.

If raves have been incorporated into the mainstream of youth culture, so has graffiti art. The "golden age" of graffiti art was the 1970s and '80s, and its capital was New York City. At the movement's height, graffiti artists "developed a grandiloquent rhetoric to explain that adorning buildings was a form of empowerment. It was, they argued, a way of reclaiming the streets for free expression, and rebelling against the concept of private property."[29] Yet, in practice, graffiti artists were equal-opportunity taggers: painting businesses, libraries, schools, monuments, abandoned buildings, and most famously, subway cars. For journalist Ariella Budick, "Graffiti's natural habitat was public space. It belonged on a subway car in motion, throwing off different versions of the same message: 'I was here'. It belonged on the side of warehouses, a collective mural on grand scale."[30] However, like raves, graffiti art later went mainstream. The Manhattan Art world embraced the genre in the early 1980s, with "showings" in fancy art galleries.[31] Today, graffiti artists are even employed by advertising agencies plugging hot youth commodities. "Uptown suddenly met downtown. Agents picked up taggers," reported Somini Sengupta in the *New York Times*.[32] In the process, graffiti became domesticated or "gentrified."[33] The death knell for New York City's subway art came in 1989 when then-Mayor Edward Koch decided to pull defaced subway cars from service until they had been cleaned, thus denying graffiti artists their public platform.[34] Increasingly, graffiti artists came to rely on photographs of their work posted online to gain fame. The audience had shifted from primarily local, to virtual, spanning the globe.

It was in this changing international context that urban exploration as a definable hobby or countercultural lifestyle emerged and flourished. That urban explorers strongly identified with the activity was confirmed in August 2005 with the death of Jeff Chapman, at age thirty-one. To his many friends and admirers, Ninjalicious's death was a stunning loss. Hundreds of people from around the world posted tributes to him and his work.[35] Many struggled with their emotions, to communicate what this one man and his mission meant to them. Words like "inspiration" and "influential" pepper the postings. He wrote with a "childlike reverence for his environment," according to Toronto's *This Magazine*.[36] He also knew how to tell a story: "Chapman had the best prose of any zine author I've read anywhere. Many zinesters are clever, of course, but Chapman wrote with a 19th century literary journalist's attention to detail; nothing escaped his notice."[37] A large number of people also revealed how they stumbled onto the Infiltration website in the late 1990s and realized that they were not alone: they belonged to a global network of young men and women interested in exploring the underside of the urban environment. "His magazine with his precise writing and photography may have single-handedly brought all of UE fans together and formed a community," wrote Finn from Texas.[38] Another thought Chapman "bettered all of us, and society as a whole, by inspiring us to an activity – maybe even a lifestyle – that opens minds."[39]

Urban exploration's journey from an underground youth movement to the mainstream followed much the same path as graffiti and rave. The growing popularity of the hobby can be measured in the flurry of recent popular interest in urban exploration. UE has been featured in the plots of several popular television shows such as *Crime Scene Investigation* (*CSI*), *CSI: Miami*, and *Law and Order*; CBC Radio docudramas; supernatural or horror movies; novels like David Morrell's *Creepers*; a five-part documentary on the Discovery Channel; and there are a number of digital eulogies to demolished mills and factories on the Internet.[40] The best-selling *Weird U.S.* alternative travel guides published by Barnes and Noble, recently made into a television series by the History Channel, are yet another indication of the creeping commercialization of the hobby. Jeff Chapman's book, *Access All Areas*, released in 2005, has also sold well.[41] Urban exploration, it seems, has hit the mainstream on both sides of the Canada-United States border.

Toronto filmmaker Robert Fantinatto was so impressed by what he found at <www.infiltration.org> – the "granddaddy of all [UE] websites" – that he produced the 2005 DVD *Forgotten Places: Urban Exploration, Industrial Archaeology and the Aesthetics of Decay*. This forty-three minute, independently produced film attempted to provide an insider's viewpoint on the urban exploration movement. In his Toronto *Globe and Mail* review of the DVD, however, Dave LeBlanc expressed his surprise at what the DVD did not document: "It's unconcerned with when these factories closed, what they manufactured, or where they're located (most are in Toronto, for the record)."[42] Fantinatto justified this inattention to context as necessary in order to produce a "generic place that's in everbody's town." He wanted the film to speak to anyone in the world. The resulting universalized aesthetic of abandonment resembles the one conveyed by <implosionworld.com> and other industrial demolition sites.

This interest in abandoned spaces is, of course, nothing new. Most people's childhood memories, I suspect, include journeys of "exploration" into the surrounding natural and built environments. I can recall my own childhood fascination with the massive, grey, concrete grain elevator that loomed over our working class neighbourhood in Thunder Bay, Ontario. The neighbourhood was our playground, so our curiosity led us to "discover" many of its secret nooks and crannies – though this did not include the still-active industrial site itself. We were taught never to trespass on railroad or industrial lands. To hammer home the point that these were dangerous places for children, all the kids in the neighbourhood were paraded before a neighbour who had lost his leg to a passing train.[43] He showed us the stump and told us that this was what would happen if we went where we weren't supposed to go.

While my early childhood memories are from the 1970s, before the devastating recessions of the early 1980s and early 1990s, urban explorers belong to a generation of North Americans who never knew the post-war boom. They grew up in towns and cities that were, or were not as the case may be, making the transition to a post-industrial economy of service and high technology. Abandoned mills and factories had become a conspicuous part of the urban landscape. When asked, several members of the Urban Explorer's Resources forum indicated that their "first time" urban exploring took place at age seven or eight in an abandoned place located near their childhood home. They did not know that what they were doing was called "urban exploration" – the term had not yet been invented.[44]

What then differentiated the urban explorer from the common trespasser? In responding to this frequently asked question, urban explorers note that they have adopted a code of conduct, and, much like advocates of rave dances and grafitti art, are motivated by larger historical and philosophical concerns. In fact, urban exploration was part of a larger effort to reignite childhood wonderment and reconnect us to the towns and cities in which we live. Urban exploration appeals to mainly young adults who are unhappy with the "spatial homogeneity" and commercialism of the modern city.[45] Unlike trespassers who are motivated by profit or mischief, urban explorers – we are told – don't harm the places they explore. They love these spaces.

For Ninjalicious, urban exploration was a rare authentic experience. Humans are "designed to explore and to play," he said.[46] Urban exploration was "free, fun and hurts no one. It's a thrilling, mind-expanding hobby that encourages our natural instincts to explore and play in our own environment. It encourages people to create their own adventures, like when they were kids. Instead of buying the pre-packaged kind. And it nurtures a sense of wonder in the everyday spaces we inhabit or pass by that few history books could ever hope to recreate."[47] He lamented the fact that in most cities, parking lots had replaced common areas, and every square inch was becoming commercialized. Cities should be for citizens.

"Genuine urban explorers," Ninjalicious declared, "never vandalize, steal or damage anything – we don't even litter. We're in it for the thrill of discovery and a few nice pictures."[48] The movement's mantra, "Take only pictures and leave only footprints," originated in the code of ethics promoted by Ninjalicious, and echoed the slogan of forest preservationists in Canada and the United States. He was almost "evangelical about the virtue and value of exploring cities, preaching ethics that encouraged trespassing but forbade theft, vandalism and even littering."[49] In one form or another, this code is invoked on virtually every urban exploration website. The Montreal club, for example, states that its members will not tag, steal, or vandalize, if for no other reason than it "helps preserve the environment for future explorers to enjoy."[50] Many urban explorers also claim that they never "break and enter," but merely entered when the opportunity arose.

This ethical code has been widely accepted – at least rhetorically – within the movement. It is commonplace for urban explorers to assert the prohibition against vandalism and tagging in their online narratives. This prescription goes largely unquestioned on the websites. It was what defined the movement and distinguished it from other activities. As a result, several urban explorers expressed their outrage when their hobby was represented as little better than pilfering, in an episode of the hit, crime-fighting TV program *CSI: Miami*, that aired in 2006. In the storyline, two young urban explorers kick down the door of an old hotel in search of souvenirs – only to find two dead bodies. This was "not exactly what we do," said one outraged viewer. "True explorers," noted another, respected the sites they visited.

Just how important the ethical code was to the collective identity of urban explorers became apparent when one young man, new to the forum on the Urban Explorers' Resources website, posted an account of how he climbed the water tower at a closed pulp and paper mill to spray-paint a green smiley face: "We were making it pretty, it's old, neglected, we turned an old hunk of metal into 150 feet of towering sarcasm."[51] The posting received a hostile response from other list members. One Chicago man responded that "A big green smiley face isn't 'pretty.' You guys could have painted a mural on that water tower and I wouldn't approve. It wasn't yours to paint."[52] A woman from West Virginia agreed, "There is nothing cool about painting up a building. I don't even like when the city pays someone to paint something on a building. But when you tag an old site that is just wrong." Several list members suggested that the tower climber should get off the online forum. According to one, "I hope you didn't have the intention of becoming a full member of this site."[53] Despite urban exploration's criticism of the over-regulated city, vandals and taggers were not welcome in the movement. They did not follow the script.

If their hobby was good clean fun, urban explorers also emphasized the idea that their activities served a higher purpose: namely, to record abandoned buildings before they are demolished or converted to other uses. Much of this documentation takes the form of photographic images and narrative descriptions of what they saw, posted online. "I explore and take photos because I'm curious," said one man from Atlanta, Georgia.[54]

Sam Knowlton of the *Lawrence Journal-World*, who accompanied an urban exploration team in Kansas City in 2005, asked one of the enthusiasts, Kelsey Lutz, why she does what she does. Lutz replied that she was a photographer: "You're almost documenting history by the pictures you take and the things you see – knowing sometimes buildings are on a demolition schedule and that they're not going to be there and you're probably going to be one of the last people that sees it."[55] Team members could not decide what was more appealing to them, "the fun of the mission or the knowledge that they contribute to the global UrbEx network" by posting their photographs online. Another group member asserted that they conducted extensive background research "to find everything we possibly can about the history of the location and what it was used for – and interesting facts – so what we are able to share will have the most whole historical picture we can offer." The team thus committed "all it sees to memory and film."[56]

These narratives are fundamentally stories of discovery and possession: the "conquest of places" where one should not be.[57] "Take notes and make maps," advised Urban Explorers Net. "It makes the trip much more interesting, and it will help your recollection when you set up that fancy website about your exploits." The comparison with the "exploits" of the age of discovery is at its most explicit in *Jinx Magazine*: "Exploration serves no purpose when its results remain obscure; Leif Erickson found the Americas half a millennium before Columbus, but his discovery failed to reach influential ears, and so is a footnote."[58] The "records" of urban exploration, "like any exploration," are therefore self-published in magazines (zines), email list serves, and on the web.

Beyond thrill-seeking, it seems clear that urban explorers believe that by recording their observations in words and images, they are preserving history. This educational or historical justification for their activities also serves to distance them from everyday trespassers. "Forgotten and abandoned corners of the world's cities suddenly are rediscovered," noted the editors of *Jinx*, who then drew a troubling historical analogy to describe the difference between a trespasser and an explorer:

> With *Infiltration* magazine, then, the urban explorer truly parted
> company with the mundane trespasser. Ninjalicious became
> an explorer when he faithfully published his observations and
> enriched posterity by them. The trespasser, by contrast, always

consigned his story to silence; he, like the base Indian, threw a pearl away richer than all his tribe.[59]

The "base Indian" as a trespasser on his own land is an analogy that reeks of class and racial bias. In the context of deindustrialization, one might expect that many of the "mundane" trespassers were local youths – the sons and daughters of many of the same men and women who once worked in the abandoned mills and factories. The urban explorers, by contrast, were more likely to come from successful white-collar families living in the suburbs, or in other towns or cities altogether. None of the urban explorer narratives that I read – and I have read hundreds – provided any indication that the storyteller had ever been in a working mill or factory. More to the point, perhaps, there was no indication that their parents had, either. So these were not the sons and daughters of mill and factory workers. *Jinx*'s historical analogy may therefore be appropriate, but not in the way that the magazine's editors obviously intended. In effect, the explorer-trespasser dichotomy is an invention. It is a rhetorical device used to justify an illegal activity and to distance middle class explorers from working class trespassers.[60] According to the *Boston Globe*, it "comes down to trespassing with style."

NARRATING INDUSTRIAL RUINS

Wealthy tourists have long shown the tendency to view themselves as travellers, and everyone else as tourists. As Jonathan Culler observed, "the desire to distinguish between tourists and real travellers is a part of tourism – integral to it rather than outside it or beyond it."[61] The same holds true in urban exploration. Consider, for example, this comment made by an exploration group based in Vancouver: "In cities all around the world, there are people who refuse to let themselves be herded about like the rest of the sheep. These places choose to step outside the norm, and venture places few would tread." The explorer/tourist sensibility was an overwhelmingly romantic one, placing value on feeling, imagination, and the "authentic" experience.[62] Colin Campbell made much the same point. For him, the romantic movement "ushered in a new hedonism in which the stimulation of the emotions or feelings became one of the most valued pleasures."[63] Romantics "elevated the pleasures of the imagination to a higher moral plane," encouraging the "sanctity of the deeply personal response to nature."[64] In sum, romanticism focused on "the intensity of emotion and sensation, on poetic mystery rather than intellectual clarity, and on individual hedonistic expression."[65]

The aesthetic categories of the picturesque and the sublime are particularly useful in helping us to understand the magnetism of industrial ruins. The picturesque was a softer aesthetic, entailing idyllic natural landscapes that looked "like a picture."[66] Historian Patricia Jasen credits the romantic sensibility for encouraging "an appreciation of those scenes in which landscape and history, especially in the form of ruins and graveyards, were blended together."[67] Archaic and medieval ruins fascinated the nineteenth-century tourist in search of the picturesque. There was nothing gentle, however, about the sublime in the natural landscape: mountains, ravines, cascading water, and great waterfalls. These places were valued for the intensity of the experience. For Jasen, "the sublime meant being swept away by the beauty and terror of some natural phenomenon – being transported (however briefly) into another realm of being or consciousness." The evocative power of sublime places has long been a selling point to tourists.

Of course these insights into romanticism and tourism can be applied to urban exploration. The search for the sublime in the built environment is at UE's very core. While the sublime was usually associated with dramatic features of the natural landscape, such as Niagara Falls, the category was sometimes applied to the built environment. In the late-nineteenth and early-twentieth centuries, for example, commentators frequently invoked the sublime in their descriptions of North America's massive mills and factories. An industrial landscape "threatened the individual with its sheer scale, its noise, its complexity, and the superhuman power of the forces at work."[68] The working mill or factory evoked "fear tinged with wonder" from visitors. In turn, the great industrial districts of Cleveland, Chicago, and Detroit engendered fascination and revulsion. North Americans groped "toward a new language and new visual representation to capture the new forms and light of the new sort of landscape."[69] David Nye called this sense of awe the "technological sublime."

The same sense of wonder accompanied deindustrialization. In March 2004, Ninjalicious explored the interior of the closed "Canada Works" of the Steel Company of Canada (Stelco) in Hamilton, Ontario. The narrative begins with a short history of the "mammoth" finishing mill since it opened in 1913, and mentions, without explanation, that the mill closed in 1984. The narrative then turns to the "mission" itself. Ninjalicious, who is accompanied by three friends, records his impressions on first seeing the inside of the mill. The "huge rusting hulk" looked on the verge of collapse," but he was startled by the size and beauty of the place – this was "truly decay at its finest." The narrative follows the four explorers as they pass through the flooded basement (where they are almost electrocuted), the burnt-out room, the peeling paint room, "and other tourist attractions," before they venture upstairs to the second floor and the roof. Danger lurks everywhere in the narrative. After they make their way across the hazardous second floor (the "least favourite part of the trip" and "certainly the riskiest"), the narrative ends with the group's re-emergence on the street: "I was happy when we made our way over the skyway, down the stairs, and back to solid ground. We cheerfully made our way back out to civilization shortly afterwards."[70]

This particular exploration narrative is illustrated with eleven photographic images, taken, presumably, by Ninjalicious himself. The first image is of a worn "PRIVATE PROPERTY" sign on the chain-link fence outside the plant. The playful caption reads: "This sign had rusted so much that it was hard to read, but I think it said 'All Welcome, Love Stelco.'" The rest of the photographs are taken in the mill's interior. These evocative images show light streaming down from holes in the roof, illuminating the wrecked interior below. Several large pieces of equipment are recorded, as is the signage. The captions comment on the aesthetics of the place: "chaotic elegance," "mammothy," as well as the new uses put to the obsolete equipment – a "few older and bulkier toys have been left behind for explorers."[71]

The website of Urban Exploration Montreal offers a better understanding of the form and meaning of more typical urban explorer narratives. The Montreal group relies heavily on photographic images. The text is often little more than extended captions or vignettes arranged around this visual tour. The narratives contain no historical context of any kind and virtually no information about the function of the buildings. The team of enthusiasts focused their comments on the aesthetics of the buildings. We will follow the group's exploration of the Canada Malting Plant in the St. Henri district, and the O'Keefe Brewery downtown. The two sites stand tall in the group members' minds, for their "sheer size and decay."[72]

The Canada Malt plant, described as a "huge, extremely decayed, former malt processing plant," is one of Montreal's most "notorious spots, thus making it a very popular destination for beginning explorers, graffiti artists," and others. They ventured inside the "looming, monolithic building" expecting the "best," and got it. What they found were "precarious stairs and ladders," "prehistoric soda cans," "serpentine wire hanging from the ceiling," "flaming graffiti," and "Ahh. Decay. *blissful sigh*." They gazed at the surrounding working class neighbourhood from the top floor of the building, "feeling not unlike kings surveying our lands." For them, the Canada Malt Plant was "massive, deteriorating, dangerous, cold and FUN!"

Their visits to the O'Keefe Brewery, which stands behind the city's downtown planetarium, inspired similar enthusiasm. It was, they wrote, "where we first discovered the pleasures offered by an abandoned building of this size." The building remained mostly intact, and "visitors to this historic industrial monument will get to see a lot of the equipment and furnishings as they once were." On their first visit, the explorers were surprised to discover a rest stop and "guest book" in the heart of the building. They also found evidence of a rave. Evidently they were not the first people to visit the place. The building nonetheless provoked in them "a lingering sense of awe. Awe that man could build something so large, and abandon it so quickly. Awe that our past is so quickly and completely lost… and that you have been lucky enough to have been offered a glimpse of it." Adopting the voice of the tour guide in their exploration narrative, the young men bade visitors "Welcome to the O'Keefe Brewery."

What can we learn from these visual tours of industrial ruins? All three stories are fundamentally about what the narrators thought and saw while on their journeys of discovery. We can therefore think of them as travel narratives. The genre of the travel narrative contains several standard features, including the traveller protagonist (the narrator), and the travel itinerary as plot. Danger (whether real or imagined) has always been an important plot device in travel narratives involving "exotic" locales. It serves to accentuate distance and difference – setting the intrepid narrator apart from the rest of the crowd. Because travel narratives frequently take the form of a search for knowledge or experience, the photographic images incorporated into each narrative provide "proof" that the urban explorers were in fact there. At its worst, the search for abandoned mills and factories worthy of exploration is analogous to the sport of hunting – and the photographs are little more than pictorial trophies.[73]

What Ninjalicious and the others fail to include in their narratives is just as significant. They say very little about the history, function, and physical layout of the mills being explored. Indeed, they seem to have only a vague idea of what went on inside. Hamilton's "Canada Works" is a case in point. Bill Scandlan, one of my oral history interviewees, worked briefly as a machine operator in the mill during the Second World War, before entering the service. He returned to the plant in 1946. According to him, the Canada Works on Wellington Street North actually consisted of two divisions. The West Mill contained mainly "wire, wire cleaning, galvanizing and the nail operations," whereas the East Mill produced mainly wood screws.[74] Many of the men who worked at the mill during the early years lived in the surrounding north end neighbourhood. Here is Scandlan's description of the mill's interior as it was then:

> The mill was filthy. It had wooden floors. There were three levels. The bottom level was where there was the nail storages and nail packing: a very noisy, dirty place. The first floor was the heavy nail machines. That was what made 2½″ common, 4″ common, shingling/roofing nails. And big spikes. It was so noisy you had to wear cotton batten in your ears. There was no protective equipment – if you didn't do that, why you could lose your hearing.... Many of the senior people who had worked in the noise many years had gone deaf.[75]

Bill Scandlan went on to discuss the 1946 strike and the place of the steel-workers at the Canada Works in this early labour struggle. It is unfortunate that none of this rich history made it into Ninjalicious' travelogue. The little historical context that did was limited to the date that the Canada Works opened, and the remark that Stelco produced "a heck of a lot of shells to help destroy German industry" and "a lot of ingots" to build up Canada's. The Canada Works actually produced neither. If Ninjalicious had had the opportunity to hear Bill Scandlan's story before entering the shuttered mill, there is little doubt that he would have seen it with new eyes.

Despite their stated desire to record places before they vanish, urban explorers are more interested in aesthetics than history. The narratives are little more than an impressionistic collage of observations and feelings. We learn more about how these abandoned buildings make the narrators feel, than about their history and function. The stories thus serve to sacralize abandoned mills and factories and to mythologize them as "ruins." For example, Ninjalicious's attention is drawn to the beauty of the ruined interior of the building, the resurgent vegetation, the gargantuan size of some of the rooms, the disorder, the danger, and the extent of decay. It is a sensually charged place; a place of magical unseen forces. The site is likewise set apart from the outside world in his narrative. It is a wild zone of strange noises, darkness, and hidden danger.

So, for urban explorers, industrial ruins are sites of danger, disorder, decay, and feeling. They emphasize the danger, whether real or imagined, from rusty debris, rotten stairwells, holes in the floor, asbestos, toxic chemicals, sharp objects, and other hidden dangers. There was danger in potential human encounters too: police, security guards, criminal gangs, the homeless, as well as disenfranchised youth. Most of the stories are littered with such references. Danger sometimes even shaped how urban explorers organized their thoughts. After each mission, for example, the six "agents" in Urban Exploration London identified the hazards encountered and the general condition of the site.[76] For their part, the "Wraiths" in Vancouver went so far as to organize their missions into three colour-coded categories based on risk level: green (low), yellow (moderate), and red (high).[77]

Urban explorers, in turn, frequently represent disorder by inverting the meaning of factory signage and by noting the visual collapse of old work hierarchies. Virtually every visual tour of an abandoned mill or factory includes at least one photograph of a sign telling workers not to do this or that. These signs remind us that mills and factories were once highly controlled and hierarchical places. Every element of production was designed to work predictably, with precision. The signs took on new meaning, however, once the building was abandoned. Many urban explorers found "something comical about remaining signatures of hierarchy and authority" in abandoned places.[78] These traces of redundant power could no longer be taken seriously as there was no one there to "listen and obey." Disorder was also signalled in the deteriorating condition of the building. For some the image of an elevated foreman's hut that had collapsed onto the shop floor below signified the elimination of old hierarchies. In jumping to this conclusion, however, they overlook the larger political message embedded in the ruins: the corporations were loyal to no one and no place. Far from signalling an end to old work hierarchies, industrial ruins provide dramatic testimony to their enduring power.

The third theme that runs through the stories of urban exploration relates to the wild. Urban explorers regularly compare industrial ruins to the natural world. Andrew Henderson, for example, compares the giant ovens that he discovered in the Claycraft Brick Factory in Columbus, Ohio, to "caves."[79] These abandoned buildings are everything the modern world is not: exotic, wild, primitive, and "enmeshed in sensation." Abandoned areas are part of a wild zone that exists on the margins of the modern post-industrial city: "Ruins are sensually charged with powerful smells, profuse and intrusive textures, peculiar and delicate soundscapes, as well as perplexing visual objects, juxtapositions, and vistas, all at variance with the sensually ordered world outside."[80] For geographer Tim Edensor, to walk through unpoliced spaces like industrial ruins was to "experience the collapse of boundaries in which the outside and inside merge, and nature mingles with culture." In fact, "Factories are places in which raw nature, extracted from its environment, is then transformed into something else, but in the ruin, nature appears in less adulterated form."[81] Industrial ruins are points of transition.

Because industrial ruins are in a state of liminality, the past is everywhere present. Industrial ruins are haunted realms that "seethe with memories."[82] The allegorical representation of remembered loss is evidenced in the temporal flux of urban explorer narratives. The deep rupture in time is reflected in the poetic mystery of apparitions and hauntings. As Tim Edensor suggests, "The urge to seek out the ghosts of places is bound up with the politics of remembering the past and, more specifically, with the spatialisation of memory and how memory is sought, articulated, and inscribed upon space."[83] There are, likewise, no temporal restrictions in the narrative written by "Throckmorten," of his/her visit to the derelict Canada Malting Plant next to the Toronto Island Airport's ferry dock:

> A damp hush falls upon the darkened corridors. An occasional distant metallic clang is deadened by the whisper of still air. Layers of peeled paint crackle under foot like autumn leaves; this being the only noise to break the constant silence that blankets, everything. With a description like that, it's hard to imagine that at one point in time, the very spot I stood was once abuzz with activity. A hellish roar would have prevailed as machines churned; intense overhead lights would have cast an irritating glow upon the surrounding mechanical labyrinth. Every time I venture into one of Toronto's many abandoned industrial

buildings, these thoughts always cross my mind. It seems absurd that somewhere in the past, these places were home to hundreds of workers, for decades at a time, 365 days a year.... Now it's all gone, and the empty and neglected monuments stand as reminders to all of us that everything comes to an end.[84]

The abandoned building bore the physical traces of the people, processes, and products that were once there. These "intersecting temporalities" stimulate "involuntary memories" that are unpredictable and contingent.[85] For Tim Edensor, these memories are embedded in the materiality of industrial ruins themselves and transmitted to visitors through sight, smell, and even touch: "Being haunted draws us, always a bit magically, into the structure of feeling of a reality we come to experience, not as cold knowledge, but as transformative recognition."[86] In effect, for urban explorers one of the chief "values" in visiting industrial ruins is the intensity of emotion and sensation that these places inspire in them.

More often than not, these middle class narrators adopt the hushed voice of a nineteenth-century European adventurer exploring a strange and exotic land. Like the "white men in the jungle" of the colonial era, these modern-day travellers are drawn to and repelled by the primitive. Unlike those early travellers, urban explorers do not need to cross great geographic distances – the abandoned mill or factory could be a ten-minute drive from home. And still, these narrators leave the impression of having travelled far. This is significant. Urban explorers may not have travelled great physical distances, but they have travelled great social distances.[87] To enter an abandoned site is, in some small way, to cross an imaginative divide separating the perceived post-industrial present from the industrial past. The use of words like "civilization," and "primitive," renders this line visible. Ninjalicious's exit from Hamilton's derelict Canada Works is thus cast as a return to civilization.

THE POLITICS OF URBAN EXPLORATION

What, then, are the politics of urban exploration? How do we frame urban explorers' desire to seek out abandoned industrial sites and to record their experiences in images and words? Does the aesthetic of deindustrialization resist notions of progress or does it merely reaffirm them? To answer these questions we need first to look at urban exploration's connection to cultural geography. Several cultural geographers have recently trumpeted the political potential of urban exploration to reclaim our cities for people, and of industrial ruins to subvert notions of social "progress."

In the first instance, a recent issue of the academic journal *Cultural Geographies* (2005), edited by David Pinder, examines how artists and academics can use urban exploration as a means of democratizing urban space. "Toyshop," a Brooklyn-based artist collective, for example, has sought to exploit "opportunities for play and subversion" through street art.[88] Artists, cultural workers, activists, and urban adventurers who want to explore the sensual meaning of urban-ness gathered in the New York neighbourhood in May 2003 for the "Psy-geo-conflux" festival and conference.[89] David Pinder makes a direct link between the French situationists of the 1950s and the psycho-geographers of the 1990s and 2000s. The early work of radical geographer Bill Bunge is another point of reference. Bunge sought to map daily problems and inequities in his "expeditions" to the inner cities of Toronto and Detroit during the 1960s and 1970s.[90] Yet these efforts to explore the meaning of urban-ness are far more community-based than the more narrowly aesthetic approach adopted by the urban exploration movement.[91]

By contrast, the aesthetics of deindustrialization, and their political import, are central to the research of British geographer Tim Edensor. In *Industrial Ruins: Space, Aesthetics and Materiality*, Edensor rejects the "conventional reading" of the landscape of deindustrialization that sees dereliction and ruin as signs of waste. For him, these are wild places of tremendous beauty and freedom. As you might expect from someone whose research evolved out of his enthusiasm for visiting industrial ruins over a thirty-year period, Edensor pays tribute to the "aesthetics and materiality" of these spaces. In fact, the author's gaze is so similar to that of Ninjalicious and other urban explorers that *Industrial Ruins* can be usefully read as an extended urban exploration narrative.

Like those of other explorer narratives, the politics of Edensor's *Industrial Ruins* are often ambiguous. In the introduction, for example, he lists twenty-seven towns and cities where he personally encountered industrial ruins. He then informs the reader that "this is the last time I shall refer to their location, for the argument of the book would be less pertinent if they were accompanied by this superfluous geographical information."

But to whom are they superfluous and why? Certainly not to the men and women who worked in these closed mills and factories. Edensor is engaged in the mystification of former industrial sites, transforming them into mythic ruins. In universalizing his gaze, Edensor strips these former industrial sites of their history and their geography just as surely as the departing companies, entrepreneurs, and trophy hunters stripped the sites of their assets. Edensor would no doubt disagree. In reminding us that nothing lasts forever, he believes that the sight of ruined industry raises questions about the "persistent myth of progress." These industrial ruins thus "tempered the optimism of modern industrial development."[92]

Is Edensor right in suggesting that industrial ruins rebuke visions of progress? Or do they reify them? In my mind, the melancholy regret that permeates the urban explorer narratives does not constitute political resistance to the changes underway.[93] The changes may be lamented, but they are almost never questioned. Instead, industrial ruins act as a reminder of what was, and reinforce the already overwhelming sense of inevitability that accompanies economic change. While nostalgic responses to traces of another time should not be condemned for their sentimentality, they are more likely to confirm notions of progress than to subvert them. Much like the rituals and representations surrounding industrial demolition, the representation of industrial ruins usually affirms the inevitability of change. In fact, most urban explorer narratives are little more than adventurous play.

The story of Ninjalicious's 2001 visit to the abandoned Fisher plant serves to demonstrate just how apolitical these narratives could be. The plant is located in an "area full of old (mostly abandoned) factories and old (mostly abandoned) houses" in Detroit.[94] If the factory was Fisher Guide, as I suspect, it was the home plant of Gabriel Solano, one of my oral history narrators (see chapter 5). According to Ninjalicious, the plant was "absolutely wide open," with dozens of "easy entrances" right off the street. Not surprisingly, the plant had been

> . . . stripped pretty thoroughly, to such an extent that we couldn't really determine what each of the five floors we investigated had been used for. We did find some neat toys, like a little automatic track that seemed designed to pull cars through a tunnel in the manner of many amusement park rides, a movie theatre, and some huge vats of something or other.

After walking through the barren factory, Ninjalicious and his partner enjoyed a nice picnic on the roof of the building. That summer afternoon, the Fisher plant was their playground.

Perhaps, as a result, it was only natural for Ninjalicious to assume that those living nearby would see the site in the same way he did. The "kids who live in the houses immediately across the street," he daydreamed, "must have some awesome games of hide and seek." This may very well be true, yet there is no mention of the crime-ridden neighbourhood. Nor is there any acknowledgement of the hard times that followed the plant's closing. The fact that many of these neighbourhood kids would have had fathers who worked there, was lost on him. It is remarkable that urban explorers almost never ask why mills close. Nor do they reflect on the social impacts. These lie beyond their field of vision.

If capitalism has been left largely alone by urban explorers, governments have not been so lucky. A *Toronto Star* review of Ninjalicious's 2005 book, *Access All Areas*, described it as "a practical guide to indulging one's curiosity while gently subverting the structures of authority."[95] In fact, the government is the chief villain in many of the stories being told. Tim Edensor makes a similar point when he observes that industrial ruins stand as testament to government arrogance:

> Industrial ruins deride the pretensions of governments and
> local authorities to maintain economic prosperity and hence
> social stability, and give the lie to those myths of endless
> progress.... Instead, ruins demonstrate that these processes
> are inexorably cyclical, whereby the new is rapidly and
> inevitably transformed into the archaic; what was vibrant is
> suddenly inert.[96]

It is noteworthy, here, that Tim Edensor makes no attempt to hold companies accountable for their actions. How about the pretensions of corporate capitalism? For Edensor and other urban explorers, the city was over-regulated and over-policed. The movement's insistence on its "right" to access any area of the city relies heavily on the discourse of individual rights, which sometimes verges on libertarianism. Expressing a common viewpoint in UE circles, the Wraiths in Vancouver declared that "We feel it is our right to see these places."

This point is not lost on some "internal" critics within the urban explorer community. For example, Burlington, Ontario's Michael Cook, whose *nom de plume* is Kowalski, wondered how urban exploration differed from tourism: "It's a pastime practiced by people who would otherwise be bored or find something to do."[97] For him, urban exploration was nothing more than urban tourism. Kowalski noted that the large numbers of photographic images found on urban explorer websites provide "the same visual shorthand for abandonment and decay."[98] Most of these photographs, he wrote, do not say anything more than the "empty picturesque": they are "empty recastings of a small number of angles on the picturesque and have come to be valued in and of themselves within the urban exploration community." Another critic, "Elizabeth," similarly argued that urban explorers consume the "little differences in landscape" for their own enjoyment or profit. Once drawn to unconventional places in search of an authentic experience, urban explorers look around for good photo ops. She called for a re-examination of "our motivation for poking around in crumbling buildings and nasty factories."[99]

CONCLUSION

Writing this chapter has forced me to examine our own motivations in writing this book. Is *Corporate Wasteland* all that different from the urban explorer narratives we've looked at? After all, we, too, toured the region in search of the aesthetics of deindustrialization. The resulting iconography of dereliction, arranged in a series of photo essays (chapters 5–9), is consistent with the images found on urban explorer websites. There are images of wrecked and derelict machines, resurgent nature, ruined interiors, and mammoth factory exteriors. We were sometimes swept away by the beauty and terror of the industrial ruins we visited. Yet there are important differences. First, unlike most urban explorers, we are not particularly interested in telling the story of our own adventures in the Rust Belt. Nor will you hear much about how these industrial ruins made us feel. There is obviously some of this, but we are more interested in how others view sweeping economic changes. We approach the landscape and memory of deindustrialization from many different vantage points, urban exploration being one.

Yet the discourse of urban exploration is not monolithic. Urban explorers are drawn to abandoned industrial buildings for any number of reasons. Some seek out the transgressive thrill of going places where they are not supposed to go. Others are just curious. No matter what their individual motivation, the exploration narratives posted on urban explorer websites provide a valuable window into how some white, middle class North Americans in their teens and twenties viewed deindustrialization at the millennium. Most exploration narratives follow a familiar script. They tell the story of the explorer's journey to an unfamiliar place that feels like another world or another time. Like tourists in search of the pleasures of the imagination, urban explorers value the intensity of emotion and sensation that these abandoned sites afford them. Their sense of awe can frequently be heard in their hushed tones, and their attention to the aesthetics of deindustrialization. For some, industrial ruins are monuments to a vanished way of life – less a lament than a reminder. For most, these abandoned buildings are little more than post-industrial playgrounds. Nostalgia takes a back seat to the thrill of transgression.

CHAPTER 3

FROM CRADLE TO GRAVE

The Politics of Memory in Youngstown, Ohio[1]

In many ways, Youngtown's story is America's story.
– Sherry Lee Linkon and John Russo, *Steeltown USA*

Youngstown has become a symbol of how unilateral
corporate decision-making can lay waste a community...
but also a story of a new beginning, "Shout Youngstown."
– Staughton Lynd, *Living Inside Our Hope*

YOUNGSTOWN, A STEEL TOWN OF 150,000 SITUATED IN THE
Mahoning River Valley in Northeastern Ohio, has won the dubious distinction of being the Rust Belt city par excellence. In recent years, it has been the subject of a half a dozen monographs, numerous scholarly articles, a couple of film documentaries, extensive newspaper and television commentary, and even a song by Bruce Springsteen. The broad outline of the Youngstown story is now familiar to many living outside the "steel valley." The beginning of the end came on September 19, 1977, a date known locally as "Black Monday," when the Lykes Corporation closed the massive Campbell Works. As many as five thousand steelworkers lost their jobs. This blow was followed by four other major mill closings over the next eight years.

The story would have ended there, as it had in so many other towns and cities, had Youngstown residents not resisted the mill's closure. Religious leaders, political radicals, and community activists joined together in the "Ecumenical Coalition to Save the Mahoning Valley." Their energetic efforts to reopen the Campbell works under community ownership kept Youngstown in the national spotlight for two more years. At first, the movement met with some success. It succeeded, for example, in convincing the U.S. Department of Housing and Urban Development to fund a feasibility study written by Gar Alperovitz, a liberal economist affiliated with the National Center for Economic Alternatives, in Washington, DC. Yet the administration of President Jimmy Carter balked at the high price tag to modernize and reopen the mill – $394 million in federal loan guarantees as well as a $15 million grant.[2] In the end, appeals to community resonated in the Steel Valley but failed to sway the Carter administration. The Campbell works stayed closed.

Disillusioned by the experience, Youngstown community activists and steelworkers elected to change their tactics when other mill closures were announced in 1979 and 1980. The head offices of U.S. Steel in Pittsburgh and Youngstown were briefly occupied, and Staughton Lynd, a historian turned lawyer, brought the company to court. Some good came out of the fight. For the first time, the idea of using eminent domain as a tool to force companies to sell closed mills and factories began to be seriously discussed. Companies that refused to sell closed plants would now face the prospect of local government seizing industrial property for a public purpose: jobs.[3] Until then, eminent domain powers had been regularly used by municipalities wanting to expropriate residential property for the public good, usually for slum clearances and highway extensions. Though ultimately unsuccessful, Youngstown's refusal to die was seen as something new. Youngstown was headline news, putting the city at the centre of the deindustrialization debate in the United States.

The theoretical insights offered by historian Daniel James and geographer Doreen Massey are useful in exploring the memory and meaning of deindustrialization in and about Youngstown. Just as individuals make sense of their lives through the stories they tell – what Daniel James calls the "foundational myths of the self"[4] – so, too, do communities. James notes that human communities "adopt narratives that inculcate and confirm their integrity and coherence over time."[5] Sherry Lee Linkon and John Russo call Youngstown's foundational myth its "constitutive narrative." Until the mills closed, this narrative told of the making of the "steel valley," the "cradle of steel": the industrial pioneers who built the valley's first iron forge, the shift to steelmaking, the hard and dirty work, the strikes, ethnic pride, and home ownership.[6] Yet the local uniqueness of any place, as Doreen Massey has shown, is a "product of wider contacts; the local is always already a product, in part, of 'global' forces" or "the world beyond the place itself."[7] Hence, the politics of remembering, like the constitutive narrative itself, were a product of local social relations *and* larger social, economic, political, and cultural forces. We need to explore the interaction between the local and the trans-local, the stories of loss and resistance, meaning and memory.

How, then, have Youngstown residents come to terms with deindustrialization? Do their memories of the mill closings correspond to the Youngstown story being told by popular artists based outside the region? What are the similarities and differences between the two? Why do people prefer one story over another? Who wants whom to remember what, and why? In pursuing these questions, we will turn to Dale Maharidge and Michael Williamson's haunting photo-essay *Journey to Nowhere*; Bruce Springsteen's moving ballad "youngstown"; the commemorative narratives written by local journalists on successive anniversaries of Black Monday; the erection of two local monuments to steel; the establishment of a steel museum; and finally, to Linkon and Russo's book, *Steeltown USA: Work and Memory in Youngstown.* We will approach each one as a site of memory.[8] Youngstown has been envisioned, sung, commemorated, memorialized, and otherwise remembered at the local, regional, national, and transnational scales. In looking at the interaction between these vantage points, we hope to better understand how the "Youngstown story" came to be told and why. The meaning of deindustrialization cannot be found in "local culture" alone. Though there have been several "Youngstown stories" in circulation over time and space, the story of community resistance is not the one that has prevailed. For most, the Youngstown story is about the hardship and hurt caused by deindustrialization, and by the subsequent loss of community.

ENVISIONING YOUNGSTOWN

Most North Americans "get" their history from popular culture; and very little of it directly from professional historians. To illustrate this point, consider for a moment how popular artists have influenced our understanding of the Great Depression and the Dust Bowl in the United States. The mythical flight of John Steinbeck's Joad family from drought and mechanization is familiar to us all. Stripped of their land, the Joads piled on to a truck and headed west to the promised land of California; but once there, they found more heartbreak than promise. Shortly after Steinbeck's novel *The Grapes of Wrath* became a best-seller in 1939, 20th Century Fox studios rushed a film adaptation of the novel into production, and folksinger Woody Guthrie recorded the song "Tom Joad" on his 1940 album *Dust Bowl Ballads.*[9] The Joad family's saga had become America's. Today, few would deny that the work of these artists has profoundly shaped how we look back on those hard times. It therefore stands to reason that future generations will likewise understand deindustrialization in the 1970s and 1980s through the prism of popular culture.

The most significant effort to envision deindustrializing Youngstown came from two west coast reporters, Dale Maharidge and Michael Williamson. Their *Journey to Nowhere* began when their city editor at the *Sacramento Bee* – "a hobo of sorts himself" – asked them to investigate reports of formerly blue-collar, "middle class" people riding the rails.[10] It was the early 1980s and North America was in the worst economic downturn since the Great Depression. The two young reporters, both in their early twenties, set out to understand "what causes formerly middle class people to wind up living on the street."[11] Williamson, now a staff photographer for the *Washington Post*, later recalled that the "idea was not just to show homeless people in shelters and soup lines, but to answer as journalists where they came from. And eventually we found we had so much material, it screamed to be a book."[12] There is no doubt that the resulting story of loss and displacement is an immensely powerful one.

Except for their decision to begin their journey in Youngstown, Ohio, Maharidge and Williamson claimed to have had "no specific plans other than to head aimlessly west, as do many of the jobless."[13] Yet *Journey to Nowhere* strikes a familiar chord, as they travelled down the same road taken by Steinbeck, Ford, and Guthrie a half century earlier. By following in those footsteps, Maharidge and Williamson hoped to provoke compassion, and concern to change society and rekindle the New Deal idealism of the 1930s:

> Our model for chronicling the contemporary hard times was the Great Depression, from stories told by our elders and from what we'd read. In the 1930s, despite conservative undercurrents, programs were created – and citizens found compassion – to change society. A half century later our goal was to be among those educating the public about the disenfranchised. We believed Americans wouldn't tolerate growing class divisions – if only they knew what was going on.[14]

Theirs was clearly not a journey to nowhere. Rather, in adopting the plot structure of *The Grapes of Wrath*, these particular travellers had a map and a reason for being on the road. It is a story with a clear beginning, middle, and end.[15]

The authors justified their decision to begin their three-month journey in Youngstown, Ohio, by claiming that the city "typifies the agony of dozens of Midwestern cities." The resulting photographs of demolished steel mills reveal the enormity of the catastrophe that befell the region. Joe Marshall and his twenty-nine year-old son, Joe Junior, were photographed surveying the rubble of what was once the Ohio Works: "They point. They look. They remember." The Marshalls were shown to have deep roots in the Steel Valley, making their displacement all the more devastating. A series of photographs taken inside the closed Brier Hill mill – resembling those eerie underwater photographs taken inside sunken vessels – revealed a place suspended in time: tools littered the floor; iron ladles were scattered about; and goggles and shoes lay still where they were left on the final day.

What are the politics of *Journey to Nowhere*? Who or what sank these mills? Maharidge and Williamson suggest that workers blamed industrialists, and industrialists blamed the workers. They all blamed imports. But, the authors add knowingly, "much larger forces" were at work.[16] What were these mysterious forces that escaped the attention of Youngstown steelworkers and mill owners? According to them, it was nothing more than a "changing world." America, it seems, had entered an "age of uncertainty" that was to be "ruled by computers and high technology." Apparently, there was nobody to blame for deindustrialization. It just happened.

This ambiguous message is reflected in their treatment of the story of resistance in Youngstown. For example, Williamson photographed an empty meeting room where a podium stood naked beside a row of chairs arranged neatly behind a table. A banner on the wall behind read: "Family of USWA 1375 Solidarity Works." Yet the point of the photograph seems to be quite the opposite. We are told that few "rust bowl" towns had escaped deindustrialization and that "no one seemed to have an answer. So the town dies." Herein lies the fundamental contradiction in *Journey to Nowhere*. In their effort to spark the same kind of "progressive populist outrage" that was "seen in the 1930s," Maharidge and Williamson imply that solidarity, in fact, does not work. The story of loss and victimization, key to generating middle class compassion for displaced workers, had, oddly, produced a political message that implies that resistance to plant shutdowns was futile.

The book's middle and end are largely indistinguishable from the journey that the Joad family "made" some time ago except that, in these postmodern times, it was the authors themselves who made it. In a chapter entitled "Yankees in the Promised Land," they relate the stigma attached to being a Yankee in Houston, Texas. When they arrived in the southwest in a beat-up car with Ohio licence plates, they were met with public hostility and police repression. In their words, they were treated like "some northern industrial refugees." From Houston, the duo headed down Route 66 to the farming areas of Southern California – the literal end of the narrative road. Throughout their journey, the authors cast the emerging underclass in the role of Tom Joad: a "strong breed" of "survivors" who could be hailed as "unchristened heroes." In inviting the reader to identify, does Maharidge and Williamson's journey of loss and victimization provide the basis for their desired collective action?

SINGING YOUNGSTOWN

While Maharidge and Williamson memorialized the Youngstown story in photographs and words, Bruce Springsteen remembered it in his music. Born in Freehold, New Jersey, in 1949, to a bus-driving father and a mother who worked as a legal secretary, Springsteen has become one of the most popular musicians of his generation. No other North American musician is as closely identified with the common man.[17] He achieved this connection through his use of class-conscious lyrics, as well as his ability to trigger an emotional response in his listeners. "You can't tell people what to think," he once explained. "You can show them something by saying, 'Put these shoes on, walk in these shoes.' People then recognize themselves in those characters whose lives on the surface seem to have no relation to theirs."[18] Shared feelings, rather than thought, provided the basis for solidarity and identification.[19]

The appearance of *the ghost of tom joad* in 1995 was no exception. The album owes much to Woody Guthrie's *Dust Bowl Ballads* (1940) for its subject matter (the dispossessed), its somber tone, its politics, its title, and its ballad "the ghost of tom joad." Every song on the album invites identification with the downtrodden and the destitute. Springsteen's recurring message was that the new times were just as hard as the old.

Both Guthrie and Springsteen used popular culture to address social injustices in the United States.[20] Musicologist Bryan Garman has shown that these influences came together in the "hurt song," which "summon[ed] a history of pain and suffering to consciousness, reopen[ed] the wounds that fester beneath our layers of ideological gauze, and offer[ed] the hope of a healing process based on collective action and communal relationships."[21]

In personalizing their politics, these artists hoped to forge a unity of interest between their listeners and their subjects.

Bruce Springsteen wrote his song "youngstown" almost by chance when *the ghost of tom joad* was nearing completion in 1995. As he tells it, one sleepless night he pulled *Journey to Nowhere* down from his living room shelf and read it from cover to cover.[22] In writing and performing "youngstown," Springsteen drew heavily from *Journey to Nowhere* for inspiration and stories. Like the book, the song's words linger on the sense of loss felt by displaced Youngstown steelworkers. The first verse establishes the long tradition of steelmaking in the Mahoning Valley and how it produced the cannonballs that "helped the Union win the war."[23] The second and third verses shift the focus to the steelworkers themselves. Blame is placed on "them big boys" who did "what Hitler couldn't do." This sentiment comes almost directly from Joe Marshall Senior as quoted in *Journey to Nowhere*. Verse four then projects the Youngstown story onto the entire Rust Belt where "the story's always the same." It is here that outrage creeps into Springsteen's lyrics:

> Now sir you tell me the world's changed
> Once I made you rich enough
> Rich enough to forget my name.[24]

In this, Springsteen went far beyond Maharidge and Williamson's "changing world." The political message that he delivered was far less ambiguous, even if the emphasis on loss and victimization remained the same. In the song's final verse, Springsteen lamented the loss of community, and lost masculine pride in hard manual labour. The spirit behind this song is deeply pessimistic and it ends in resignation and bitterness.[25]

Just how much the Youngstown story had changed since Black Monday can be seen by comparing Springsteen's lyrics with those of an earlier song by Tom Hunter, a little-known San Francisco singer-songwriter. Hunter wrote "Back to Work in Youngstown" in 1978, inspired by the local struggle to reopen the steel mill. Each of the four verses deals with an element of the local economic situation. As Hunter noted: "When I'm performing the song in coffee houses or church meetings I can see the indignation rise in people as I sing the first verse. It's good to know you can affect people that way with your music."[26] Hunter begins with Black Monday and identifies the chief villain: the Lykes Corporation (the parent company of Sheet and Tube). But the song is really about the community's defiant reaction to this crisis, as revealed by Hunter's account of the religious response.[27] He goes on to claim that Youngstown represents the "same old story" of conglomerates and communities in conflict, and ends the song with the defiant shouts of "Save our valley!" that could be heard "all around town." The song became an anthem of sorts for the Ecumenical Coalition, sung repeatedly at meetings and public rallies.

From today's vantage point, these two songs appear so dissimilar that it is hard to believe that Springsteen and Hunter were singing about the same place. Nowhere are these differences in tone and content as clearly expressed as in each song's refrain:

We're going back to work in Youngstown,
We're going back to work today,
We're going back to work in Youngstown,
And we're doing it in our own way.
    (Tom Hunter, "Back to Work in Youngstown," 1978)

Here in Youngstown
Here in Youngstown
My sweet Jenny I'm sinkin'd down
Here darlin' in Youngstown.
    (Bruce Springsteen, "youngstown," 1995)

Whereas the first refrain communicated a story of community resistance predicated on hope, activism, autonomy, and defiance, the second shifted attention to the disillusionment and stagnation that followed the closure.

What accounted for this changing emphasis? Obviously, the stories of resistance and of loss were separated by seventeen years of hard times. Hunter sang "Back to Work in Youngstown" at the outset of the crisis when local activists believed they could reopen the plant under community ownership. By contrast, Springsteen returned to a deindustrialized valley where resistance had failed. It was evoked by a reporter in 1995:

Wander along the east bank of the Mahoning River, and you will see the remains of a lost civilization. Strange, silent hulks of steel litter the land, some still defiantly thrusting their corroded arms toward the sky.... This lost culture has just been unearthed by an archaeologist named Bruce Springsteen.[28]

The transformation of the event into a symbol has erased many of its details; for outsiders Youngstown is arguably no longer a clear and vital memory, but a vague idea forever stuck in time.

After the release of Bruce Springsteen's *the ghost of tom joad*, and critical acclaim for "youngstown," *Journey to Nowhere* was reprinted with a new introduction written by Springsteen, and the inclusion of the lyrics of three songs from the album: "youngstown," "the new timer," and "the ghost of tom joad." While the first two songs were directly inspired by Maharidge and Williamson, the inclusion of the third provides yet another indication of the profound influence of dust-bowl imagery. The compression of time and space in the collective memory of economic displacement, combined with the blurring of boundaries between fiction and non-fiction, contributed to the emergence of this master narrative. The lingering memory of the Great Depression has clearly provided a template for popular storytellers who cast displaced industrial workers as the dust-bowl refugees of the 1980s. This narrative has been invoked so often in relation to industrial decline that displaced "Okie" farmers and "Yankee" industrial workers have become fused in popular imagination. Their version of the Youngstown story was therefore derived, in large part, from a fictional account of the Joad family written in 1939. It is fitting then that Dale Maharidge has called Springsteen a musical Steinbeck, adding that it was "amazing how accurately he's captured in those few words the whole spirit of Youngstown, both the pride and the hurt."[29]

COMMEMORATING YOUNGSTOWN

How then do Youngstown area residents remember the mill closings? Can the "whole spirit of Youngstown" be contained in feelings of pride and hurt? Has the story of resistance been lost? Few dates hold as much meaning to Youngstown residents as does September 19, 1977: Black Monday. My first research trip to the Mahoning Valley happened to coincide with the twentieth anniversary of the closing of the Campbell Works. For the better part of a week, much of the front page of the local newspaper, the Youngstown *Vindicator,* explored the meanings and consequences of Black Monday:

Steel used to be synonymous with Youngstown and most of the Mahoning Valley, but 20 years after the fall of the steel industry here, steel production is dramatically less visible. In the absence of the pouring smokestacks and brightly burning furnaces that once gave life to the Valley, recovery has been slow from Black Monday – September 19, 1977 – the day that set off the collapse of Youngstown steel.[30]

It was for this reason that Black Monday was widely regarded as the darkest day in Youngstown history.[31] It marked the beginning of the end.

At first, the memory of Black Monday was bound up with the continuing efforts to reopen the Campbell Works.[32] The first anniversary of Black Monday was accordingly a day of "as much protest as it was ritual." A prayer service at Gate 14 of the Campbell Works, organized by the Ecumenical Coalition, was followed by a noon-hour rally in the city's downtown.[33] A torch was lit as a symbol of hope for the thousands of steelworkers put out of work. Those attending the prayer service heard the Reverend C. Edward Weisheimer say that this torch was a "light to illuminate the past and show the way to the future."[34] The darkness that descended on the Steel Valley that Monday in September, enveloped his speech:

Soon the fires of the furnaces went out. A shadow was cast over the community threatening the welfare of families, schools and economic stability.... Yet, the light did not go out in the hearts and souls of people. The light of faith in the Mahoning Valley and the determination to overcome the threat has blazed a new consciousness in the community.

Hope rather than despair typified this first commemoration.

The continued optimism of local residents in 1979 was recorded in the *Vindicator*'s special four-part series of articles. The weeks and months following Black Monday, readers were told, "bristled with predictions, all of them dark, for the Mahoning Valley."[35] However, the worst of these fears did not materialize. While subsequent instalments examined the difficulties faced by laid-off steelworkers, readers were told of the promising revitalization efforts already underway in Youngstown. Even so, the source of this promise was no longer found in the Ecumenical Coalition.[36] As this early effort faded into the background, other development projects emerged.

Three years later this optimism had vanished altogether. The closing of three more mills, and the spectacular failure of most of the diversification schemes, had cast a pall over the valley. Thus, when the *Vindicator* ran another four-part retrospective – "Black Monday: Five Years Later" – that dark day in September now seemed to mark the end of the area's steelmaking era:

> The blast furnaces at the former Youngstown Sheet & Tube Co's Campbell Works have been cooling for five years. Those at Sheet & Tube's Brier Hill Works and US Steel Corp's Ohio Works have been dismantled. Except in a few cases, the old Steel Valley mills are shut down – no matter who owns them. It's easy these days to believe that the steel era here is really gone.[37]

In part one of this collaborative effort, the newspaper wondered how an industry so much a part of the history of one community could "simply cease to be or move away?" This was followed by a series of articles that explored the meaning of the cultural and economic destruction of the area: "Black Monday. The day that nullified the past, upset the present and forever changed the future of the Mahoning Valley."[38] A new sense of inevitability now infused the memories of mill closings, as they were said to have "fallen like metal-clad dominoes."[39] Indeed, a new Youngstown story of falling population, rising crime, and burgeoning welfare rolls was also taking hold.

Even though a glimmer of hope remained in the various redevelopment initiatives underway in 1982, the Steel Valley's history gave ample reason to doubt.[40] To make its point, the *Vindicator* pointed to the failed efforts of the Ecumenical Coalition: be it "noble experiment" or "socialistic delusion." These comments revealed how the Coalition's attempt to reopen the Campbell Works was coming under increasing public criticism in the early 1980s. An oral history project conducted at this time by Youngstown State University confirmed this falling-out. Youngstown Mayor Phillip Richley, for example, saw the Coalition's campaign as an "exercise in futility" that did not make "a great deal of business sense."[41] Even though the interviewer appeared to agree with this assessment, public criticism of the Ecumenical Coalition was more a whisper than a shout.

The tenth anniversary of Black Monday in 1987, one mill closing later, saw one hundred area residents gather in intermittent rain at Gate 14, the site of the 1978 prayer service, to remember the mill's closing.[42] In sharp contrast to that earlier gathering, it had an "air of a memorial service." It was reported that some in attendance "echoed old, bitter themes, blaming corporate greed for betraying a community." Others called on those gathered to look to the future. Campbell Mayor James J. Vargo was one of those who wanted to put the past behind him: "You've got to sell the future; you can't sell the past. The past belongs to the past. Let's build the buildings of the 21st century here and tear these mills down." Given the decade of uncertainty and job loss that followed Black Monday, Vargo's appeal is easily understood. According to another observer, the Campbell Works' black smokestacks "still point skyward from the floor of the Mahoning Valley, like giant spikes driven into the heart of a community."[43]

While the empty mill was a visible reminder of what was lost, far less clear was the heightened criticism of the community's attempts to keep it open. Once a strong supporter of the Ecumenical Coalition, the *Vindicator* now featured the views of critics. Thomas Cleary, for example, a former Youngstown Sheet and Tube vice-president, and the only member of the Board of Directors to oppose the closing, blamed the coalition's failure on "out-of-towners" caught up in social movements. Similarly, another company manager cited in retrospect said the religious leaders meant well, but they raised "false hopes and diverted attention" from more serious projects. The discrediting of the Ecumenical Coalition was all but complete by the twentieth anniversary of Black Monday. The story of resistance persisted, but its underlying message had shifted from one of defiance to one of failure.

MEMORIALIZING YOUNGSTOWN

The changing Youngstown story could be seen in other ways. Most people living in deindustrialized communities such as Youngstown look back fondly to a time when industry was humming. Others look back in anger and resentment. Public memory – defined by historian John Bodnar as a "body of beliefs and ideas about the past that help a public or society understand both its past, present, and by implication, its future" – is contested between advocates of different versions of the past.[44] How the loss of industry is memorialized is therefore subject to challenge and change. Nowhere was this as true as in Youngstown, Ohio.

The residents of the Youngstown area celebrated their nation's bicentennial in 1976, with a time capsule to be reopened a century later. Inside this capsule – an ingot mould donated by Youngstown Sheet and Tube – the town's citizens left an assortment of artifacts to represent the prosperity and pride of their blue-collar community.[45] In keeping with the oft-repeated story of how the Valley came to be settled, the memorial was situated near the site of the Hopewell Furnace, built in 1806 by Daniel and James Heaton, the first iron furnace west of the Allegheny Mountains.[46] Its archaeological remains have long been the focus of preservation efforts. "This humble birthplace," claimed the president of the local historical society, "has touched the lives of all residents of Mahoning County."[47] It was only natural, then, that the new monument/time capsule should be located nearby and that it should be given the name "Hopewell."

Nobody in attendance that day could have realized how soon, and how dramatically, life in the valley was about to change. Like other deindustrialized areas, the Mahoning Valley has largely failed to make the transition into the new post-industrial economy. Just one year after the nation's bicentennial, the Hopewell Memorial – like the valley it commemorated – had fallen on hard times. The grass lawn was left unmowed and the flagpole stood empty. There was already a dusting of rust around the capsule seal. Even the optimistic words inscribed on the capsule's plaque – "steel has provided the means for growth and prosperity in this Steel Valley community for many of our nation's 200 years…" – now rang hollow.[48] Hope had turned to despair.

The other major tribute to the steelmaking heritage of the Mahoning Valley took the form of a sculpture, christened "The Steelmakers." The idea for this public monument also originated before Black Monday, when the Youngstown Area Arts Council commissioned an internationally known artist. George Segal's tribute to the heritage and working spirit of Youngstown took the form of a sculpture depicting two steelworkers testing the content of a "heat" of steel in an open-hearth furnace.[49] Segal modelled the steelworkers after two real-life Youngstown residents – Peter Knobly Junior and Wayman Paramore – and incorporated parts of an open-hearth furnace salvaged from the now closed Campbell Works.[50] Commenting on the new sculpture, Wayman Paramore said, "I'm not representing me, I'm representing all the men who came into steel and worked in steel, past, present, and future." But, like many of these men, Paramore had lost his job. Four area mills had closed during the three years it took Segal to complete his piece.

As if to confirm the arrival of the post-steel era, this bronze sculpture erected in front of Higbees Department Store in downtown Youngstown as a "fresh new symbol" of the area's steelmaking past, proved to many, instead, to be an unwelcome reminder. At a time when the area was staggering from mill closings, there were grumblings that the $150,000 could have been better spent.[51] When one of the two life-size figures was uprooted after only four months on the job, and placed on the curbside as if hitchhiking out of town, it was not replanted for another eight months. On account of constant acts of vandalism, the city eventually decided to put the two bronze ironworkers in store for safekeeping. The Steel Valley without steel had become a "cruel irony."[52]

For Dr. Louis Zona, Director of the Butler Institute of American Art, the piece's ill-treatment could be explained by the unfortunate clash between the sculpture's creation and the closing of the mills. "It was the timing," he said. "It was going to be a tribute to the steel industry and it wound up being a memorial. It became a symbol of all that was negative in terms of what the steel industry had supposedly done to us."[53] And yet Zona was baffled by the antipathy the sculpture provoked, asking, "What is there to dislike about two men captured doing what they did to make an honest living?" Since 1991, the steelworker monument has enjoyed a new life in its location outside the Youngstown Historical Center of Industry and Labor, where there are few passing residents to disturb it.

EXHIBITING YOUNGSTOWN

The pride and hurt felt by Youngstown residents have also been on display inside the town's steel museum. It is no coincidence that the campaign to open the Youngstown Historical Center of Industry and Labor began shortly after Black Monday. It came to fruition fifteen years later, in 1992. As a branch museum of the Ohio Historical Society, Youngstown's steel museum, as it is known locally, had to negotiate local and national assumptions about the history of the Mahoning Valley.[54]

The development of this museum reveals much about Youngstown in the years following Black Monday. As mills began to close, some area residents hoped to salvage something from the wreckage. Much of this attention was focused initially on the Jeannette blast furnace, a part of the Brier Hill works built in 1917. Its owner suggested in 1979 that part of the soon-to-be-closed plant might be used as a museum. State Senator Harry Meshel, a key proponent of a steel museum, was aware that steelworkers wanted jobs and not a mausoleum. As a result, he declared that a steel museum at the site was only feasible if the efforts to save the mill failed.[55] To avoid any misunderstanding, Meshel and the Ohio Historical Society met with the Ecumenical Coalition and the United Steelworkers union. Once the plant closed in December 1979, local efforts to preserve the Jeannette blast furnace intensified.[56] These attempts ultimately failed, in part because of the high cost of renovation (including asbestos cleanup), and because there was no groundswell of public support for the project. Even so, many lamented the day in January 1997 when the "Jenny" blast furnace was finally demolished.

Instead of a "working" steel museum, Meshel and the Ohio Historical Society proposed a purpose-built museum situated in a non-industrial area of the city, between the depressed commercial downtown and the campus of Youngstown State University. Completed in 1989, the $4.2 million museum building, designed by famed architect Michael Graves, received international attention. The building's award-winning design incorporated various elements of classic mill and factory architecture, making liberal use of brick materials, and incorporating a smokestack-type structure.[57] Readers of *Progressive Architecture* were told that Graves "looked beyond the city's recently built mills to 19th century factories that incorporated residential elements. Likewise, his building is synthetic, a landmark with references to human habitation and the industrial process."[58] The architecture of the museum building therefore represented a universalized image of industry.

It very nearly came to symbolize something altogether different. Troubling financial problems dogged the early development of the steel museum, preventing the installation of a permanent exhibit until 1992, three years after the building was completed. An October 1989 article in the national newsmagazine *Newsweek*, entitled "The (Empty) Steel Museum," dubbed it a "stillborn monument to a dying industry."[59] The steel museum was, *Newsweek* added, "just what the rust belt needs: another empty steel plant."[60] Eventually, however, funds were found and the museum's permanent exhibit opened to the public.

The architectural design of the museum reflected the Ohio Historical Society's original intention to tell the tale of the rise and fall of the industrial heartland.[61] Far from being only a steel museum, it would tell the stories of Ohio's auto, textile, aluminum, and steel industries.[62] This broad perspective taken by the state agency ran counter to the desire of some local residents to pay special tribute to the demolished Steel Valley. Donna DeBlasio, the society's local co-ordinator, for example, was quoted in the *Vindicator* as saying that the project would allow young people to gain first-hand experience with steelmaking.[63] A 1986 editorial echoed this hope:

> As for the museum itself, its role upon opening... unfortunately, will not be celebrating a vital, thriving steel industry, which gave the Mahoning Valley life, vitality and character for many decades. No, because of the industry's demise, the museum's importance will come in perpetuating for future generations a knowledge of steelmaking, its equipment and history, and particularly in honouring the memory of the men and women whose sweat, skill and muscle made the steel and developed the valley. Besides enriching the city's architecture, the museum will define an era that's seared in the minds and hearts of many who want their descendants to know and appreciate their roots. By harbouring our history and artifacts, the building can add to the lives of us all.[64]

The wish to keep the area's steelmaking past alive, if only in a museum setting, thus animated many local supporters of the museum project. Yet the geographic and thematic scope of the exhibit remained an open question until April 1990, when the exhibition floor plan revealed that the focus would be on Youngstown.[65]

The permanent exhibit's script – "the blueprint for what the museum will depict through artifacts, models, graphics and language" – tells the stories of steelworkers, their families, and a "rust belt" community, through a variety of techniques, including oral history.[66] That this story would make room for the mill closings was, however, not confirmed until three months later in July 1990. For Donna DeBlasio, the deindustrialization of the Steel Valley had to be dealt with. Failure to do so, she cautioned, would be "like talking about the Civil War and not talking about slavery. It's ugly, but it did happen."[67] The curatorial team nonetheless hoped to avoid "passing judgement" on the mill closings.[68]

In the completed exhibit, "By the Sweat of Their Brow: Forging the Steel Valley," visitors to the steel museum are taken through a circular space composed of five sections, "each of which reconstructs a physical environment from industrial Youngstown, from the interior of a 1920s worker dwelling to a contemporary steel-plant gate house."[69] The exhibit ends in a small, darkened room where visitors are confronted by the falling blast furnaces in a massive black and white photomural covering two walls.[70] In this imaginative re-enactment, visitors are separated from the dramatic image by a barbed wire fence, recreating the sense of helplessness felt by local residents forced to watch their own unmaking.[71]

The story of loss and victimization represented in these falling blast furnaces dominates the room. However, if visitors turn their backs on the fence and the image on the walls they find a small television monitor showing excerpts from "Shout Youngstown," a 1983 documentary about the town's defiant response to mill closures. The video was being played without audio during my first two visits (and at an almost inaudible level on my third), but this may have been intentionally ironic. A small glass cabinet located in the middle of the room contains a "Save Our Valley" bumper sticker, a protest button, and a brief reminder that in response to the mill closings, "community religious leaders organized the Mahoning Valley Ecumenical Coalition. The coalition's efforts to reopen the plant were unsuccessful." The Black Monday wall panel, situated beside the video monitor, helps visitors to make sense of industrial decline. After noting the shock felt by everyone in the valley, the panel's text concludes that:

> In the years that followed, the American steel industry became less centralized and many individual plants were downsized. Large integrated mills that had employed thousands were replaced by mini-mills that employed hundreds. The Mahoning Valley was transformed, too, into a less industrial region.[72]

But the exhibit fails to hold anyone responsible for the mill closings.[73]

The local reaction to the exhibit has been decidedly mixed. Museum officials blamed low attendance figures on the lingering anger of many Youngstown residents towards the steel companies.[74] Contrary to expectations, local residents were reluctant to deal with these painful memories. Even so, the steel museum's exhibit has struck a chord with some visitors. One local commentator who moved to the Youngstown area in the late 1980s admitted that he once felt like a "late arrival at a theatre who shows up only to find the performance is over." The permanent exhibition allowed him to better understand what his friends and neighbours had lived through. For him, the museum was nothing less than "our Holocaust Memorial":

> A large part of it evokes horror and shock and loss that the
> Valley must have felt beginning in 1977.... Watching those blast
> furnaces get torn down must have been like staring in disbelief
> as someone bursts into the living room, carts off all the furni-
> ture and then leaves you, stunned and helpless and alone, in
> the middle of the floor. You wonder how you can get on with life
> after experiencing such devastation. The museum doesn't tell
> us how to cope and move on. It's strictly a look back – and not in
> anger at the unfairness of life, nor with misty-eyed backpatting
> that glosses over the facts. The exhibit is built – solid as Valley
> steel – out of a simple desire for the truth, tempered with a deep
> sense of justifiable pride in the way we were and the durable
> things we made.[75]

How then does the steel museum's permanent exhibit compare with the Youngstown story being told by popular artists based outside the region? Visitors to the steel museum are given mixed messages. While the image of the falling blast furnaces of the Ohio Works shares much in common with the Youngstown story told by Springsteen, and Maharidge and Williamson, the local emphasis on Black Monday and local resistance to the closings persists on the margins of the exhibit. But rather than an explanation, the exhibit offers visitors a "look back" at the pain and loss felt by displaced industrial workers.

ROMANTICIZING COMMUNITY

In 2002, twenty-five years after "Black Monday," Linkon and Russo published their highly original and thought-provoking book, *Steeltown USA: Work and Memory in Youngstown*. Directors of the innovative Working Class Studies program at Youngstown State University, they examine the conflict over representation of Youngstown's steelmaking past and its deindustrialized present. The "local culture" – the physical landscape, written words, visual images, sculptures, film, song, and oral history interviews – is read for what it tells us about what people remember and why. The focus is therefore on the "before" and the "after" – as there is remarkably little included on the momentous years between 1977 and 1985. With this, the shift from the politics of mill closings, to the cultural meaning of deindustrialization in their aftermath, is complete.

Place and memory are central to Linkon and Russo's analysis. They contend that place is integral to individual and civic identity-construction. Landscapes are never static, but are constantly changing. The authors effectively mine this changing landscape for meaning. Steelmaking was much more than a source of wages and work. It represented an "important element of community life, a source of identity and solidarity, an activity that brought pride and fulfillment to individuals and the community."[76] Indeed, Youngstown's rise as a steel town "can be seen as the community's 'constitutive narrative,' the story that provided a unifying image of the meaning of this place for most of the twentieth century."[77] At the same time, the authors are careful not to allow this unifying tale to mask deep social divisions, both before and after the mill closings.

The mill closings shattered Youngstown's self-confident image of itself. Linkon and Russo examine the production of an image of Youngstown as a place of loss and failure. The struggle pitted those who contended that Youngstown's steelmaking past had to be forgotten before people could look to the future, against those who argued that Youngtown's industrial past had to be acknowledged and accepted before people could move on. These two conflicting visions resulted in a series of public clashes, including a failed attempt to preserve the Jeanette blast furnace from demolition. Until residents take pride in their past, Linkon and Russo suggest, Youngstown has no future. "Community lost" provides the narrative arc.[78]

Central to the discussion of memory in *Steeltown USA* is the communitarianism of Robert N. Bellah. In *Habits of the Heart: Individualism and Commitment in American Life*, Bellah argued that communities have a history and that they are constituted by their past.[79] For Linkon and Russo, then, a "real community" is a "community of memory; one that does not forget its past."[80] Communities of memory thus "continually retell their stories, and this process creates a sense of shared history and identity, out of which develop vision and hope for the future." In effect, the past provides a context of meaning for the present. Memory is thus presented as a significant arena of conflict in post-industrial Youngstown.

The "community of memory" idea is a promising one. But must community be local? There is no reason to assume that the community of memory formed around the steel mill closures in Youngstown was confined to place. Unlike closings elsewhere, Youngstown's agony, as well as its resistance, was splashed onto the front pages of newspapers around the world. That a large number of "outsiders" have made their pilgrimage to Youngstown is indicative of a circle of memory wider than the authors appear willing to consider. There is a tendency, instead, to draw a line between a local "us" and a non-resident "them." Despite the authors' recognition of a plurality of sometimes conflicting viewpoints in Youngstown, and the book's nationalizing title, there is ultimately only one community, and it is local.

Yet Linkon and Russo's tendency to romanticize community is not unusual. Ever since the publication of Barry Bluestone and Bennett Harrison's seminal *The Deindustrialization of America: Plant Closings, Community Abandonment and the Dismantling of Basic Industry* in 1982, New Left academics and activists have conceived of the struggle over deindustrialization in the United States as one pitting "capital" against "community." In this formulation of the problem, local communities do battle with global capital with predictable results. A similar localism runs through Jefferson Cowie and Joseph Heathcott's *Beyond the Ruins: The Meaning of Deindustrialization*. In fact, in their contribution to this path-breaking volume, Russo and Linkon rely again on the static notion of "the community." The threatening "others" or "outsiders," in this context, are not the faceless capitalists of old, but rather the non-resident cultural producers who give Youngstown a bad name. At times, this argument verges on urban boosterism.

This equation of community with locality is a reflection of the persistence and proliferation of the community discourse since the 1960s. Historian Christopher Lasch once noted that local associations have proliferated because leftist intellectuals and students were repulsed by the nationalism of the Vietnam War era. He termed this love affair the "cult of the little community."[81] Community is almost always invoked, as Miranda Joseph argues in *Against the Romance of Community*, as an "unequivocal good, an indicator of a high quality of life, a life of human understanding, caring, selflessness, belonging."[82] Community is likewise presented as an "organic, natural, spontaneous" occurrence that emerges in times of crisis or tragedy. The romantic discourse of community implies that community is somehow autonomous of capitalist society.

But are community and capital truly opposites? Take, for example, sociologist James Overton's findings on Newfoundland after the cod moratorium of 1992, indicating that the community discourse, in this case "community economic development," provided ideological cover for a provincial government committed to downsizing the state via privatization, spending cuts, deregulation, and social policy "reform."[83] We need to look more closely at how community is employed, and why. In the end, what Linkon and Russo offer is an investigation of the local community side of this "community versus capital" equation. Workers, their unions, the steel companies, the state, and the wider debate about deindustrialization are all peripheral to the story being told here. Consequently, *Steeltown USA* fails to explain Youngstown's place in the wider discourse about the meaning of economic change. Why does "Youngstown" – which has come to signify as much a moment in time as it does a geographic location – loom so large in the popular imagination?

CONCLUSION

While Youngstown remains a potent symbol, its meaning has changed over time. Indeed, there have been several Youngstown stories told over the last three decades. During that time, the Youngstown story has gone from one of defiance and resistance, to one of victimization and loss. There are two variants to the story now being told, depending on the vantage point. On the one hand, popular artists from outside the area have used *The Grapes of Wrath* as a template. In this version, the ghost of Tom Joad lurks everywhere. On the other hand, local commemorative activity, monument building, the permanent exhibition of the steel museum, and local scholarly production focus primarily on the disastrous effects of deindustrialization in the Mahoning Valley, while taking the time to mention that resistance failed. Despite these differences in national and local perspectives, the political strategies remain essentially the same. By making the political personal, opponents of plant closings, and local residents, hoped to make people care. The resulting story of "community lost" presents residents as innocent and passive victims in the face of dislocation.

There are many ironies at work here. Wanting to inspire collective action in the future, liberal artists, journalists, and curators have overlooked collective action in the past. Yet in stressing the loss felt by Youngstown residents, and in losing the story of resistance and defiance, these artists have unintentionally reinforced the paralyzing sense of inevitability surrounding deindustrialization. Treated like an advancing weather front, the "gales of creative destruction" have taken on a natural quality. It just happened. Yet if the changing Youngstown story is any indication, the political strategy of stressing victimization over resistance, and loss over defiance, may be politically self-defeating, as well as historically inaccurate.[84]

PART II

ORAL HISTORY AND PHOTOGRAPHY

"The Mill," Sturgeon Falls, Ontario

CHAPTER 4

OUT OF PLACE
The Plant Shutdown Stories of
Sturgeon Falls (Ontario) Paperworkers

Places as depicted on maps are caught in a moment; they are slices through time.

— Doreen Massey

SHIFTING OUR ATTENTION FROM "ARTISTS," "URBAN EXPLORERS," and "spectators," and turning towards the plant shutdown stories told by displaced workers themselves,[1] we can ask ourselves some hard questions: What does "economic change" mean to those who pay the social and economic price? How do people and place change as a consequence of a mill's closure?

Sturgeon Falls, Ontario, is a small, French-speaking mill town of six thousand, located between Sudbury and North Bay in northern Ontario. It is typical of the single-industry towns that dot the Canadian Shield.[2] The town's corrugated paper mill was the centre of local life for more than a century. The decline of the mill came gradually, with one production line after another falling silent over a thirty-year period. When the future of the mill was cast into doubt in the early 1990s, Sturgeon Falls' residents rallied to save it. With the generous support of the Ontario New Democratic Party government, and a million dollars raised locally, the mill was converted to produce 100 percent recycled paper.[3] Its future seemed secure until American-owned Weyerhaeuser purchased MacMillan Bloedel in 1999, and with it the Sturgeon Falls operation. The paper mill closed three years later. Raymond Marcoux explained the closing this way: "They got everything in a box.... Eventually they will sort out what they want and discard what they don't want."[4] The Sturgeon Falls mill and its workers were taken out of the box, bagged, and left out on the curbside for pickup.

To carry out this case study, we conducted sixty life course interviews with former mill workers and managers, their spouses, and municipal officials, between 2003 and 2006, as well as nineteen follow-up interviews.[5] The first interviews were conducted while attempts to reopen the mill were still underway. They continued as the mill was being demolished in 2004, and ended when all that remained was an empty field and a hole. At first, many people declined to be interviewed and others chose to remain anonymous. This reaction was very different from what I had experienced interviewing men and women who experienced job loss elsewhere, back in the 1970s and '80s. The open wounds left by the closure in Sturgeon Falls continued to fester and many people just did not feel like talking about it. Some said that they would not be able to contain their anger. Others were afraid that they would say something that might jeopardize the continuing efforts to reopen the mill. No one wanted to be *the one* who convinced Weyerhaeuser not to sell the mill to another owner. "People are afraid to speak up," admitted Mike Lacroix, the vice-president of Local 7135 of the Communication, Energy and Paperworkers Union of Canada (CEP).

The plant shutdown stories recorded in Sturgeon Falls reveal a deep disconnect between mill workers and their families on the one hand and the larger locality on the other. Weyerhaeuser's decision to close the mill displaced people not only to the economic periphery, but to the cultural periphery as well. In addition to revealing the sundering of local community, the plant shutdown stories expose the limits of class solidarity beyond the locality. Many Sturgeon Falls workers spoke bitterly about the "ho-hum" reaction they got from unionized Weyerhaeuser workers in other parts of Canada. In an era of continental free trade and global trade liberalization, their appeal to the nationalist sentiments of Canadians failed to stir the politicians, or the people, to action. The story of the mill's closing played itself out on the local pages of the West Nipissing *Tribune* and the *North Bay Nugget*, not the nationally circulated *National Post* or the Toronto *Globe and Mail*. In contrast to Youngstown, journalists from around the world did not stream into town. Despite the best efforts of the mill workers and their union to generate media interest, few people outside the immediate area would ever hear of Weyerhaeuser's drastic decision.

Central to my analysis is the concept of place. Place identity is, according to geographer Doreen Massey, constructed out of a particular constellation of social relations, meeting and weaving together. When the places that define us change we ourselves change. Recent studies have shown that the old tendency to cast the political struggle against deindustrialization as pitting "community" against "capital," hid a far more complex, local struggle over power and place identity. Industrial towns are not homogenous places, and longstanding class divisions often intensify in the aftermath of major mill and factory closings. If place attachment is a symbolic bond between people and place, this bond is often severed at times of sudden social or economic upheaval.[6] People then attempt to recreate these attachments by remembering and talking about the places where they have lived and worked.[7] Narration is central to this process.

Through her examination of the politics of place, Kathryn Marie Dudley has found that we tend to view the shift from industrialism to postindustrialism, in linear or evolutionary terms. Yet from a cultural standpoint this is not an orderly or a smooth transition. The closing of the Chrysler (AMC) auto assembly plant in Kenosha, Wisconsin, in 1988 "dramatized a deep cultural antagonism that has long divided the city of Kenosha." For blue-collar workers, the closing of the auto plant represented the end of an era. For white-collar workers, on the other hand, the plant closing was seen as progress. Several of Kenosha's teachers, for example, expressed their hope that their working class students would now take their schooling (and thus their teachers) more seriously.[8] The "new Kenosha" that arose from the ashes banished the town's working class to the past and put workers in their place: that "place" now being on the margins of local politics and culture.[9] Economic restructuring makes liminality a pervasive experience among displaced workers and their families.[10]

Oral sources are a particularly rich source for historians interested in memory and meaning. I have been interviewing displaced industrial workers about job loss since the mid-1990s. Long-service workers have all spoken with a great deal of emotion about their strong attachment to people, place, and product. This strong attachment to the industrial workplace and to workplace communities has struck some commentators as surprising. From a middle class perspective, mills and factories are alienating and polluting places. For some, they are nothing more than "dark satanic mills." For others, industrialism is simply passé and therefore subject to fits of nostalgia.[11] At conferences I have occasionally faced intense questioning about the "nostalgia" and "romanticism" of plant shutdown stories.

There is of course a real danger of falling into the trap of "smokestack nostalgia" – an empty lament for lost industry that assumes unity, and silences conflict and resistance. Displaced workers *do* look back on their lives before the mill's closing through gold-tinted lenses. Why not? Their lives *were* often better. If displaced workers can be forgiven a touch of nostalgia, there is a far greater danger when historians trade in nostalgia for the purpose of generating sympathy for the "victims" of economic change. Nostalgia empties out history's meaning and, ironically, serves to depoliticize the past.[12] Yet there is also a danger in middle class academic audiences assuming that the warm memories of working people are *nothing but* nostalgia. This, too, serves to depoliticize – and to effectively silence a group of already marginalized men and women. At its worst, it belittles working people's attachments to their work and their cultural worlds. For example, in their recent introduction to *Beyond the Ruins: The Meaning of Deindustrialization*, Cowie and Heathcott called on labour historians to avoid smokestack nostalgia: "We have to strip industrial work of its broad-shouldered, social-realist patina and see it for what it was: tough work that people did because it paid well and it was located in their communities."[13] To maintain that work typically meant more than this bleak happenstance, these authors seem to be saying, is to deal in "broad-shouldered, social realist" image-making. We reject this assertion.

PLACE IDENTITY IN A WORKING MAN'S TOWN

Working at the mill was once central to the economic and social life of Sturgeon Falls. The history of the mill and the history of the town were, for many, one and the same. When the first pulp mill opened in the 1890s, the town thrived. When Abitibi Pulp and Paper closed the mill from 1932 until 1947, the town was devastated. Old timers such as Ken Colquhoun recall seeing tens of thousands of logs being run down the Sturgeon River past the closed mill to Lake Nipissing, where they were taken across the lake and fed to a sawmill in Callandar.[14] The town of Sturgeon Falls only came back to life when the mill reopened after the war. In 1947, the corrugated paper line restarted. In 1951, the mill diversified into hardboard, and in 1956, into platewood. The 1950s were thus remembered as a "happy period" by many interviewees.

The mill's smokestack and water tower physically dominated the town, and loom large in the oral narratives. Several interviewees noted that they could see the mill from the windows of their homes. "Smoke has been coming out of those stacks for as long as I can remember," said Mike Lacroix.[15] It was also the best-paying job in the area and the largest employer. "If you have to earn a living," said Marc Côté, "it was the best."[16] When Denis Mac-Gregor first walked through the gate in November 1972 at age eighteen, he thought that he was set for life.[17] Sturgeon Falls was quite simply a "single industry town," Pierre Hardy stated.[18]

The mill was treated as an actor in these oral narratives. Virtually everyone referred to it simply as "the mill." When asked about entering the plant gates for the first time, several narrators spoke of the time when "the mill" called to offer them a job. "My Mother told me, 'The mill called,'" remembered Raymond Marcoux.[19] It is noteworthy that almost no one referred to the mill by its corporate name. "Weyerhaeuser" was used in its most narrow sense to describe the company – an outside entity that controlled the mill, and therefore, their destiny. In part, the distinction drawn between the "company" and the "mill" may have been due to the fact that Weyerhaeuser owned the mill for just three years before closing it down. MacMillan Bloedel, the previous owner, operated the mill for only twenty years after purchasing it from Abitibi in 1979. As a result, most of those interviewed had worked for three corporate bosses during their time in the mill. For these worker-narrators, this was their mill, not the company's.

There was a palpable sense of pride expressed in the plant shutdown stories. One salaried interviewee (who wished to remain anonymous) noted that "We were making a good product. It was well recognized in the market." Photographs taken during these celebrations and preserved in the mill newsletter attest to this pride in the mill's efficiency and profitability.[20] Almost everyone emphasized that the mill continued to make money until the end. Marcel Boudreau even referred to it as "that little gold mine on the Sturgeon River."[21]

Though the paper mill offered the highest wages in the area, it also generated social divisions along class and language lines. For much of its history, English-speaking managers recruited from outside the region ran the mill. Even though its labour force was drawn mainly from local, French-speaking Roman Catholics who made up the overwhelming majority of the area's population, English was the language of work inside the mill. There were few French-speaking mill managers until the final years of operation. The workplace community that took root here was a class community, reinforced by gender and language, and it grew up – to some extent – in opposition to the Anglo-Protestant management of the mill.

This social division was most apparent in the oral history interviews conducted with Wayne LeBelle. University educated, with a degree in sociology, and a keen interest in the history of the region, Wayne LeBelle has written several books documenting the history of Sturgeon Falls and the surrounding townships.[22] Originally from Kapuskasing, Wayne moved to Sturgeon Falls in 1967 to become a reporter for the *North Bay Nugget*. In Sturgeon Falls, he said, "you only got one place to go and work and that is the mill."[23] In a series of interviews, LeBelle emphasized the monopolistic hold that the Anglo mill managers – brought in from outside, and dwelling apart in company homes in the "compound" beside the mill – had on the indigenous French-Canadian community. In his view, this was a form of economic colonialism that made people dependent. As a result, the company and its English-speaking managers acted like they owned the place. According to LeBelle,

> The mill became their mother, their father, their accountant, their priest, their banker, their mortgager, their, their, their. It became like their whole life. And many people never left town [during lengthy layoffs]. Maybe never became the people, got to be what they could have been. There could have been more doctors, more lawyers… but a lot of people just chose to go to the mill with their lunch pail. It really was very hurtful… that was the way it has been for a hundred years. They would work in the mill and they would cut pulpwood.[24]

The mill may have created jobs, but it "had a very crushing force on the French-Canadian population here."[25] In LeBelle's mind, the mill was a destroyer of people.

Henri Labelle, Mill Worker, Sturgeon Falls, Ontario

This interpretation is supported to some extent by a public controversy that erupted in the early 1970s, when local Franco-Ontarians demanded a high school of their own. Unbelievably, the only high school in Sturgeon Falls was English. Faced with these demands, Cam Barrington, the long-time plant manager, threatened at a public meeting to close the mill, rather than pay the higher school taxes that would result from the proposal.[26] Many in Sturgeon Falls were outraged, and a protest march descended on the mill the following day. Upon seeing the approaching column, Ed Fortin, the mill's personnel manager, and one of the few Franco-Ontarians to have made it into the ranks of management, turned to Barrington and said, tongue in cheek, "They've come to get you."[27] The crisis passed when a French-language high school was established after all, but the authority of the English managers would never be the same again.

If language reinforced class divisions in Sturgeon Falls, gender served to bridge them. There was a deep sense among former mill workers that Sturgeon Falls was a working man's town. The forest industry is a male-dominated sector to be sure; the fundamentally gendered nature of forestry towns is evident in the oral history interviews.[28] Percy Allary, for example, told us that "You spend more time with the guys at work than you do with our own family."[29] It was a place where blue-collar men drove pickup trucks and went to work with a lunch bucket and workboots.[30] The mill workers were family men for the most part. Only a handful of women worked in the mill office. Those women who found part-time work in town, usually in the service sector or in the town's hospital or schools, were deemed to be on the margins of the town's economic life. Randy Restoule summarized it this way: "There are teachers and the hospitals, but the reason why they are there is because of this mill."[31] Ruth Thompson was the mill manager's secretary until Weyerhaeuser took over. In her narrative, she makes a distinction between "company people" (salaried staff) and "workers" (union wage earners) as well as between "company people" and the two "company girls."[32] The male breadwinner ideal, at least discursively, reigned supreme in Sturgeon Falls.[33]

The connection to the mill ran deep in many families. These bonds were so strong that interviewees frequently referred to themselves as "mill families." The reason for this is not difficult to find. "Our dads worked there... we worked there... our kids worked there in the summer," Marc Côté recalled.[34] Lawrence Pretty's father had worked in the mill since it reopened in 1947. "He worked his life in there and I worked mine," he told us.[35] "I went into work and stayed there. Thirty-eight years later I came out."

The mill also had a policy of hiring employees' sons and daughters for summer jobs. Once in the plant, these students had an inside track for permanent employment. Sons followed fathers into the mill, and sometimes, as in the case of Ruth Thompson's son, followed mothers as well. Mill employment was effectively closed to other families. Over time, it became an increasingly insular workplace community, disconnected from the wider locality. Thus the saliency of the everyday term – "mill families." Marcel

Boudreau fondly called it "our little mill," but the "our" in this statement was getting smaller and smaller.[36]

MEMORIES OF LOSS AND RESISTANCE

Pride in work and service, and anger at Weyerhaeuser for closing the mill, collided in the thirty-year ring. Denis MacGregor, a machine tender, put in his thirty years and received in return a ring symbolizing his loyalty and service. Denis got his ring on November 11, 2002, and he got his "walking papers" on December 6, 2002.[37] The problem was that the service ring for men was emblazoned with a large "W" for Weyerhaeuser. In an interview with Kristen O'Hare, Denis expressed his feelings about the ring, and about the company:

> I usually wear that [thirty-year ring], but the guys at the mill give me a hard time. But I say, "Hey, I earned that." So nobody is going to tell me if I can wear it or not. I could take the insignia off, maybe I would because I really hate those guys. I don't hate the States. I hate Weyerhaeuser.... What do I think about Weyerhaeuser? Is that what you want to know? I hate them with a passion. They have changed my way of life. They don't give a shit about us and like they said, it was a "corporate decision" and it's easy for a "corporate decision" because it is in Washington. They don't know us.... I wear this [thirty-year ring] because I am proud to wear it. Not because it is Weyerhaeuser, but it's thirty years of service – good service. They made me live for thirty years. I can't take that away from them. But Weyerhaeuser wasn't with us for very long and I think that is why they did it that way. Had they been able to let us go within two months [of buying the plant in 1999] they would have done it.[38]

Denis's story reminds us that the mill may have been owned by Weyerhaeuser, but workers who spent a good deal of their lives inside its walls were strongly attached to the place, and developed what could be described as a proprietary interest.

When a mill or factory closes, job loss is a collective experience. This is especially true in a single-industry forestry town. For Mike Lacroix, the local union vice-president and twenty-four-year man, it was a like a family: "We were born and raised together. We worked together every day. It's hard to see your other family suffer."[39] He added that: "Our lives and our children's lives have been ripped away.... I've left the best years of my life back at the mill...we've all left part of our lives there."[40]

The ordeal began at eight o'clock in the morning on October 8, 2002, when the company convened a meeting at the community centre in neighbouring Cache Bay, a predominantly English-speaking community. Interviewees recall that this was a particularly cold autumn morning. Expecting trouble, the company had engaged a private security firm to be present. Many of the workers were unimpressed. One interviewee, who wished to remain nameless, recalled that the company had "some goons in the audience. They thought there would be a riot." It sent a nasty message to everyone present. An out-of-town official from Weyerhaeuser made a brief announcement that the mill would close on December 6th and directed workers to pick up a personally tailored package that detailed what each would receive in terms of severance pay. In the question period that followed, the company made it clear that it would not sell the plant "at any price." This uncompromising position was bitterly resented by all the mill workers interviewed.

Not surprisingly, the announcement came as a shock. Wayne Pigeau, at age twenty-six one of the youngest employees, told the *Tribune* that those working the night shift speculated about what would be announced that morning.[41] They knew it had to be something big, as the company announced it would shut down production for the day. Many of those interviewed thought Weyerhaeuser would announce a layoff. Several others thought that the company might announce the mill's closing, but not for a few years' time. Nobody expected the company to announce that the mill would shut down just two months later for good. One employee after another told us that the mill was busy till the day it closed. Weyerhaeuser had an "evergreen" contract to supply all of its corrugated medium until the following summer. The company had three corrugated paper mills, but the other two were located in the United States. To stop production when it did, Weyerhaeuser reportedly had to pay a stiff penalty to the customer. Naturally, this did not sit well with the mill workers.

After the announcement, the Sturgeon Falls workers were "like Zombies" for the next eight weeks.[42] To keep production going until the end, Weyerhaeuser offered them a $5,000 bonus. However, as Pierre Hardy noted, the bonus came "with strings attached": it was tied to production and safety. If there were three recorded "safety incidents," or accidents, Hardy said, the payment would be zero: "Some bonus! Talk about stress!"[43] Small accidents were therefore left unreported. Any talk of occupying the plant in protest was also quashed; the workers would have lost their bonus. Nobody was willing to lose this cash. It would come in handy over the coming months and years. In effect, Mike Lacroix sighed, the bonus bought their silence.

Memories of the final shift were sometimes painful, sometimes wistful. The mill closed on December 5th, a day earlier than planned. The atmosphere was subdued. "We were kicked out after lunch," said Wayne Pigeau. "Guys began filing out after they were told to leave."[44] Percy Allary recalled that everybody brought in some food for a "big feast." Photographs that were taken that day show workers gathered around the last roll of paper produced by the mill, and then signing their names to it. Allary took a final walk through the mill, and at 12:30 p.m. management told them to go home. Marcel Boudreau recalled that other guys had tears in their eyes. Not him. "I took what was mine and left," he said. Yet he described his last shift as a "good shift":

> It was a Thursday. I started my long weekend. I had worked the
> Wednesday, Thursday. We were on twelve-hour shifts. I was done.
> My relief was in at twenty to seven. I went down, took my shower,
> emptied my locker. Went upstairs, emptied out my locker there.
> I had three lockers to empty out. I walked out of the mill at 7:30.
> I got to the end of the driveway, at the end of the mill property.
> I turned around and took a look. Steam was coming out of the
> stacks as it always did. Turn around and that was it. I haven't
> been back in the mill ever since.[45]

Pierre Hardy's description of his last shift in the mill was broadly similar to other people's accounts: "It was a long shift, put it that way." Pierre did not want to shut the paper machine down. "There was no way I was going to do it. Get some other guys to do it.... I am not going to shut the machine down. Get someone else to do your dirty work."[46] But, as it turned out, his last shift was not the mill's last, so it was somebody else's job. "Thank God!" he exclaimed. He did go back, however, to see the last roll and to take some

Old Grinder Foundations, Sturgeon Falls Mill

pictures. He cut off a sheet of the paper and wrote "last shift" on it. On his locker he wrote, "'I'll be back,' just like Arnold," he laughed.[47]

The median age of the mill workforce was between forty-seven and forty-eight. Ten of the workers, aged fifty-five to fifty-eight, were caught in the "three year zone" and had to accept a rolled-back pension in order to retire immediately. "That hurt," Raymond Marcoux said.[48] Those unable to retire expressed their fear for the future. A profound sense of loss permeated the oral testimonies. Marcel Boudreau, like many others, once thought that he had a job for life: "I can remember lying in bed and wondering what the hell I was going to do. I had a grade twelve education. It took me six years to do it.... When I got hired in the mill I was told by the guys that were working there that 'this was a job for life. You just have to put up with the layoffs in between.'"[49]

Resistance was also a key theme. The national CEP union declared Friday, December 6th, a day of action. Six Sturgeon Falls workers were sent by the union to speak to workers at other Weyerhaeuser-owned mills in Canada: Pierre Hardy was sent to Miramachi, New Brunswick; Louis Benoit to Kamloops, British Columbia; Renald Robert to Prince Albert, Saskatchewan; Rene Lebel to Edson, Alberta; and Marcel Boudreau to Dryden and Ear Falls, in northwestern Ontario. There they met with local trade unionists and participated in informational picket lines. Pierre Hardy was kind enough to let us photocopy the written text of his speech to Weyerhaeuser workers in New Brunswick. It reads in part: "I am here to give the Sturgeon Falls mill a face and a voice and ask for your support. This is an organization that has NO values, NO vision, and NO commitment to the people or the environment – just the opposite of what they preach. For those of you that work for Weyerhaeuser, don't be fooled, you may next."[50] This was a prescient warning.

By all accounts, the men received a mixed reaction. Even though the Kamloops local of the CEP donated $1,300 to the Sturgeon Falls workers, it was the story of the cool reception that Marcel Boudreau got at the plant gate in Dryden that circulated most widely within Sturgeon Falls. This is the story that is told and retold. It went something like this: The union sent Marcel Boudreau to carry the message of union solidarity and defiance to Weyerhaeuser's paper mill in Dryden. At the plant gate, however, Boudreau received a disheartening response to his appeal. Most of the paperworkers that he encountered in Dryden simply shrugged their shoulders and said that the company was treating them well. Boudreau could not get anyone to say anything bad about Weyerhaeuser. They were indifferent to the plight of Sturgeon Falls. "Better them than us" seemed to be the reaction of many. The account ends with the storyteller, often pausing for dramatic effect, saying that five hundred Dryden workers were laid off by Weyerhaeuser in October 2003. The moral of this story is clear. The mill workers wanted us to draw the same conclusions they had: it was foolhardy for the workers in Dryden to believe that Weyerhaeuser would treat them any better than they had treated their employees in Sturgeon Falls. This was a heartless American company that was loyal to no one. The story communicates how Marcel

Boudreau and the other mill workers felt in the absence of union or class solidarity. They felt isolated and alone.

While Pierre Hardy, Marcel Boudreau, and others were pleading their case in forestry towns across Canada, one hundred and fifty people gathered in Sturgeon Falls to protest the closing. They marched on the closed mill carrying signs and banners declaring "Weyerhaeuser, free Sturgeon Falls" and chanting "Free the mill. Free the mill. Weyerhaeuser go home."[51] Among the dignitaries in attendance that morning were the vice-president of the national CEP, the President of the Ontario Federation of Labour, the mayor, as well as the local members of the provincial and federal legislatures. Yet what is surprising is how few town residents attended the rally. With 140 workers losing their jobs, one would have expected a larger turnout. Wayne LeBelle rightly noted that "You never saw a whole bunch of community people out there supporting them." This public protest, and the even smaller ones that followed, was attended almost exclusively by mill workers and their families. In this light, the *Tribune*'s headline – "West Nipissing Marches" – seems like an overstatement.[52]

The union's picket line went up at the plant's main gate on Monday, December 9th. In the days and months that followed, Marcel Boudreau, who lived nearby, arrived regularly at seven in the morning with seven or eight picket signs.[53] As the first to arrive, he was in charge of setting up. A core group of ten or fifteen attended every day, while a couple dozen others showed up less regularly. What of the others? Some found work in Sudbury or North Bay. A few moved away. The stalwarts offered a variety of reasons. Perhaps as a reflection of the changing gender division of labour within many mill families, Marcel Boudreau said that one man couldn't come out because "his wife wouldn't let him go on the picket line."[54] Those who did show up, however, were defiant. Looking back, Marcel smiled and said that he "drank an awful lot of coffee last winter."[55]

Pierre Hardy was another regular, arriving soon after Marcel. For the first two or three weeks there was no fire to keep the picketers warm. One day someone brought a barrel. The fire kept the men warm during the frigid winter months. Pierre Hardy started it each morning and stayed until noon when there was a shift change on the picket line and another crew took over. Marcel Boudreau insisted he never set the fire, because he was "never cold." Asked why not, he replied: "I had a purpose. I had a reason for getting up. I wanted them to see my face."[56] More to the point, Marcel wanted the "mill babysitter" from Weyerhaeuser to see him walking that line. "It was one of those things that has to be done," he explained. Boudreau was bearing witness: "When guys were showing up for work I was already there. I was there before they were. I wanted them to see my face. I wanted them to know that I'm not going anywhere."[57]

The men on the line spent the cold winter months of January, February, and March, as well as the spring months of April and May, contemplating their futures. If the picket line provided these men with time to think, the line was also a space of daily confrontation, as the mill workers temporarily blocked the vehicles of Weyerhaeuser office staff from entering by the front gate. Mike Lacroix recalled that there were several incidents on the picket line with vehicles trying to force their way through. Passing cars would often honk their horns.

In retrospect, Pierre Hardy wished the picket line had been set up on the other side of the mill, facing the main highway. As it was, the mill's main gate faced the town itself. The advantage of the highway side, he mused, was that this would have been far more embarrassing to the company, as hundreds of cars passed by each day.[58] The main gate, however, was a more natural location. It was where the mill workers themselves filed in each morning. It was also where the "mill babysitter," to borrow Boudreau's phrase, would see them.

While the fight continued, the CEP campaigned to save the mill. They issued press releases, and undertook court action. To bolster their case, the national and local unions wrapped themselves in the Canadian flag. The press releases issued by the union, and their public utterances during these months, teemed with nationalist indignation. On November 29, 2002, for example, the union announced that it had initiated a political action campaign to "focus national attention on what happens when a large American corporation is allowed to exploit the resources of a small Canadian town out of sheer greed."[59] The public comments of the leaders of CEP Local 7135, recorded in the *Tribune* and the *Nugget*, pushed the same buttons. In February 2003, for example, local union president Denis Senecal called on the Ontario government to intervene: "Is he going to let American companies dictate how to do business in Ontario? This is not only our fight…it's the province's fight."[60] The anger directed at Americans was deeply felt. It had become personal. The plant shutdown stories of the majority of the mill workers bristle with nationalist barbs. Many are convinced that a Canadian company would have done things differently. Several interviewees even suggested that the mill would still be in operation had Mac-Millan Bloedel not been acquired by American-owned Weyerhaeuser. The picket line continued until June 2003, but it was becoming clear that the mill could not be saved. Demolition began in June 2004.

One of the most painful topics discussed in the oral interviews was the demolition of the mill. Restoration Environmental Contractors, based in southern Ontario, was given the contract to demolish the 300,000 square foot facility as well as to provide environmental abatement.[61] The reaction of the interviewees to the mill's demolition was mixed. Hubert Gervais visited the site every day in order to document the demolition with his camera.[62] He took thousands of images. Marcel Labbé also watched the demolition crews at work, but from his car parked outside the fence.[63] The mill's smokestack had special significance for Marcel: "What we're watching is the chimney. You know the tall chimney. When that goes down that will mean something because that's where we worked. It's bad."[64] Ruth Thompson, agreed: "It was a little mill. It was like another era gone by. Now, it is going to be torn down just like part of your life is being ripped away. That's how I felt."[65]

Even so, not every former mill employee wished to witness the demolition. Several of the workers were repelled by the sight. In fact, Pete Hardy has avoided setting his eyes on the mill ever since they began tearing it down. "I wanted to see the mill as it was," he told me.[66] This was not an easy task in a town as small as Sturgeon Falls. Other workers looked, but did not like what they saw. Randy Restoule found it hard to watch Weyerhaeuser removing equipment.[67] Mike Lacroix told us that his father still swears every time he passes the mill site, such is his anger.[68] In one final act of resistance, Mike Lacroix successfully, if only temporarily, halted demolition in July 2004 when he filed a complaint with the Ontario government stating that the demolition company was not following proper procedures in removing asbestos from the building.[69] To counter this bad-news story, a spokesperson for the demolition company attempted to explain it away by saying: "There's a lot of negative public feeling and animosity about the closing, and now demolition, of this plant, by former employees in the community."[70] No kidding.

DISPLACED TO THE PERIPHERY

When Weyerhaeuser closed the corrugated paper plant, mill workers and their families continued to believe that the paper mill remained at the economic and cultural heart of the town. To them, it was a mill town. They were convinced that its closing would be a disaster not only for themselves, but for Sturgeon Falls as a whole. In letters to the editor and in published interviews with the media, they warned that the closing would result in businesses shutting down, lower house values, an exodus of young people, and would put into question the future of the town itself. The mill's closing is "like taking a page out of history and closing the book," said Marc Côté. "When you shut something like that down you take a little bit of the heart of the town."[71]

The mill's closing has had a devastating economic impact on most of the mill families. There were few jobs to apply for in Sturgeon Falls, and fewer still for middle-aged men with a high school education. "Who wants to hire a fifty-year-old with no trade?" asked Pierre Hardy. Even before the mill's closing, the town's unemployment rate stood at 16.3 percent, far higher than the rate that then prevailed in Ontario.[72] In part, the high rate was the result of the end of hardboard production at the mill, which had resulted in the layoff of 150 workers. If Sturgeon Falls was a working man's town before the mill closing, it now threatened to become a "retirement town" or an "old age home."[73] There was also a gender dimension to the changes underway. The major employers in the town were now in the public and retail sectors – two areas that traditionally employed women. As a result, it was sometimes easier for women to find work than it was for former male breadwinners.

If families struggled with the economic consequences of job loss, life seemed to go on without the mill. Many mill workers expressed genuine surprise when the mill's closing did not have the devastating economic effect they had always expected. House prices did not plummet; businesses did not close overnight. At first, J.P. Charles, a former reeve of Springer Township, thought that the mill's closing would be "tough" on Sturgeon, but remarked that "the town is busy."[74] The town's proximity to North Bay and Sudbury allowed residents to commute to jobs located east and west. The effects were most obvious to residents when it came to the town's finances. "It's a massive revenue loss," said the town's chief administrative officer, Jay Barbeau.[75] The mill had generated $700,000 in direct revenues annually: $150,000 for municipal garbage removal, $200,000 for water and sewerage services, and $350,000 in taxes. The municipality responded by raising taxes.

Dismantling the Paper Machine Room, Sturgeon Falls Mill

Despite the mill's central place in the lives and memories of the mill workers and their families, its economic and cultural centrality had eroded over time. Over a thirty-year period, one production line after another was halted, until only one remained. The workforce went from a peak of 700, to just 140 at the end. As each production line fell silent, younger workers were laid off. For many years, one interviewee remarked, "the place was really unsteady. There was no guarantee of a good future here." Brian Lafleche could attest to that. He was laid off in 1969 when the platewood mill closed, but was eventually called back, only to lose his job again in 1972. At this point, he'd had enough, and he went into sales.[76] The closing of the hardboard plant and the corrugated paper machine's shift from virgin wood to 100 percent recycled paper in 1991, was particularly difficult. The mill's workforce was cut in half, and the mill lost its longstanding connection to the surrounding rural townships which provided the wood. Gerry Stevens, a former mill superintendent, remembers what it was like walking through the plant in the final years. Entire sections of the mill were abandoned.[77] As the years wore on, Brian Lafleche noted, "the mill diminished."[78]

The mill's closing did not have the impact it would have, had it closed thirty years earlier. "It would have devastated the town," said Lafleche. In the early days, "the mill would have been *the* employer in the town. If the mill closes the town is dead, that used to be the saying."[79] Others agreed with this assessment. It had not made "the kind of impact that you would think," mused Wayne LeBelle.[80] While the mill continued to be a key source of tax revenue for the town, its centrality in the lives of many local families was long past.

By 2002, the 140 remaining mill workers found themselves isolated. "A lot of people were envious of us for working there," Pierre Hardy pointed out. Lawrence Pretty could also remember people saying to him "'Oh, because your dad worked there that's why you work there.'" The distinction drawn between "mill people," "mill workers," or "mill families" on the one hand, and "townspeople," or "the community" on the other, ran through the oral narratives of mill workers and their spouses. When the mill closed, it was believed that the envy of some residents turned to glee. Marcel Boudreau, for example, was convinced that many townspeople "felt we were too well paid for what we did. I know for a fact that there is a number of people who were quite happy to see the mill shut down and have us all lose our jobs. 'Welcome to the real world.' Jealous people."

But how did Sturgeon Falls residents not closely associated with the mill really feel? Did they embrace the socio-economic and cultural changes underway? There was, of course, a wide range of responses. What is clear from the evidence collected is that the mill was no longer the dominant economic and cultural force in the town. It had lost its centrality. The gradual decline of the mill's workforce was offset to some extent by employment growth in the public sector. A new local office of Statistics Canada employed 250 and the hospital another 238. At the same time, the mill's ties to the surrounding rural townships were cut when the mill shifted its fibre furnish from wood to recycled cardboard in the early 1990s. Until then, the mill relied almost exclusively on area farmers and sawmills for its supply. Wayne LeBelle put it bluntly when he said: "For us in Field [a small village near Sturgeon Falls], it means nothing. For the majority of West Nipissing it means nothing." It only meant something to those who lost their jobs. To everyone else, even locally, it "means very little." Hammering home the point, he continued: "It sounds like a huge tragedy and it is for some individuals. It is a big smack. In the bigger picture of West Nipissing it's not. The world does not revolve around Sturgeon Falls. It does not. Ask all those questions in Verner, in Cache Bay."[81] However harsh this assessment may be, it is hard to ignore. In many respects, Sturgeon Falls had ceased to be a "mill town" even before the mill closed in December 2002. The town's shift away from industry had occurred gradually, over several decades. The mill's closing simply marked the completion of this long-term process.

And yet, this economic and cultural shift had largely escaped the notice of the mill workers and their families. Time and again, the men and women interviewed expressed their genuine surprise that the closure of the mill did not have a more visible effect on Sturgeon Falls. "It doesn't appear to have affected the town too much," observed Marcel Labbé. Others thought that townspeople would be surprised when the situation eventually worsened. "People don't truly understand the impact on the community," cautioned Mike Lacroix. In this context, mill workers could not help but feel that the town that they knew was dead. For Randy Restoule, "The writing was on the wall. We just didn't see it.... We were sold out."[82]

Several of the mill workers drew a contrast between the local community's energetic response to the threatened closure of the corrugated paper mill in 1991, and the inaction of 2002–2003. The town council focused its energy on purchasing the mill's hydroelectric generating plant, not on saving the mill itself. According to Marcel Boudreau, the "community sure pulled together to try to do something then. But they didn't do a goddamn thing to do anything about it this time around. I'm not ashamed to say it either. I walked the picket line all winter last year. I would say there was not much help from our local councillors here." As far as Pierre Hardy is concerned, "the community never did anything for us... [19]'91 and 2003 it is like night and day." Several workers suggested that the West Nipissing *Tribune*, the bilingual weekly newspaper serving the locality, was far less supportive of the mill workers and their efforts to reopen the mill in 2003, than the *North Bay Nugget*. "We had more backing from North Bay than we had from Sturgeon," recalled Mike Lacroix. "I don't know why. Even the *Nugget*, they came over and covered the stories. Our own people…they wouldn't. Why aren't you backing us? We are trying to keep this place going to make money for the community."[83]

While the reasons for the changed response to the mill's closing are many and complex, three points need to be kept in mind. First, the old town council of Sturgeon Falls – which would have been ready "to fight to the death for its 'industry'" – had been amalgamated in January 1999 with the adjoining townships.[84] The new municipality of West Nipissing had a very different style and focus and was no longer wedded to the mill. The political players had changed. Second, in the ten or eleven intervening years the mill's workforce had declined from 300 to 140. With these diminished numbers, it became possible to imagine a Sturgeon Falls without the mill. This was still not the case in 1991–92. Finally, the successful effort to keep the mill open in the early 1990s by converting the mill to recycled paper, only to have it close a decade later, sapped the town's will to resist. Several interviewees spoke of an "exhausted" community unable to respond to Weyerhaeuser's decision to shut down.

The oral narratives are supported by a series of letters to the editor published in *The Tribune* between October 2002 and March 2003. At first, the voices of mill workers and their families predominated. However, starting in March 2003, other residents began to challenge the legitimacy of their claims. At issue in this debate was nothing less than who had the right to speak on behalf of Sturgeon Falls and the "community."[85]

In their efforts to mobilize public opinion and state power (if only the municipality), the mill workers and their supporters appealed to place attachment, nation, and the environment. Shortly after the closing was announced, on October 22, 2002, Bruce Colquhoun, a mill worker, urged the "whole community" to respond as it had in 1991 when the mill's future was last threatened. He appealed to local "community" sentiment and challenged those who would not defend place:

> This closure doesn't just affect us who work at the mill. It will
> have a great impact on everyone here. There is a lot of money
> generated into our economy that will be lost. Families will be
> forced to move away, because, let's face it, there sure isn't much

OCC Recycling Area. Sturgeon Falls Mill

work around here to be found. Property values will decrease drastically, and property taxes will increase because of the lost taxes from the mill. There are a few people who laugh at us, because we've "had it so good for so long." Laugh all you want, but what is the town without the mill? We will ALL soon find out, won't we.

Bruce Colquhoun's community of identification, however, was not tied exclusively to place. He also saw the mill's closing as a matter of concern to all Canadians. This nationalist appeal was made explicit when he challenged Weyerhaeuser's refusal to sell the mill as a going concern: "Typical Americans. And they wonder why they are hated throughout the world. They are going to tell us Canadians what to do with our mill."[86] He thus appealed to two communities of identification at once – one national and the other local.[87]

The letter from Jane Hardy, the spouse of a twenty-seven-year man, invoked the same two themes. Published on December 10, 2002, a few days after the mill closed, the letter blamed "American corporate greed" for the closure and noted that the mill's profits had been diverted to the company's headquarters in Washington State, USA. Once again, the nationality of the employer loomed large in Hardy's mind:

> Is it because this is a multinational American company, that
> they can just lock the door and pack up, return to the States
> and carry on their business as usual? Should they be allowed to
> operate in this manner? They have left their wreckage scattered
> all over Sturgeon Falls, Ontario and area, and this will never be
> forgiven or forgotten! Is this the American way of doing business
> in Canada?"[88]

She went on to write that when Weyerhaeuser announced the mill's closing on October 8th, "those Americans might as well have dropped a bomb on Sturgeon Falls." With the image of Americans dropping a bomb, Jane Hardy neatly shows just how intertwined national and local identities had become. In the post 9/11 world, one would be hard-pressed to find a more loaded analogy than the one employed by Hardy.

If place attachment and national sentiment were not sufficient motivators to readers of *The Tribune*, Colquhoun and Hardy added a third reason to care: the environment. Now, it might seem surprising that paper-mill workers would invoke the environment in their own defence. It is common knowledge that paper mills are among the worst polluters of the environment. But as Jane Hardy noted in a subsequent letter, this mill was "unique" insofar as its source of wood fibre was recovered paper, rather than virgin wood and sawmill waste. As a result, it was a relatively clean mill, and reduced the waste flowing into Ontario's landfills. Bruce reminded his readers that only a short time earlier the mill produced its one millionth ton of recovered paper: "That is 1 MILLION TONS of material that has been diverted from landfill sites. 1 ton is 2,000 pounds. That's a lot of paper and cardboard. We are a 100 percent recycling mill. I am surprised that environmental groups haven't come forward yet."[89]

Not everyone in Sturgeon Falls, however, agreed with the mill families. Vera Charles, for example, wrote a toughly worded letter in response to Jane Hardy: "There has been much boo-hoo-ing and feeling sorry for ourselves, which is mostly due to a big lack of understanding of how a business operates."[90] Weyerhaeuser was not a "charity," she asserted. It would not be easy for workers to find new work, "but these are the realities of modern life." Charles then suggested that the mill workers had no cause to complain as, unlike non-union, or part-time workers, they have been "employed for years at salaries most of us can only dream about," and received severance pay, career counselling, and "eventually, pensions!" Mill workers, she said, should "count their blessings" and be "thankful to receive such benefits when they are out of work." Adopting the same rhetorical device that Jane Hardy used against the female spokesperson of Weyerhaeuser, Vera Charles went on to say:

> "Corporate greed," says Jane Hardy, that's exactly right! That is what for-profit businesses in a free market are all about, and for that matter, most individuals as well.... Rather than whining, complaining, and shame shaming Weyerhaeuser like little children, we would do well to take our share of the responsibility and learn from this. Have we not watched as other single-industry towns suffered the same misfortune? Did we not know that plant closures, layoffs, and cutbacks are common in our time, and that an individual now passes through five careers in a lifetime...? Instead of bemoaning what we lost, we should think positively about where to go from here. Other towns have bounced back; so can Sturgeon Falls. It seems to me that the enormous amount of energy spent in outrage and grief could be channelled to better use elsewhere.[91]

While few other letter writers would be as uncompromising, Charles was not alone. Others urged readers to put the town's industrial past behind them. "Now let's accept the reality of the situation and move on," said Mike Parsons.[92]

The desire to move on was expressed repeatedly in the oral interviews conducted with people outside the orbit of the mill families. Several of these interviewees believed that the changes resulting from the shutdown would ultimately be beneficial to Sturgeon Falls. Interviewed in July 2004, Ronald Beauchamp, a key figure in the West Nipissing Economic Development Corporation, who contributed to the saving of the mill in the early 1990s, now concluded that he was representing:

> ... [the] interest of the municipality which is not exclusively
> the interest of employees. The employees would have liked
> for us to buy the mill, but that is not in the best interest of
> the municipality. To buy a mill that will not be producing. Or,
> that there are too many question marks. It's a world market.
> Nobody came forward with the expertise. People would say,
> "Look at Tembec." Well when the employees bought Tembec,
> the managers were there to buy into this. Here, all we had were
> the employees. They were telling us "OK, that machine is fine."
> "That machine." That is not the problem. The problem is the
> world market. Can we sell this product? Can we compete in the
> world market? So there was a lot of friction between the munici-
> pality and the employees.

The interests of the town and the mill employees had become decoupled. The end result of the mill's closing, he said, will be "very positive." As for the mill site, there was "nothing to do" with the mill buildings. They had to be demolished:

> I was convinced there was nothing to do with that plant. It was
> just too old. You are not going to put a $200 million, modern
> machine inside an old building whose foundation was built a
> hundred years [ago]. If you are going to buy a Rolls Royce the
> building [of] a new garage is not a problem. You are not going
> [to] park the Rolls Royce in an old garage that is going to fall.
> There are much better properties in the area for building a new
> plant where there is no underground pollution. Where you have
> access to services. There is just no logic to building a new mill
> where the old one is.[93]

If the mill site had no future as a site of industrial production, it did have other uses. It was "prime real estate" for tourism, Beauchamp said. "By the river, there are all kinds of possibilities. So our objective was not to save the old mill." In his view, a park should be built in its place.

Beauchamp's vision was in large part adopted by the Community Adjustment and Recovery Committee (CARC), headed by Royal Poulin, a leading Progressive Conservative Party supporter in the area. The committee was asked to identify the opportunities for development and to fund selected projects. In June 2003, CARC produced a report entitled "Let's Grow Together." Sturgeon Falls' future, it reported, was to position itself as a commuter suburb for North Bay and Sudbury, to make Sturgeon Falls a family-oriented wilderness destination, and to develop specialized retailing.[94] This report represented a massive redefinition of place, just six month after the mill closed. Even though efforts to reopen the mill persisted, the town's leadership had already turned its back on the town's industrial past and embraced its post-industrial future. In effect, the mill families had lost their central place in the economic and cultural life of the town. They were now outsiders looking in. Reflecting on the legacy of the mill, Wayne LeBelle told me: "Drive around town and say, 'OK. What is the legacy they left behind? What did they leave behind? They're going to leave behind some flat territory. They are going to leave behind a big huge parking lot.'"[95] It is as if the mill had never existed.

CONCLUSION

What does the future hold for Sturgeon Falls, the mill workers, and their families? What becomes of a "mill town" once the mill is gone? Whose town is it? It is impossible to answer these questions for certain. Time will tell. When asked about the future of Sturgeon Falls, former mill workers continue to struggle with the idea that there is a future for Sturgeon Falls without industry. Randy Restoule spoke for many when he said: "I think we do need an industry here. We can't just be a bedroom community for North Bay and Sudbury. We need an industry to be our base, a tax base."[96] The town's location within commuting distance of Sudbury and North Bay has certainly saved it from the dismal fate of more isolated towns with no industry. The town's tourism strategy is also proceeding apace. The unfolding Sturgeon Falls story, like that of dozens of other deindustrialized towns and cities across North America, is one of liminality – being caught betwixt and between. It is also one of contestation.

If the physical evidence of more than a century of paper production has already been largely erased, former mill workers risk losing their past in another way. In the course of demolishing the mill, Weyerhaeuser shredded most of the mill records, and shipped the remainder to the United States, where they are off limits to researchers. Except for a scattering of records secreted away in peoples' basements, and a handful of photographs donated to the local museum, a century of production records has effectively ceased to exist. It is as if the mill's history was being demolished too. This deeply offended several interviewees. In the words of Hubert Gervais: "I think they should have come to us, the two historians, Bruce Colquhoun and myself, because there are a lot of files, old files, that they threw out, which was part of history. Boxes and boxes and boxes…they threw out an awful lot when they closed the mill. I just couldn't believe it…. Boxes and boxes of our history. Why didn't they leave it here?"[97]

"The Bone Yard," Fisher Guide, Detroit, Michigan

CHAPTER 5

GABRIEL'S DETROIT

I FIRST MET GABRIEL SOLANO AFTER HE RESPONDED TO A
February 1998 appeal for "plant shutdown stories," placed in the *Detroit Sunday Journal*, a weekly newspaper published by the striking employees of the
Detroit News. Like several of the others who responded to the announcement, Gabriel had a burning desire to tell his story. And what a story it is! A
longtime employee of General Motors, Gabriel has experienced three separate plant closings in his lifetime. The closing of his "home plant," Fisher
Guide in southwest Detroit, had the most crushing effect on Gabriel and
his family. He was never the same again. Until his death in 2005, he counted
himself one of the "I-75 Gypsies" working in GM's Pontiac plant. These are
the folks who have closed out plants up and down Interstate 75. Not only
were these plant-closing veterans alienated from the company, they felt let
down by their union as well. In its broad outlines, then, Gabriel's plant shutdown story was typical: an eloquent denunciation of capitalist greed and
union indifference.

Gabriel also profoundly influenced the photo essay, as he agreed to
guide us around Detroit in June 2003. When we arrived, we found Gabriel's
southwest Detroit neighbourhood slowly bouncing back from the ravages
of the 1980s and '90s. Here we juxtapose passages from Gabriel's 1998

interview, with photographs taken that hot summer day. Except for the opening photo of Gabriel, taken in the abandoned shell of his former plant, the photo essay follows the sequence of "stops" selected by Gabriel. Gabriel's Detroit includes closed auto assembly and parts plants, abandoned and struggling steel mills, and an abandoned excursion boat that once took workers and their families for a blue-collar getaway. All of the images reflect Gabriel's lifelong association with General Motors, one of the world's largest corporations.

The first stop was at a former GM parts supplier, which closed in the 1980s. The plant was located on Central Avenue, formerly a bustling thoroughfare between busy Michigan and Jefferson Avenues in the heart of the factory district. We then proceeded to Gabriel's former Fisher Guide plant, which closed in the late 1980s. The image of the interior is taken in a smaller structure where metal stamping took place. Gabriel called it the "boneyard." David's use of infrared film brings this dead space momentarily back to life in a ghostly glow. Since the mill's closing, the empty space appears to have been used as a chop shop by car thieves.

Next, Gabriel took us to the struggling Great Lakes Steel mill on Zug Island, where his father had worked until his retirement. The mill – pictured from the former site of Detroit Coke, which was shut down for polluting the environment – strongly resembles a World War II battleship. This photo visualizes Gabriel's own use of the nautical metaphor of a sinking ship to describe mills and factories going down. The next stop on our journey was to the resting place of the Columbia. With its sister ship the St. Clair, the Columbia once took workers to an island amusement park. "That was our big cruise," recalled Gabriel. As a child, he remembers watching the ship's powerful pistons, and eating popcorn and cotton candy: "You felt like somebody on that boat." There were no first- or second-class seating areas – working families had the run of the boat. For Gabriel, the pistons were a metaphor for Detroit itself: it was a "working boat." No longer. Today, the ship stands still and the island amusement rides have been demolished to make way for luxury condominiums.

We then turn to a series of photographs of the McLouth steel mill in the downriver community of Trenton. As we stood outside the fence watching David climb atop a railroad trestle, Gabriel noted that "if you worked for McLouth Steel you were king, you were on top." This story helps explain why employees tried to keep the mill going, but ended up losing everything,

Great Lakes Steel, Zug Island, Michigan

in 1995. The sight of an upturned helmet on top of an overgrown telephone booth serves as an apt symbol. Our day ended outside a six-storey former GM automotive assembly plant. There was no need to search for Detroit's deindustrialized landscape. It is everywhere. Like Gabriel himself, Detroit has been beaten and battered. Yet in spite of everything, they have survived: Gabriel continued to work for GM, and Detroit remains an industrial metropolis.

GABRIEL SOLANO: My name is Gabriel Solano. I was born and raised in Detroit, Michigan. I come from a blue-collar family. My dad was a steelworker for Great Lakes Steel. A union man. Put in his thirty years. He has since passed. My mom is still alive. I come from a rather large family. There's ten brothers and four sisters.

I grew up in southwestern Detroit, which is a predominately blue-collar part of the city. The factories were the prevalent workplace: Cadillacs, which is GM, Fleetwoods, which is GM, and Fisher Guide, GM. As I grew up I had hopes of college, but the factories, the lure, the money.... We found them to be the "golden nugget." And it was! I started off after high school, working for GM the "business of businesses." We were partners. We were going to do this for life – this thirty-year ambition.

So, as time wore on, I chose to become a good worker: be on time, come in every day, build the product the way they wanted it built.... I got married while I worked in the shop. We had a child. We moved out to the suburbs. The big dream was on. Full boat. Full course. I bought the GM product: the car, the truck, the house in the suburbs, the new baby, the new furniture. And then [smiles and laughs] the dream came crashing down.

∎ ∎ ∎

STEVEN HIGH: What was it like growing up in that neighbourhood? Can you tell us any stories that capture the spirit of the place?

GABRIEL: To watch the people go to work. To watch my Dad get up. To see this just was mesmerizing because this was what America was about. This was what we all worked for, to make corporations their money so we could get on with our lives. People tended to their houses. Everyone was part of the community. Community was whole and it was wholesome. Church was a necessity. You had to belong to a church in order to belong to the community. And to see this wholesomeness was like, this is life. This is what we live for. And I enjoyed it. I enjoyed it. I enjoyed going to work. I enjoyed being with my co-workers because this is what we lived for....

And this was taken away. To see the abandoned houses popping up, to see the storefronts closing, to see the devastation of the joblessness because the small shops fed the big shops. It was like a domino effect. It was an effect that didn't hurt just me, it hurt the guy in the small shop. Because we all worked as one; and to see this community start going down the tubes, down the drain. Devastating. It was devastating. Because this was what I called home, this was what I still call home because I never left.

∎ ∎ ∎

STEVE: What was it like working in this plant? What was your job in the plant?

GABRIEL: When I first hired in at Fisher Guide, I can still remember this day, they took me to this part of the plant I had never been. They had these gigantic presses. These presses were as big as hell.

The man says, "Here's some rubber gloves and here's an apron." And there's this bin of steel plates. And he says, "You stack them for the guy who has to feed them."

I'm bending over and as quick as I can stack them, he would feed them into that press. And I said, "Is this the way to make a living?"

∎ ∎ ∎

Gabriel Solano, "I-75 Gypsy," Detroit, Michigan

I want to relate this story. It's an interesting one. They shipped me over to the West Plant (which is Plant 5) two weeks before they're shutting it down [smiles]. So I get there and the fore-man gives me this "You're here to do the job,' and I mean, he's

gung ho! And I'm looking at him like "I just got a free ticket on
the Titanic." It's already hit the iceberg. It's three-quarters sunk
and you're telling me to strike up the band? And I said, "Can
life get any worse and then I meet you?" So he read me his riot
act about what we have to do for this plant and it is going to
shut down in two weeks. Mind you, this is at Christmas time.
I'm like, "Is this for real?" It is real. So, "You're absolutely right,
which way is the life boat?" At which point I said, "You have to
have fun with this." And I made it fun. I was around a bunch of
workers who had never been to a plant closing. I had already
closed two.

STEVE: What was the second one you closed?

GABRIEL: It was a Livonia trim shop. I was there briefly. I think
it was the Lusitania and then I got on the Titanic, so one got
torpedoed and the other hit the iceberg. I was rather enlight-
ened because I had now become calloused and I understood
what was going on. To watch some of these other workers who
would threaten to bring in gun. The "I hate everyone" mentality.
It was understood. I had seen it. I had felt it. I had done it. Been

The Columbia Sitting Idle, Detroit, Michigan

there. Well it was one hell of an irony because it was Christmas time and I can remember this day so vividly, because I was taking notes, because I wanted to feel this even further down the road.... I can still remember so vividly: "Attention! Attention!" Then, they put out flyers and posters: "Free hot dogs, pops, popcorn in the cafeteria. Please come down." I said, "Hey, I'll look at the freebies." So I go down there and...you could see the anger. You could see the hurt. You could see the anxiety. And you could see most – the fear. They started playing Christmas music over the PA. I think, "Strike up the band – the Titanic is going down." So we get in line and the plant manager and all of his cronies are passing out hot dogs and pop. And they're so damn cheerful and they're taking pictures. So he hands me a hot dog – so I dropped it on the floor. He says, "Here's another one." So I throw it against the wall. He says, "Do you have an attitude?" And I started laughing and I says, "That's ironic that you should ask me that. Here you are shutting our plant down, putting us out of work. You're playing Christmas music. It's at Christmas time. I should be happier than a pig in you-know-what?" I says,

"No. No. This is what I think of your hot dogs. A matter of fact, this is what I think of you." At which point they said, "Call Security. We don't want him in here because he is disrupting the other employees."

I said, "No, you don't have to call them. I'll leave. But I just want you to know how I feel, and it's genuine. Been through a lot to have to do this, but this is my respect to you...the same respect you gave me." It was a hell of an irony. Christmas music, free hot dogs, plant closing at Christmas time. So here I am on the Titanic and I'm thinking, "Aw, jeez, I've been too kind."

■ ■ ■

I actually went down to the Solidarity House [UAW headquarters]. It was the most striking thing. This gentleman came out of the door in a nice suit. And I could see he had been working steady. And here I am, losing the farm. And he was not even letting me past the front door. He kept me in the lobby and did not even invite me into his office.

And it hurt because these are the people that my father had taught me to be proud of and to be part of. And I am still part of them in my heart. Because once you become a union man, you are always a union man. Come hell or high water, and I was in some high water and I was in hell. It was devastating because he kept me way out there in the lobby. He didn't even ask me to sit down. He was more ready to go to lunch than to talk to me and give me an embrace, a shoulder to cry on. Give me some authentic feeling like "Hey, hang in there. It's going to happen."

At which point I never went back because I knew what I was up against. The local stopped talking to us, the international kept us at bay. I gave up.

■ ■ ■

STEVE: What was the mood in the plant while this was going on? How did people deal with it? How did people react?

GABRIEL: You see it coming but you don't believe it.... You live eight hours at home, you sleep for six hours, and then you live at the plant for eight hours. It is one third of your life. So, for ten or fifteen years you've lived one third of your life in this facility. You see the train coming, you're on the track, it's going to stop. It's

The McLouth Steel Mill from Trestle, Trenton, Michigan

not coming. You hear the whistle and you feel the vibration...and then next thing you know you've just gotten run over. And you still don't even believe it after its run over you, and a hundred cars have run past. It's the darndest thing.

• • •

STEVE: What do you lose when you go through a plant shutdown? You lose income of course, but what else do you lose?

GABRIEL: I lost a part of me. Me as a person who said, "I have a goal. I have a dream. I'm setting forth on it and I'm going to give 150 percent."

To come home and say "I no longer have a job." The wife looks at you. You're looking at this baby. You're looking at this house and you're realizing that something is missing and it's a part of me. I don't so much feel that I was missing GM but I was missing a part of me. Something internal. It's hard to explain because it's an emotion. It's a feeling. Because it took all those years to build this emotion and this feeling and then it's not there. So you end up with a blank in your life. There is a blank. Yes there is.

• • •

STEVE: Why "I-75 Gypsies"? Who are you?

GABRIEL: Thank you for the question. Thank you. We are the people who shut down plants up and down I[interstate]-75. That's why we call ourselves the I-75 gypsies. We have no home plants. We are very hardened people. We are very thick-skinned but we were also very good people because we've been at all the battles in the war called the automotive industry. To meet one you'll meet the most wonderful person. . . . There's like four or five hundred of us there [in the Pontiac auto plant] and they stuck us all damn near in the same building.

We're neat because everyone has a story. They're beautiful stories. They're stories of hurt, of fear, of anger, of loss, of gain. The whole rollercoaster. What's ironic is that when they ship us to another facility, we are treated as though we were I-75 gypsies. We're taken in but we're treated differently. This is from our own UAW.

Perfect example, we came out of a layoff, a lot of us, plant shutdown, layoffs, we all meshed in at this facility. They took us in only because they needed, as they say in the business, "bodies." We happen to be that. They gave us "1-7-85" plant seniority, so a gentleman with corporate seniority of twenty-five years walks in with 1-7-85: January 7, 1985. He can't hold a day shift because an in-plant person has more seniority. Except the ironic thing [is] you're a UAW member but you're a lower-class member. I think about that and it bothers me. . . . A person can have twenty-five years UAW time, but can't receive a ring due to the fact that they've been designated in the bylaws of the local agreement that you must have twelve years and one day in that facility. Second-class UAW citizens once again... Something small means a lot of the men.... I brought up to the international about "When will we be able to incorporate our seniority into the plant?" "Won't happen." So we maintain this ugliness ourselves. It's an irony. Although we all have fifteen, twenty-five, twenty-eight years, we don't have what is called a "home plant."

STEVE: What are some of the plants that people closed out? Where did your friends work?

GABRIEL: [claps] Well, let's start. The list is long and furious. Let's go. Fleetwoods, Cadillac on Clark Street (a lot of wonderful people from those two facilities), my home plant Fisher Guide, Ford Street, Willowrun (beautiful people came out of Willowrun), Flint... We've got people from Flint...people from Ohio, you name it: Indiana, Wisconsin. You name it we have them there: approximately four hundred to five hundred of us. There will be more [with] the closing of Buick City.

Nipissing Refinery, Cobalt, Ontario

CHAPTER 6

DEINDUSTRIAL
FRAGMENTS

IN SHARP CONTRAST TO GABRIEL'S DETROIT, CLOSED Canadian mills and factories are often hidden and hard to find. On our road trips through southern Ontario, David and I found scattered, abandoned, industrial sites. These isolated ruins do not constitute a landscape per se. Many former industrial sites have been demolished and replaced by donut shops, strip malls, and cinema complexes. Others have retained their industrial character. In 2003, only in Welland did closed mills cast a shadow over an entire town. Atlas Steel shut down two months after Stelco closed Welland Tube.[1] Over six hundred Canadians lost their jobs. More typical, however, was the auto town of Windsor, where we succeeded in photographing only two abandoned mills (several Windsor auto plants – including Chrysler's Pilette Road plant – have since closed, displacing hundreds of workers). Interviewee Peter Wirth, a tool-and-die maker, for example, worked at the Canada Motor Lamp plant, later owned by Rockwell International. The other abandoned industrial site is the Riverside Brewery building, built in 1923, and closed in 1935 when a competitor purchased the company. In the decades that followed, the building was used as a warehouse, before being abandoned altogether.[2]

Wallaceburg, Hamilton, and Cobalt also appear in the photographs. The former Canada Dominion Sugar Company mill represents one of the three "anchor" industries of Wallaceburg, a short drive from Windsor. The other two were the glass and brass industries. The plant processed sugar from the surrounding area until 1960, when falling trade barriers allowed cheap Cuban sugar into Canada. Much of the original plant – most notably the powerhouse and stack – were demolished fifteen years ago. What remains is being used as warehousing, and as an industrial park for small firms.[3]

The Nipissing Refinery in Cobalt is one of the abandoned mining sites that dot Canada's provincial northlands.[4] The refinery has a fascinating history. Opened in 1948 with the assistance of the U.S. Army, it refined cobalt extract during the early decades of the Cold War. Later, it was converted to refine silver. Since then, the mill has had many more lives, but now stands empty.

Dominion Sugar, Wallaceburg, Ontario

Hamilton, by contrast, has so far been able to retain its steel industry. Both the Steel Company of Canada (Stelco) and Dominion Foundries
(DOFASCO) continue to operate integrated steel mills in the city. A study of
local plant closings turns to other, more peripheral, industries such as automotive, agricultural machinery, glass, twine, textiles, shoes, shovels, foun-
dry-work, and so on. The interviewees represent a broad range of Hamilton
workers. Dorothy Routenburg, for example, worked much of her life in the
International Harvester twine mill. When the mill closed in 1970, male co-
workers were able to transfer into other company operations in Hamilton,
but not the women. At the time, women were confined to designated job categories. Union seniority lists formalized this gender division of labour within
industrial complexes. Dorothy was therefore out of luck. Male interviewees
also struggled to find work. John Livingstone, an immigrant from Scotland,
worked at True Temper, a maker of shovels. Although the plant employed
only some 150 people, he had numerous family members working with him.
The closing of the mill in the 1980s thus had a disproportionate impact on
his family. Not surprisingly, given the high rate of foreign ownership of
the Canadian economy, many of the interviewees directed their anger at
American companies that closed plants in Canada. The nationalism of Ed

Lawrenson, a former employee of Bendix Automotive in Windsor, proved typical. Bolstered by Canadian nationalism, interviewees emphasized collective resistance to plant closings to a far greater extent than those interviewed in the United States. The story of Allen Industries in Hamilton, told by David Christopherson, then the local UAW president, now a member of Parliament in Ottawa, is emblematic of this Canadian story of collective resistance.

DOROTHY ROUTENBURG

TWINE MILL, INTERNATIONAL HARVESTER, HAMILTON, ONTARIO [CLOSED 1970]

DOROTHY: I decided to buy a house. Don't ask me what on. I phoned this real estate guy and asked him about a house. He took me down and showed me this house on Superior Street. And all I had was five dollars in my purse, going out to look at a house. I have nerve, I'm telling you.

I liked the house. And he said, "How about a down payment?" I said, "Well, not tonight, we'll have to talk this over. I'll see about it." I went into work the next day and I wanted that house but I thought, "How can you get a house for five bucks?" My foreman then was Scotty Wilcox, so I went in and talked to Scotty and I told him that I had to have a house. He agreed with me. And, well, he knew everything about me and I never missed a day of work or anything.... He said, "Go over and see the credit union." I said, "I got nothing in the credit union to buy a house." He said, "I'll give you time off from work. Go on."

So I went over...and talked to the guy. He said, "You hardly have any money in here." I said, "I know, but I want to buy a house." So he told me, "You got more nerve than anything I've ever seen.... Well, if you can get somebody to co-sign for you, I'll give you the money for the house."

I went back in to see Scotty. Talked it over with Scotty. Scotty says, "I'll tell you what I'll do. I'll sign for you. Where's the papers?" I had the papers all ready. I says, "Here they are." He says, "Oh my God, you've got nerve!" He signed them. I went running back.... They gave me the money for the down payment on the house and gave me a thousand dollars more so I could get into that house. I never missed a day off of work. I worked in there and I got that house paid for.

STEVEN HIGH: Quite the foreman who would co-sign your loan!

DOROTHY: Yeah. Yeah. And I told Scotty, I says, "I won't stay home. I suppose I'm dying I'll come to work." And I did. I seen the days when I was so sick that I thought I should have.... I went in and I went to work and I got my house paid for. Five-buck house, I always called it. That was all the money I had.

STEVE: That's a great story.

DOROTHY: That's what you call nerve. Going to look at a house as if you had a million dollars hanging onto your purse.

• • •

Brantford made twine. That was McCormick. And we used to do Brantford's work and put it out. And Brantford made us use their cards. Which wasn't fair... I used to stick my tickets in and put my name on it. Well, I was up at my brother's [who owned a farm] and – you'll hardly believe this – I was up there, and Norm was telling me he was buying Brantford twine. He wasn't buying Hamilton. And I said, "You are...are you...?" So we were out in the field and he opened this bag up. And I said, "Let's see that." So I looked down in the bottom. "Whose name's that?" And he said, "That's you!" I said, "I made that twine. They're making that twine in Hamilton. That's not Brantford."

STEVE: So you'd write your name on it?

DOROTHY: On the card. On the little sticker card and I shoved it in the bag. "Inspected by Dorothy." You'd seal it all over and it was in that bag. And he didn't believe it. And I said I did that for every one that I put out for Brantford. I figured Brantford's not going to get the credit for this twine. And they said, "Don't put nothing in there. Only Brantford." And I thought, why should they get it?

STEVE: Why do you think they closed the mill then?

DOROTHY: Too much opposition. They were making twine in the States. To Chicago. So they just put us right out of business. Yeah. Yeah. It was an American plant. You can't fight the Yankees. You know what they say: "Them damn Yankees."

JOHN LIVINGSTONE

TRUE TEMPER, HAMILTON, ONTARIO [CLOSED 1987]

STEVE: When they decided to close the Saltfleet plant, how was that announced to you? Do you remember the day that they made the announcement?

JOHN: Oh, yeah. They took us down and told us that the plant would be closing at the end of that year. So we had a meeting: the executive and I. And we just said they've made their minds up, so let's just do a closure agreement. Saltfleet closed in 1987 with a closure agreement.

They were willing to give you a couple of dollars here and a couple of dollars there and that was it. We added to the pension multipliers. Plus, the medical was extended. And we received a good severance package. I got about $11,000 severance. Some guys got $22,000. The pension agreement was good for some, not for others.

I had twenty-two years service, but I got two years added on in the closeout agreement.... I'm here waiting for retirement now. It's a bad thing when you lose your job. As I said, you lose your dignity too. I didn't, but a lot of people do....

PETER WIRTH
TRUSCON AND CANADA MOTOR LAMP [ROCKWELL], WINDSOR, ONTARIO [CLOSED 1960 AND 1975, RESPECTIVELY]

PETER: It was good [coming to Canada Motor Lamp after Truscon Steel closed its Windsor plant in 1960]. Some new guys; a new bunch of guys in there.

STEVE: Is that right across the street from Dominion Forge? It's still there, right?

PETER: Yeah, falling apart [laughs]. They got to pull it down pretty soon because somebody had set fire inside there. It was a good plant when we were there.

STEVE: Was it one big open space?

PETER: Yeah, right to the back.

STEVE: How was it laid out? You'd walk in the front door?

PETER: Front door is [to] the office. Factory workers would come in the side.... We [tool-and-die makers] were in the back, southwest corner in the tool room. You had a large press room and a small press room.... Good place to work.

Interior, Canada Motor Lamp (later Rockwell), Windsor, Ontario

ED LAWRENSON

BENDIX AUTOMOTIVE, WINDSOR, ONTARIO [CLOSED 1980]

STEVE: When you go through a shutdown, what do you lose in that kind of experience?

ED: Well, I can remember coming home the day they announced it. I was twenty-seven years old with a couple of kids. I didn't have a mortgage – I was renting. I wasn't making great money. So I tell you I was scared. I was scared, boy. I thought man, what am I going to do? I had been there ten years. Just the thought of going out and looking for another job was unbelievable, devastating. You kind of have to build yourself up. You get that worthless feeling. It was scary. I was scared....

And then...the company "supposedly" lost our employee records. We couldn't even apply for pogey. They moved all of the paperwork to Chatham and when I went down to file, they couldn't find it. It took four months to straighten out. I had no money or nothin,' eh?

I remember the woman down at Unemployment Insurance saying to me, "You never worked there." Hey lady, don't tell me I haven't worked there. Like, Christ, I've been there ten years. But she was adamant: "You've never worked there before."

• • •

Things have always been made too easy for corporations. They are allowed to come in. They make tremendous profits, ruin people's health and lives, and when things get tough, they just pack up and disappear. I can remember hearing stories of several companies: the employees left one night, went back the next morning, and the place was empty. They loaded trucks and crossed the border. Well, you have to have customs papers for that. And with equipment and loans and grants... And if things get a little tough, the first thing they'll say is "We'll go to the States."

There was a threat of "We'll pull out, we'll go to the States." Well, in my opinion, especially after Bendix... "Hey, if you're going to be like that, we don't want you anyway." We'd rather be out of work than have to live in fear of working from one week to the next, from one year to the next. That's not a way to live....

I honestly believe the people of Canada have been shafted. They've had the wool pulled over their eyes and these corporations laugh right in our faces.

BOB RICE
NIPISSING REFINERY, COBALT, ONTARIO [CLOSED SEVERAL TIMES]

NOTE: *The following exchange followed Bob Rice's (a former mill manager) recounting of how the plant's planned reopening in 1975 came to naught, when a police investigation found that the new owners had no intention of carrying out the plan. It was a scam designed to defraud the government of thousands of dollars in regional development monies. Promised their old jobs back, eighteen refinery workers had invested time and money preparing the site.*

STEVE: The eighteen guys must have been heartbroken.
BOB: They were used to it. It is the story of Cobalt. Boom and bust. Boom and bust. Boom and bust. It has been going on like that for

a hundred years because the people coming up from Toronto and Ottawa, New York, or wherever, used the romance of the mining town and the romance of a people to their advantage.

DAVID CHRISTOPHERSON
ALLEN INDUSTRIES, HAMILTON, ONTARIO [CLOSED MID-1980s]

STEVE: How did you find out about the closure?
DAVID: The usual way it happens: rumours floating around for the longest time; people trying to decipher what's on crates and invoices that are coming in. Strange people walking through the plant looking very worried or very decisive or very analytical and weren't just studying for the usual reasons.... It was all under a cloak of secrecy. The rumour mill was churning.... Of course we had nothing in the collective agreement for closures because it's like getting a clause to insure you from a meteorite hitting. There's no reason to put it in there. There was also little or no legislation in place to govern it either....

• • •

They [the management of Allen Industries] would not even talk. They would not even talk. So we began to mount pressure by the usual means: resolutions to the labour council, picketing outside, letters from Bob White, who is now president of the Canadian Labour Congress. And, of course, the point was "You're not even going to meet?" Eventually that pressure led to a meeting and we did our homework....

[We] created a team and sat down and we were ready to start working: as we would with any other set of negotiations. This was the normal way you'd prepare. The company just walked in and sat down, listened to us...and they said, "We've heard what you've had to say. We'll get back to you." Alright. We were hoping they'd be a little more prepared than that. But alright. And then pushed them for a time frame. In the meantime, they hired one of the best, and most ruthless (in my opinion) company labour lawyers around. I don't know how the man slept at night. I honestly don't. But anyway, they went away and after the agreed period of time...they just said, "We

have nothing further to negotiate." And of course…they hadn't done anything. They were obviously just playing us for time and they – and some of us were just apoplectic that this was their attitude – weren't moving. Their response was, "You wanted a meeting, you got it. You wanted us to listen to what you say, we listened. We told you we would respond and our response is 'We have nothing further to say.'" So I mean we were cranked. It's so unreasonable and so unbelievable that we never planned for them to come in and be that ruthless.…

Our strategy was to find ways to get them to give us some kind of an offer, but we really didn't have a legal leg to stand on. We aimed to force them. The provincial and federal governments were next to useless. They made a few noises, but they didn't do anything. They didn't see it as part of their responsibility. It was very much laissez-faire business politics: "Well that's the story folks. That's just the way the business world works and gosh its too bad that those nice people are being hurt, but hey, we can't do anything." So they were no help at all. What we ultimately decided was that we had to hit them in their pocketbook. And the reality was that they hadn't done their planning very well. The announced closure was out, but they had to keep producing

Abandoned Farm Implements Factory, Hamilton, Ontario

in order to honour their contracts. Somehow they had it in their minds that these little working people will be good enough to continue as they always had, right up to the end, and quietly jump off the cliff and go away. Now we didn't quite see it that way....

We need to have an impact to get the message through, but we didn't want to do something that was so dramatic that we had them decide it was better to shut it down. We had to find a way to be an effective irritant that was enough of an irritant to affect their decision, but not enough to have them take a decision [to depart early].... If we just took over the plant and shut it down, there was a good chance they were going to [go].... Instead, what we decided was a campaign where we had people wearing badges – the local made them up...and people would pin them on – they were of all shapes and colours and all they said was, "I'm blowing the whistle on Allen Industries." Then we issued everybody – as they were going into work on the first day of the campaign – with a whistle. The instructions were given very quietly, and we hoped enough to cover us should legal action take place, but we were in dangerous water anyway. It was no time for the leadership to get nervous. The plan was that as soon as you had enough distance and distraction from your foreman or supervisor, you'd blow the whistle. That's all you did – you blew the whistle. Now there were other things happening, which to this day I still don't fully know [who was behind them]…. It was amazing how many breakdowns they had, and how many products turned out just a little off what they should have been. Funny how that happened. But the main one was a psychological game. Our whole point was to force them to negotiate. That's all we wanted.

At the same time that this was going on, we had the usual picketers outside, and we had people coming in from other plants with the broader message of "You owe it to us to sit down and talk." But the main strategy inside the plant was just to drive them absolutely crazy. Every time you didn't have to work, you didn't, but this was not an acknowledged "slow down." It was an individual thing…. All day long you had all these whistles going off all over the place. Day after day after day and they couldn't stop it. And we had the public behind us. There was just enough going on, enough trouble, it was interfering with their ability to get their product out. But again we hadn't crossed the line where they said, "Look, its better to just wash our hands of this place." We drove the supervisors crazy with those bloody whistles. It was driving our people nuts too, but not in the same way because it was their fight. And our people felt good because through it all we felt so hopeless. It was like what it must be like for a scientist to face new viruses when AIDS first broke. Where they sit down and say, "What do we do?" We had to do something. By engaging our people, without realizing it at the time, we were also giv- ing people hope. Because they were fighting and at least doing something. And they had the support of the community and the broader labour movement, but we made sure it was still locally run…. At the end of the day, we did get a settlement…. There was finally something…. We won the recognition and the right of workers to get something more than a pink slip.

Refinery Gear, Cobalt, Ontario

Coal Tipple, West Virginia

CHAPTER 7

KING COAL
The Coal Counties of West Virginia

WEST VIRGINIA HAS ALWAYS BEEN AN OVERWHELMINGLY rural state. In 1990, two-thirds of the population remained rural.[1] However, unlike other rural states, West Virginia was heavily industrialized. Men came to work in the West Virginia coal mines from far and wide. Residents of mining communities therefore had diverse origins, and included large numbers of African-Americans, as well as immigrants from Italy and Eastern Europe. Despite these racial and ethnic differences, a powerful sense of class solidarity was forged in the "mine wars" of the early twentieth century.

The history of coal mining in West Virginia, as elsewhere, is one of struggle and conflict. The efforts of the United Mine Workers of America (UMW), formed in 1890, to organize the state's coalfields, met with fierce resistance. Mill owners employed the hired guns of the Baldwin Felts Detective Agency to evict union families from company housing. Local sheriffs usually did the bidding of mine owners. Sid Hatfield, the chief of police of Matewan, proved to be an exception. A hero in life, Hatfield became a martyr in death for the miners' union, when he was gunned down on the steps of the McDowell County courthouse in Welch. His story is featured in a film named after the town of Matewan.[2]

In Canada, mining companies were sold mining rights, but not the land itself. In West Virginia, by contrast, natural resource companies control two-thirds of all private lands. As a result, the state has many classic "company towns" where the mine owned the housing, the general store, and virtually all other places of business. Before World War I, nearly 80 percent of mine workers in southern West Virginia lived in company-owned towns.[3] In McDowell County, only 7 percent of the land was given over to farming – but many miners' families had substantial gardens. A few companies, such as the U.S. Steel Corporation, even developed model towns.[4]

Yet most mining towns in McDowell and Wyoming counties, as elsewhere in West Virginia, were no kind of model. In 1943, U.S. Secretary of the Interior Ickes assigned Richard L.G. Deverall to investigate a wildcat strike that halted coal production in the area. Deverall reported on the mining camps in the vicinity of Welch, particularly the Elkhorn Valley, which had a population of 94,000 and seventy-three mines in operation.[5] He indicated that most of the company towns in the area were built around the mine. They are, he reported, "impossibly dirty, containing no grass and are devoid of any recreational activity of any kind." Similarly, prices at the company store were "outrageously high," and many miners were in debt.[6] "The miner is therefore chained to the company town," he concluded. Deverall also noted

Glen Rogers, West Virginia

that coal companies were dumping slag from the mines wherever they saw fit – scarring the landscape.

Coal used up people and place. In their haunting book, *Coal Hollow*, Ken and Melanie Light make the point that the coal companies once treated miners and their families like slag.[7] While company control over towns gradually diminished in the post-war era, the industrial and residential ruins pictured in this chapter originate in this period. Coal-mining towns have been devastated by reduced employment stemming from a combination of technological change and mine closures. Between 1950 and 1970, the number of coal miners in the United States dropped an astounding 75 percent. In West Virginia, the number of coal miners fell during that period from 127,304 to 40,513.[8] The number had dropped to just 24,000 by 1990. The loss of so many unionized jobs has resulted in high unemployment, mass out-migration, and the abandonment of once-bustling mining towns. In fact, over one million people have left West Virginia since 1945.

David Lewis, by contrast, has been drawn to West Virginia for decades. He travels to the state whenever he gets the chance. For this project, he photographed the coal towns of Welch, Cass, and Glen Rogers, all located in the southern coal-mining counties. Much like Deverell fifty years earlier, David noticed the environmental legacy of mining in the area. Companies had

Peerless Coal & Coke Co., West Virginia, 1921

mined off entire mountaintops and dumped the debris into the surrounding valleys. The photographic images of abandoned storefronts, offices, and a boarding house, were all taken in Glen Rogers.

Interior Hallway, Allied Paper, Kalamazoo, Michigan

CHAPTER 8

A VANISHING LANDMARK
Allied Paper in Kalamazoo, Michigan

CLOSED IN 1998, THE OLD BRYANT (LATER ALLIED) PAPER mill in Kalamazoo, Michigan, still had most of its machinery in place when David Lewis visited the site in 2004. The mill, designed by civil engineer Dan J. Albertson, began production in 1896. Along with four other area paper mills, the Bryant mill helped make Kalamazoo "The Paper City" for much of the twentieth century. That phase ended in the 1990s when all five mills closed, displacing 1,500 workers. The local economy was further rocked by the closure of a General Motors stamping plant, and with it, the loss of another 3,500 jobs.[1] Recently, the city's pharmaceutical industry has taken a hit, with major layoffs of scientists and headquarters staff. As a sign of the times, the former headquarters building of the John Updike Company is being demolished in 2007.[2]

When David entered the charred remains of the office area of the abandoned mill, torched by vandals in 2001, he was surprised to discover dozens of now worthless Allied Paper Company share certificates strewn across the floor. One of these share certificates is reproduced in the travelling exhibition of David's work. The interior was a "joy to photograph," he recalled. One of the three mill buildings, Mill C, has since been demolished, and most of the remaining structures were slated to be torn down by December 2004. In

Allied Paper, Kalamazoo, Michigan

August 2004, demolition crews had even uncovered an illicit methampheta-mine lab in one of the mill buildings. According to Ed Finnerty, a journalist for the *Kalamazoo Gazette*, historic preservationists had lobbied to save the mills from the wrecking ball, but to no avail.[3] The powerhouse still stood in February 2007.

The story does not end here, however. The United States Environmental Protection Agency (EPA) and the Michigan Department of Natural Resources (MDNR) have compiled considerable data about Allied Paper, which had operated on this eighty-acre site since 1925. The mill left a poisoned environmental legacy. In fact, the site made it onto the EPA's national

Power House, Allied Paper, Kalamazoo, Michigan

priority list once the MDNR detected polychlorinated biphenyls (PCBs) – a likely carcinogen – in sediment in the Kalamazoo River, in 1986. The trail of contamination was traced back to Allied's Bryant Mill Pond discharges into Portage Creek. Michigan filed a complaint against Allied in 1987, demanding an immediate end to the release of hazardous substances into the environment. Tests have since revealed that an estimated 350,000 pounds of PCBs, discharged by four area paper mills including Allied, have collected in the waterways. The Allied mill site poses an unacceptable risk to human health and the environment, particularly to the 142,000 people who obtain their drinking water within a three-mile radius. To deal with this problem, the EPA

Charred Office, Allied Paper, Kalamazoo, Michigan

has designated an eighty-mile stretch of the Kalamazoo River and a three-mile stretch of Portage Creek as a "Superfund Site." Removal of contaminants began on Portage Creek in 1998, upon the mill's closing.

Bibliography

Alessio, Dominic T. "Capitalist Realist Art: Industrial Images of Hamilton, Ontario, 1884–1910," *Journal of Urban History* 18, 4 (1992), 442–69.

Altman, Irwin and Setha M. Low, eds. *Place Attachment*. New York: Plenum Press, 1992.

Anastakis, Dimitry. "Industrial Sunrise? The Chrysler Bailout, the State, and the Re-industrialization of the Canadian Automotive Sector, 1975–1986," *Urban History Review* 35, 2 (Spring 2007), 37–50.

Andreae, Christopher. "Industry, Dereliction, and Landscapes in Ontario," *Ontario History* 89, 2 (June 1997), 161–80.

Andrews, Malcolm. *The Search for the Picturesque: Landscape Aesthetics and Tourism in Britain, 1760–1800*. Palo Alto: Stanford University Press, 1989.

Angus, Charlie and Louie Palu. *Industrial Cathedrals of the North*. Toronto: Between the Lines, 1999.

Bamberger, Bill and Cathy N. Davidson. *Closing: The Life and Death of an American Factory*. New York: W.W. Norton and Company, 1998.

Barnes, Trevor J. and Roger Hayter, "Economic Restructuring, Local Development and Resource Towns: Forest Communities in Coastal British Columbia," *Canadian Journal of Regional Science* 17, 3 (Autumn 1994), 289–310.

Barthel, Diane. "Getting in Touch with History: The Role of Historic Preservation in Shaping Collective Memories," *Qualitative Sociology* 19, 3 (1996), 345–64.

Bashevkin, Sylvia. *True Patriot Love: The Politics of Canadian Nationalism*. Toronto: Oxford University Press, 1991.

Beauregard, Robert. *Voices of Decline: The Postwar Fate of U.S. Cities*. Oxford: Blackwell, 1993.

Benjamin, Walter. *Illuminations*. London: Verso, 1973.

Biggs, Lindy. *The Rational Factory: Architecture, Technology, and Work in America's Age of Mass Production*. Baltimore: Johns Hopkins University Press, 1996.

Blackmar, Elizabeth. "Modernist Ruins," *American Quarterly* 53, 2 (2001), 324–39.

Block, Fred. *Postindustrial Possibilities: A Critique of Economic Discourse*. Berkeley: University of California Press, 1990.

Bluestone, Barry and Bennett Harrison. *The Deindustrialization of America: Plant Closings, Community Abandonment, and the Dismantling of Basic Industry*. New York: Basic Books, 1982.

Bodnar, John. "Power and Memory in Oral History: Workers and Managers at Studebaker," *Journal of American History* 75 (1989), 1201–21.

Bourdieu, Pierre. "The Social Space and the Genesis of Groups," *Theory and Society* 14 (November 1985), 723–44.

———. "Social Space and Symbolic Power," *Sociological Theory* 7, 1 (1989), 14–25.

Brantlinger, Patrick, "Victorians and Africans: The Genealogy of the Myth of the Dark Continent," *Critical Inquiry* 12, 1 (1985), 166–203.

Bruno, Robert. *Steelworker Alley: How Class Works in Youngstown*. Ithaca: Cornell University Press, 1999.

Buss, Terry F. and F. Stevens Redburn. *Shutdown at Youngstown: Public Policy for Mass Unemployment*. Albany: State University of New York Press, 1983.

Calhoun, C.J. "Community: Toward a Variable Conceptualization for Comparative Research," *Social History* 5, 1 (January 1980), 105–29.

Camp, Scott D. *Worker Response to Plant Closings: Steelworkers in Johnstown and Youngstown*. New York: Garland Publishers, 1995.

Campbell, Colin. *The Romantic Ethic and the Spirit of Modern Consumerism*. New York: Blackwell, 1987.

Chatterley, Cedric and Alicia J. Rouverol. *"I Was Content and Not Content": The Story of Linda Lord and the Closing of Penobscot Poultry*. Carbondale: Southern Illinois University Press, 2000.

Cohen, Lizabeth. "What Kind of a World Have We Lost? Workers' Lives and Deindustrialization in the Museum," *American Quarterly* 41, 4 (1989), 670–81.

Connerly, Charles E. "The Community Question: An Extension of Wellman and Leighton," *Urban Affairs Quarterly* 20, 4 (1985), 537–56.

Cooper, Frederick. *Colonialism in Question: Theory, Knowledge, History*. Berkeley: University of California Press, 2005.

Cowie, Jefferson. *Capital Moves: RCA's 70-Year Quest for Cheap Labor*. Ithaca: Cornell University Press, 1999.

Cowie, Jefferson and Joseph Heathcott, eds. *Beyond the Ruins: The Meaning of Deindustrialization*. Ithaca: Cornell University Press, 2003.

Cullen, Jim. *Born in the USA: Bruce Springsteen and the American Tradition*. New York: Harper Collins, 1997.

Culler, Jonathan. "The Semiotics of Tourism," in *Framing the Sign: Criticism and its Institutions*. Oxford: Blackwell, 1988.

Cumbler, John T. *A Social History of Economic Decline: Business, Politics and Work in Trenton*. New Brunswick, NJ: Rutgers University Press, 1989.

Davis, Fred. *Yearning for Yesterday: A Sociology of Nostalgia*. New York: Free Press, 1979.

Dawson, Michael. "Victoria Debates its Post–Industrial Reality: Tourism, Deindustrialization, and Store–Hour Regulations, 1900–1958," *Urban History Review* 35, 2 (Spring 2007), 14–24.

Debary, Octave. "Deindustrialization and Museumification: From Exhibited Memory to Forgotten History," *Sociology of Education* 69, 2 (April 1996), 105–25.

de Certeau, Michel. *The Practice of Everyday Life*. Berkeley: University of California Press, 1984.

Deyo, L.B. and David "Lefty" Leibowitz. *Invisible Frontier: Exploring the Tunnels, Ruins and Rooftops of Hidden New York*. New York: Three Rivers Press, 2003.

Dublin, Thomas. *When the Mines Closed: Stories of Struggle in Hard Times*. Ithaca: Cornell University Press, 1998.

Dudley, Kathryn Marie. *The End of the Line: Lost Jobs, New Lives in Postindustrial America*. Chicago: University of Chicago Press, 1994.

Duncombe, Stephen. *Notes from Underground: Zines and the Politics of Alternative Culture*. New York: Verso, 1997.

Dunk, Thomas W. *It's A Working Man's Town: Male Working-Class Culture*. Montreal: McGill–Queen's University Press, 1991.

Edensor, Tim. "The Ghosts of Industrial Ruins: Ordering and Disordering Memory in Excessive Space," *Environment and Planning D: Society and Place* 23 (2005), 829–49.

———. *Industrial Ruins: Space, Aesthetics and Materiality*. Oxford: Berg, 2005.

Edwards, J. Arwel and Joan Carles Llurdés i Coit, "Mines and Quarries: Industrial

Heritage Tourism," *Annals of Tourism Research* 23, 2 (1996), 341–63.

Egan, Brian and Susanne Klausen, "Female in a Forest Town: The Marginalization of Women in Port Alberni's Economy," *BC Studies* 118 (1998), 5–40.

Evans, Walker. *Photographs for the Farm Security Administration, 1935–1938.* New York: De Capo Press, 1975.

Faue, Elizabeth. "Community, Class and Comparison in Labour History and Local History," *Labour History* 78 (May 2000), 155–62.

Fine, Lisa. *The Story of REO JOE: Work, Kin, and Community in Autotown, USA.* Philadelphia: Temple University Press, 2004.

Foote, Kenneth E. *Shadowed Ground: America's Landscapes of Violence and Tragedy.* Albany: State University of New York Press, 2001.

Francaviglia, Richard V. *Hard Places: Reading the Landscape of America's Historic Mining Districts.* Iowa City: University of Iowa Press, 1991.

Frisch, Michael. "De-, Re-, and Post-Industrialization: Industrial Heritage as Contested Memorial Terrain," *Journal of Folklore Research* 35, 3 (1998).

———. *A Shared Authority: Essays on the Craft and Meaning of Oral and Public History.* Albany: State University of New York Press, 1990.

Foucault, Michel. *Discipline and Punish: The Birth of the Prison.* New York: Vintage, 1975.

Fritzsche, Peter. "Specters of History: On Nostalgia, Exile, and Modernity," *American Historical Review* (December 2001), 1587–618.

Garman, Bryan. "The Ghost of History: Bruce Springsteen, Woody Guthrie and the Hurt Song," *Popular Music and Society* 20, 2 (1996), 69–120.

Gindin, Sam. *The Canadian Auto Workers: The Birth and Transformation of a Union.* Toronto: James Lorimer and Company, 1995.

Green, James. *Taking History to Heart: The Power of the Past in Building Social Movements.* Amherst: University of Massachusetts Press, 2000.

Gregory, Derek and John Urry, eds. *Social Relations and Spatial Structures.* New York: St. Martin's Press, 1985.

Greil, Marcus. *Lipstick Traces: A Secret History of the 20th Century.* Cambridge: Harvard University Press, 1990.

Guimond, James. *American Photography and the American Dream.* Chapel Hill: University of North Carolina Press, 1991.

Hathaway, Dale A. *Can Workers Have A Voice? The Politics of Deindustrialization in Pittsburgh.* University Park, PA: Pennsylvania State University Press, 1993.

Hayden, Dolores. *The Power of Place: Urban Landscapes as Public History.* Cambridge, MA: MIT Press, 1995.

Hayter, Roger, Trevor J. Barnes, and Michael J. Bradshaw, "Relocating Resource Peripheries to the Core of Economic Geography's Theorizing: Rationale and Agenda," *AREA* 35, 1 (2003), 15–23.

Herod, Andrew. "Workers, Space and Labor Geography," *International Labor and Working Class History* 64 (Fall 2003), 112–38.

Heron, Craig. "The Labour Historian and Public History," *Labour/le Travail* 45 (Spring 2000), 171–97.

High, Steven. "Capital and Community Reconsidered: The Politics and Meaning of Deindustrialization," *Labour/le Travail* 55 (Spring 2005), 187–96.

———. "Deindustrializing Youngstown: Memories of Resistance and Loss in the Decades Following 'Black Monday,'" *History Workshop Journal* 54 (2002), 100–21.

———. *Industrial Sunset: The Making of North America's Rust Belt, 1969–1984.* Toronto: University of Toronto Press, 2003.

———. "Introduction." Special Issue on "The Politics and Memory of Deindustrialization in Canada" *Urban History Review* 35, 2 (Spring 2007), 2–13.

Hine, Lewis. *Men at Work. Photographic Studies of Modern Men and Machines.* New York: Dover, 1977.

Hospers, Gert-Jan. "Industrial Heritage Tourism and Regional Restructuring in the European Union," *European Planning Studies* 10, 3 (2002), 397–404.

Ingham, John N. *The Iron Barons: A Social Analysis of an American Urban Elite, 1874–1965.* Westport, Connecticut: Greenwood Press, 1977.

Jakle, John and David Wilson. *Derelict Landscapes: The Wasting of America's Built Environment.* Savage, MD: Rowan and Littlefield Publishers, 1992.

Jasen, Patricia. *Wild Things: Nature, Culture and Tourism in Ontario, 1790–1914.* Toronto: University of Toronto Press, 1995.

Jenson, Jane and Rianne Mahon, eds. *The Challenge of Restructuring: North American Labor Movements Respond.* Philadelphia: Temple University Press, 1993.

Joseph, Miranda. *Against the Romance of Community.* Minneapolis: University of Minnesota Press, 2002.

Lange, Dorothea. *Dorthea Lange: Photographs of a Lifetime.* New York: Aperture, 1982.

Lasch, Christopher. "The Communitarian Critique of Liberalism," in Charles H. Reynolds and Ralph V. Norman, eds. *Community in America.* Berkeley: University of California Press, 1988, 60–76.

———. *The True and Only Heaven: Progress and Its Critics.* New York: W.W. Norton, 1991.

Lears, Jackson. *No Place of Grace: Antimodernism and the Transformation of American Culture, 1880–1920.* New York: Pantheon, 1981.

LeBelle, Wayne F. *Sturgeon Falls, 1895–1995.* Field, Ontario: WFL Communications, 1995.

———. *West Nipissing Ouest.* Field, Ontario: WFL Communications, 1998.

Lennon, J. John and Malcolm Foley. *Dark Tourism: The Attraction of Death and Disaster.* London: Thomson Press, 2000.

Lewis, David W. *The Art of Bromoil and Transfer.* North Bay, 1995.

———. *The Passion Pit: A Tribute to the Drive-in.* North Bay, 2001.

Lewis, Ronald L. "Appalachian Restructuring in Historical Perspective: Coal, Culture and Social Change in West Virginia," *Urban Studies* 30, 2 (1993), 299–308.

Linehan, Denis. "An Archaeology of Dereliction: Poetics and Policy in the Governing of Depressed Industrial Districts in Interwar England and Wales," *Journal of Historical Geography* 26, 1 (2000), 99–113.

Linkon, Sherry Lee and John Russo. *Steeltown USA: Work and Memory in Youngstown.* Lawrence: University of Kansas Press, 2002.

Lucic, Karen. *Charles Sheeler and the Cult of the Machine.* Cambridge: Harvard University Press, 1991.

Lynd, Staughton. *The Fight Against Shutdowns: Youngstown's Steel Mill Closings.* San Pedro, CA: Singlejack Books, 1982.

———. "The Genesis of the Idea of a Community Right to Industrial Property in Youngstown and Pittsburgh, 1977–1987," *Journal of American History* 74, 3 (1987), 926–58.

———. *Living Inside Our Hope: A Steadfast Radical's Thoughts on Rebuilding the Movement.* Ithaca: ILR Press, 1997

Mahon, Rianne. *The Politics of Industrial Restructuring: Canadian Textiles.* Toronto: University of Toronto Press, 1984.

Mairess, Francois. "La belle histoire, aux origines de la nouvelle muséologie," *Publics et Musées* 17–18 (janvier–juin 2000), 33–56.

Mann, Alan. *Gathering at the Forks: The Story of Wallaceburg.* Wallaceburg: Standard Press, 1984.

Marcus, Irwin M. "An Experiment in Reindustrialization: The Tri–State Conference on Steel and the Creation of the Steel Valley Authority," *Pennsylvania History* 54, 3 (1987), 179–96.

Marsh, Dave. *Glory Days: Bruce Springsteen in the 1980s*. New York: Pantheon, 1987.

Massey, Doreen. *For Space*. London: Sage, 2005.

———. "Places and their Pasts," *History Workshop Journal* 39 (1995), 182–92.

———. *Spatial Divisions of Labour: Social Structures and the Geography of Production*. London: Macmillan, 1984.

Massey, Doreen and Pat Jess, eds. *A Place in the World? Places, Cultures and Globalization*. Oxford: Oxford University Press, 1995.

Mawhiney, Anne–Marie and Jane Pitblado, eds. *Boom Town Blues: Elliot Lake, Collapse and Revival in a Single-Industry Community*. Toronto: Dundurn Press, 1999.

McDonnell, Greg. *Wheat Kings: Vanishing Landmarks of the Canadian Prairies*. Toronto: Boston Mills Press, 1999.

McKay, Ian. *The Quest for the Folk: Anti-Modernism and Cultural Selection in Twentieth-Century Nova Scotia*. Montreal: McGill-Queen's University Press, 1994.

Milkman, Ruth. *Farewell to the Factory: Auto Workers in the Late Twentieth Century*. Berkeley: University of California Press, 1997.

Modell, Judith and Charlie Brodsky. *A Town Without Steel: Envisioning Homestead*. Pittsburgh: University of Pittsburgh Press, 1998.

Moore, Sally F. and Barbara G. Myerhoff, eds. *Secular Ritual*. Amsterdam: Van Gorcum, 1977.

Newman, Katherine S. "Turning Your Backs On Tradition: Symbolic Analysis and Moral Critique in a Plant Shutdown," *Urban Anthropology* 14, 1–3 (1985), 109–50.

Ninjalicious. *Access All Areas: A User's Guide to the Art of Urban Exploration*. Toronto: Infiltration, 2005.

Niosi, Jorge and Henri Gagnon. *Fermetures d'usines, ou bien, libération nationale*. Montreal: les éditions Héritage, 1979.

Nissen, Bruce, ed. *Fighting for Jobs: Case Studies of Labor, Community Coalitions Confronting Plant Closings*. Albany: State University of New York Press, 1995.

Nora, Pierre, ed. *Realms of Memory: The Construction of the French Past*. New York: Columbia University Press, 1998.

Norcliffe, Glen. "Mapping De–industrialization: Brian Kippling's Landscapes of Toronto," *Canadian Geographer* 40 (1996), 266–77.

Norkunas, Martha. *Monuments and Memory: History and Representation in Lowell, Massachusetts*. Washington: Smithsonian, 2002.

Noverr, Douglas A. "The Midwestern Industrial Landscapes of Charles Sheeler and Philip Evergood," *Journal of American Culture* 10, 1 (Spring 1987), 15–25.

Nye, David E. *American Technological Sublime*. Cambridge: MIT Press, 1994.

———. *Image Worlds: Corporate Identities at General Electric, 1890–1930*. Cambridge: MIT Press, 1985.

Ohrne, Karin Becker. *Dorothea Lange and the Documentary Tradition*. Baton Rouge: Louisiana State University Press, 1980.

O'Neill, Annie. *Unquiet Ruin: A Photographic Excavation*. Pittsburgh: University of Pittsburgh Press, 2001.

Osberg, Lars, Fred Wien, and Jan Grude. *Vanishing Jobs: Canada's Changing Workplaces*. Toronto: James Lorimer, 1995.

Overton, James. *Making a World of Difference: Essays on Tourism, Culture and Development in Newfoundland*. St. John's: ISER, 1996.

Pace, Patricia. "Staging Childhood: Photographs of Child Labor," *The Lion and the Unicorn* 26 (2002), 324–52.

Pappas, Gregory. *The Magic City: Unemployment in a Working-Class Community.* Ithaca: Cornell University Press, 1989.

Pinder, David. "Arts of Urban Exploration," *Cultural Geographies* 121 (2005), 383–411.

Portelli, Alessandro. *The Death of Luigi Trastulli and Other Stories: Form and Meaning in Oral History.* Albany: State University of New York Press, 1991.

Pratt, Mary Louise. *Imperial Eyes: Travel Writing and Transculturation.* New York: Routledge, 1992.

Quarter, Jack. *Crossing the Line: Unionized Employee Ownership and Investment Funds.* Toronto: James Lorimer and Company, 1995.

Rogovin, Milton and Michael Frisch. *Portraits in Steel.* Ithaca: Cornell University Press, 1993.

Rollwagen, Katherine. "When Ghosts Hovered: Community and Crisis in a Company Town, Britannia Beach, British Columbia, 1957–1965," *Urban History Review* 35, 2 (Spring 2007), 25–36.

Rubenstein, James M. *The Changing U.S. Auto Industry: A Geographical Analysis.* New York: Routledge, 1992.

Said, Edward W. *Culture and Imperialism.* New York: Alfred A. Knopf, 1993.

———. *Orientalism.* New York: Vintage, 1979.

Salerno, Roger A. *Landscapes of Abandonment: Capitalism, Modernity, and Estrangement.* Albany: State University New York Press, 2003.

Schumpeter, Joseph A. *Capitalism, Socialism and Democracy.* New York: Harper and Row, 1976.

Serrin, William. *Homestead: The Glory and Tragedy of an American Steel Town.* New York: Vintage Books, 1994.

Shakel, Paul A. and Matthew Palus. "Remembering an Industrial Landscape," *International Journal of Historical Archaeology* 10, 1 (March 2006), 49–71.

Seed, Patricia. *Ceremonies of Possession in Europe's Conquest of the New World, 1492–1640.* New York: Cambridge University Press, 1995.

Shindo, Charles J. *Dust Bowl Migrants in the American Imagination.* Lawrence, Kansas: University of Kansas Press, 1997.

Smith, Doug. *Stickin' To the Union: Local 2224 Versus John Buhler.* Halifax: Fernwood Publishers, 2004.

Smith, Neil. *Uneven Development: Nature, Capital and the Production of Space.* Oxford: Blackwell, 1984.

Sobel, David and Susan Meurer. *Working at Inglis: The Life and Death of a Canadian Factory.* Toronto: James Lorimer and Company, 1994.

Sontag, Susan. *On Photography.* New York: Farrar, Strauss and Giroux, 1973.

Stein, Judith. *Running Steel, Running America: Race, Economic Policy and the Decline of Liberalism.* Chapel Hill: University of North Carolina Press, 1998.

Stewart, Kathleen. "Nostalgia – A Polemic," *Cultural Anthropology* 3, 3 (August 1988), 227–41.

———. *A Space on the Side of the Road: Cultural Poetics in an "Other" America.* Princeton: Princeton University Press, 1996.

Strange, Carolyn. "Symbiotic Commemoration: The Stories of Kalaupapa," *History and Memory* 16, 1 (2004), 86–117.

Summerby-Murray, Robert. "Interpreting Deindustrialised Landscapes of Atlantic Canada: Memory and Industrial Heritage in Sackville, New Brunswick," *Canadian Geographer* 46, 1 (2002), 48–62.

———. "Interpreting Personalized Industrial Heritage in the Mining Towns of Cumberland County, Nova Scotia: Landscape Examples from Springhill and River Hebert," *Urban History Review* 35, 2 (Spring 2007), 51–9.

Sugrue, Thomas J. *The Origins of the Urban Crisis: Race and Inequality in Post–war Detroit.* Princeton: Princeton University Press, 1997.

Taksa, Lucy. "Hauling An Infinite Freight of Mental Imagery: Finding Labour's Heritage at the Swindon Railway Steamshops' STEAM Museum," *Labour History Review* 68, 3 (December 2003), 391–410.

Teaford, Jon C. *Cities of the Heartland: The Rise and Fall of the Industrial Midwest.* Bloomington, Indiana: Indiana University Press, 1994.

Terkel, Studs. *Working.* New York: Pantheon, 1972.

Trachtenberg, Alan, ed. *Essays on Photography.* New Haven: Leete's Island Books, 1980.

Trotter, J.W. Jr. *Coal, Class, and Color: Blacks in Southern West Virginia, 1915–32.* Urbana: University of Illinois Press, 1990.

Urry, John. *The Tourist Gaze: Leisure and Travel in Contemporary Societies.* London: SAGE Publications, 1990.

Wallace, Mike. "Industrial Museums and the History of Deindustrialization," *Public Historian* 9, 1 (Winter 1987), 9–19.

———. "Razor Ribbons, History Museums, and Civic Salvation," *Radical History Review* 57 (1993), 221–41.

Walsh, John and Steven High. "Rethinking the Concept of Community," *Histoire sociale/Social History* 17, 64 (1999), 255–74.

Wellman, Barry and Barry Leighton. "Networks, Neighborhoods and Communities: Approaches to the Study of the Community Problem," *Urban Affairs Quarterly* 14 (March 1979), 363–90.

Westerman, William. "Central American Refugee Testimonies and Performed Life Histories in the Sanctuary Movement," in the *Oral History Reader*, eds. Robert Perks and Alistair Thomson. London: Routledge, 1998.

White, Hayden. *The Content of the Form: Narrative Discourse and Historical Representation.* Baltimore: Johns Hopkins University Press, 1987.

Williamson, Michael and Dale Maharidge. *Journey to Nowhere.* Garden City, NY: Dial Press, 1985.

Wilson, Brian. "The Canadian Rave Scene and Five Theses on Youth Resistance," *Canadian Journal of Sociology* 27, 3 (Summer 2002), 373–412.

Wyckoff, William. "Postindustrial Butte," *Geographical Review* 85, 4 (1995), 478–96.

Zukin, Sharon. *Landscapes of Power: From Detroit to Disney World.* Berkeley: University of California Press, 1991.

Oral History Interviews Cited

METROPOLITAN DETROIT, MICHIGAN
(videotapes donated to the
Walter Reuther Library at Wayne
State University)

Solano, Gabriel. Interviewed by Steven High.
February 24, 1998.

WINDSOR, ONTARIO
(videotapes donated to the
Windsor Public Archives)

Lawrenson, Ed. Interviewed by Steven High.
February 26, 1998.
Wirth, Peter. Interviewed by Steven High.
February 22, 1998.

HAMILTON, ONTARIO
(Videotapes donated to the
McMaster University Archives)

Christopherson, David. Interviewed by
Steven High. February 6, 1998.
Livingstone, John. Interviewed by Steven
High. February 7, 1998.
Routenburg, Dorothy. Interviewed by Steven
High, February 6, 1998.
Scandlan, William. Interviewed by Steven
High. February 7, 1998.

STURGEON FALLS, ONTARIO

Barrington, Cam. Interviewed by Steven
High. June 2005.
Beauchamp, Ronald. Interviewed by Kristen
O'Hare. July 8, 2004.
Boudreau, Marcel. Interviewed by Kristen
O'Hare. December 1, 2003.
Boudreau, Marcel. Interviewed by Steven
High. June 2005.

Charles, J.P. Interviewed by Kristen O'Hare.
August 10, 2004.
Colquhoun, Ken. Interviewed by Steven
High. June 2005.
Côté, Marc. Interviewed by Kristen O'Hare.
January 30, 2004.
Fortin, Ed. Interviewed by Kristen O'Hare.
August 5, 2004.
Gervais, Hubert. Interviewed by Steven
High on multiple occasions. 2004–6.
Hardy, Jane. Interviewed by Kristen O'Hare.
December 12, 2003.
Hardy, Jane. Interviewed by Steven High.
June 2005.
Hardy, Pierre. Interviewed by Kristen
O'Hare. December 12, 2003.
Hardy, Pierre. Interviewed by Steven High.
June 2005.
Labbé, Marcel. Interviewed by Kristen
O'Hare. August 18, 2004.
Lacroix, Mike. Interviewed by Kristen
O'Hare. February 4, 2004.
Lafleche, Brian. Interviewed by Kristen
O'Hare. June 3, 2004.
LeBelle, Wayne. Interviewed by Kristen
O'Hare. September 6, 2004.
LeBelle, Wayne. Interviewed by Steven
High. December 2005.
MacGregor, Denis. Interviewed by Kristen
O'Hare. June 17, 2004.
Marcoux, Raymond. Interviewed by Kristen
O'Hare. May 20, 2004.
Pretty, Lawrence. Interviewed by Kristen
O'Hare. June 22, 2004.
Restoule, Randy. Interviewed by Kristen
O'Hare. August 5, 2004.
Thompson. Ruth. Interviewed by Kristen
O'Hare. June 22, 2004.

Notes

INTRODUCTION
**THE LANDSCAPE
AND MEMORY OF
DEINDUSTRIALIZATION**

1   Annie O'Neill, *Unquiet Ruin: A Photo-graphic Excavation* (Pittsburgh: University of Pittsburgh Press, 2001). All three structures were designed by Pittsburgh architect Frederick Osterling.
2   Lindy Biggs, *The Rational Factory: Architecture, Technology, and Work in America's Age of Mass Production* (Philadelphia: John's Hopkins University Press, 1996).
3   Douglas A. Noverr, "The Midwestern Industrial Landscapes of Charles Sheeler and Philip Evergood," *Journal of American Culture* 10, 1 (Spring 1987), pp. 15–16. For more on Charles Sheeler see Karen Lucic, *Charles Sheeler and the Cult of the Machine* (Cambridge: Harvard University Press, 1991).
4   Denis Linehan, "An Archaeology of Dereliction: Poetics and Policy in the Governing of Depressed Industrial Districts in Interwar England and Wales," *Journal of Historical Geography* 26, 1 (2000), p. 99.
5   Delores Hayden, *The Power of Place: Urban Landscapes as Public History* (Cambridge: MIT Press, 1995).
6   Barry Bluestone and Bennett Harrison, *The Deindustrialization of America: Plant Closings, Community Abandonment, and the Dismantling of Basic Industry* (New York: Basic Books, 1982), p. 6.
7   Jefferson Cowie and Joseph Heathcott, eds., *Beyond the Ruins: The Meaning of Deindustrialization* (Ithaca: Cornell University Press, 2003), pp. 1–2.
8   For a critique of the historiography of deindustrialization, see: Steven High, "Capital and Community Reconsidered: The Politics and Meaning of Deindustrialization," *Labour/le Travail* 55 (Spring 2005), pp. 187–96.
9   James Guimond. *American Photography and the American Dream* (Chapel Hill: University of North Carolina Press, 1991), p. 12.
10 Michael Moore, quoted at the outset of Guimond, *American Photography*.
11 Steven High, *Industrial Sunset: The Making of North America's Rust Belt, 1969–1984* (Toronto: University of Toronto Press, 2003), p. 93.
12 Fred O. Williams, "While U.S. Let Its Plants Disappear, Canadians Protected Theirs, Author Says," *Buffalo News*, October 25, 2003, front of business section (continued on p. C4).
13 Jack Metzgar, "Blue-Collar Blues: The Deunionization of Manufacturing," *New Labor Forum* (Spring/Summer 2002), p. 21.
14 "Hearing on Plant Closing Legislation, Hearing Before the Subcommittee on Employment Opportunies of the Committee on Education and Labor," House of Representatives, 98th Congress, Second Session, 1984.
15 High, *Industrial Sunset*, p. 167
16 Report cited in Fred O. Williams, *loc. cit.*
17 Sam Gindin, *The Canadian Auto Workers: The Birth and Transformation of a Union* (Toronto: James Lorimer, 1995).

18 Jack Quarter, *Crossing the Line: Unionization Employee Ownership and Investment Funds* (Toronto: James Lorimer, 1995), ch. 6.

19 Jorge Niosi and Henri Gagnon, *Fermetures d'usines, ou bien, libération nationale* (Montréal: les éditions Héritage, 1979).

20 McLouth Steel, the eleventh-largest steelmaker in the United States (see ch. 5), was built between 1948 and 1954 to serve the steel needs of the auto industry. Because General Motors was its largest customer, the mill rose and fell with Detroit's automotive sector. The company cut its workforce in half between 1976 and 1982, eliminating two thousand jobs, before going into bankruptcy in 1987. At that time, the mill was saved by an employee buyout, only to close for good in the mid-1990s. See Sharon Zukin, *Landscapes of Power: From Detroit to Disney World* (Berkeley: University of California Press, 1991), p. 107.

21 High, *Industrial Sunset*, p. 112.

22 Anastakis credits state policy-makers for this state of affairs. The 1965 Auto Pact, he argues, opened the door to state involvement in the investment decisions of the Big Three automakers. While this argument is compelling, I still believe that political pressure "from below" was crucial in convincing politicians to adopt a very different position than that of their counterparts in the United States. See Dimitry Anastakis, "Industrial Sunrise? The State, The Chrysler Bailout and the Reindustrialization of the Canadian Automotive Sector, 1975–1986," *Urban History Review* (Spring 2007), pp. 37–50. Other articles in this special issue on "The Politics and Memory of Deindustrialization in Canada" examine the mining, fishing, and manufacturing sectors.

23 Lars Osberg, Fred Wien and Jan Grude, *Vanishing Jobs: Canada's Changing Workplaces* (Toronto: James Lorimer, 1995).

24 Ibid.

25 Industrial restructuring in Canada's forestry sector is discussed in a series of studies conducted by scholars associated with the "new economic geography." See Roger Hayter, Trevor J. Barnes, and Michael J. Bradshaw, "Relocating Resource Peripheries to the Core of Economic Geography's Theorizing Rationale and Agenda," *AREA* 35, 1 (2003), pp. 15–23; Trevor Barnes and Roger Hayter, "Economic Restructuring, Local Development and Resource Towns: Forest Communities in Coastal British Columbia," *Canadian Journal of Regional Science* 17, 3 (Autumn 1994), pp. 1289–1310; John Holmes, "In Search of Competitive Efficiency: Labour Process Flexibility in Canadian Newsprint Mills," *Canadian Geographer* 41, 1 (Spring 1997), pp. 7–25; and Glen Norcliffe, *Global Game, Local Arena: Restructuring in Corner Brook, Newfoundland* (St. John's: ISER Books, 2005).

26 Kathryn Marie Dudley, *The End of the Line*, p. 161.

27 Judith Stein, *Running Steel, Running America: Race, Economic Policy, and the Decline of Liberalism* (Chapel Hill: University of North Carolina Press, 1998), pp. 318–20.

28 For an insightful study of this process, see: Jefferson Cowie, *Capital Moves: RCA's 70-Year Quest for Cheap Labor* (Ithaca: Cornell University Press, 1999).

29 Joseph Shumpeter, *Capitalism, Socialism and Democracy* (New York: Harper and Row, 1976), p. 83.

30 Cowie and Heathcott, *Beyond the Ruins*, p. 3.

31 Kent Curtis, "Greening Anaconda: EPA, ARCO, and the Politics of Space in Postindustrial Montana," in Cowie and Heathcott, *Beyond the Ruins*, pp. 91–111.

32 Kathryn Marie Dudley, *The End of the Line: Lost Jobs, New Lives in*

Postindustrial America (Chicago: University of Chicago Press, 1994), p. xxiii.

33 Bill Bamberger and Cathy N. Davidson, *Closing: The Life and Death of an American Factory* (New York: Doubleday, 1998), p. 20.

34 David Sobel and Susan Meurer, *Working at Inglis: The Life and Death of a Canadian Factory* (Toronto: James Lorimer, 1994).

35 Milton Rogovin and Michael Frisch, *Portraits in Steel* (Ithaca: Cornell University Press, 1993).

36 Charlie Angus and Louie Palu, *Industrial Cathedrals of the North* (Toronto: Between the Lines, 1999); Greg McDonnell. *Wheat Kings: Vanishing Landmarks of the Canadian Prairies* (Toronto: Boston Mills Press, 1999). See also Sharon Zukin, *Landscapes of Power: From Detroit to Disney World* (Los Angeles: University of California, 1991); and Christopher Andreae, "Industry, Dereliction, and Landscapes in Ontario," *Ontario History* 89, 2 (June 1997), pp. 161–80.

37 For a critique of the heritage discourse, see: Robert Summerby-Murray, "Interpreting the Deindustrialized Landscapes of Atlantic Canada: Memory and Industrial Heritage in Sackville, New Brunswick," *Canadian Geographer* 46 (2002), pp. 48–62. One of the best analyses of an industrial museum can be found in Lucy Taksa, "'Hauling an Infinite Freight of Mental Imagery': Finding Labour's Heritage at the Swindon Railway Workshop's STEAM Museum," *Labour History Review* 68, 3 (December 2003), pp. 391–410.

38 Tim Edensor, *Industrial Ruins: Space, Aesthetics and Materiality* (Oxford: Berg, 2005), p. 13.

39 Here, I am reminded of a big drug bust in Canada. A closed brewery, located next to a busy highway north of Toronto, had been covertly converted to a massive marijuana-growing operation.

40 Once in a while, however, the abandoned site is integral to the story being told, as in *Brassed Off* (1996), and *The Full Monty* (1997).

41 Lowell Boileau. "The Fabulous Ruins of Detroit," <http://detroit.yes.com/interact/>. The site is reviewed by a reporter for the now defunct *Detroit Sunday Journal*. Michael Betzold, "Should of the City: An Artist Finds Beauty in Crumbling Treasures," *Detroit Sunday Journal* (17 May 1998). Another interesting website is dedicated to the "Rivers of Steel National Heritage Area" of Southwestern Pennsylvania: <www.riversofsteel.com>.

42 Cowie and Heathcott, *Beyond the Ruins*, p. 15.

43 Pierre Nora, ed., *Realms of Memory: The Construction of the French Past* (New York: Columbia University Press, 1998), p. 18.

44 Kritzman preface in Nora, ed., *Realms of Memory*, p. x; Detroit interviewee Willy Eugene Eady said that it was "a time of anger and sorrow." Interviewed by the author in February 1998. The videotape has been donated to the Walter Reuther Library at Wayne State University.

45 Ward Holland, "Piece of the Past Erased to Make Way for Future," *Thunder Bay Chronicle Journal* (Monday 18 December 2000), p. 1. The headline explaining the large photograph of the falling terminal elevator reads: "There it was – gone".

46 Sherry Lee Linkon and John Russo, *Steeltown USA: Work and Memory in Youngstown* (Lawrence: University of Kansas Press, 2002), p. 2

47 Place identity is constructed not only locally, but also in the "geographical beyond." Doreen Massey, "Places and their Pasts," *History Workshop Journal* 39 (1995), pp. 182–92.

48 For a fascinating discussion of community and labour, see Lucy Taksa, "Like a Bicycle Forever Teetering Between

Individualism and Collectivism: Considering Community in Relation to Labour History," *Labour History* 78 (May 2000), pp. 7–32.

49 Calhoun has noted that community has been employed more as an "evocative symbol" than as an "analytical tool." Craig Calhoun quoted in Taksa, "Like a Bicycle Forever Teetering," pp. 9–10. See also John Walsh and Steven High, "Rethinking the Concept of Community," *Histoire sociale/Social History* 17, 64 (1999) pp. 255–74. Elizabeth Faue calls on historians to "disentangle the levels, dimensions, meanings, and metaphors of 'community.'" Elizabeth Faue, "Community, Class and Comparison in Labour History and Local History," *Labour History* 78 (May 2000), p. 159.

50 Dudley, *The End of the Line*, p. xxv.

51 James Agee quoted in Ken Light and Melanie Light, *Coal Hollow: Photographs and Oral Histories* (Berkeley: University of California Press, 2006).

52 John Livingstone interviewed by Steven High in Hamilton, Ontario, 7 February 1998. The audio recording of the interview is available at the McMaster University archives.

53 Alessandro Portelli, *The Death of Luigi Trastulli and Other Stories* (Albany: State University of New York, 1991). See ch. 1&2.

54 Ibid.

55 Daniel James, *Dona Maria's Story: Life History, Memory and Political Identity* (Durham: Duke University Press, 2000), p. 186.

56 Studs Terkel, *Working* (New York: Pantheon, 1972).

57 Guimond, *American Photography*, p. 6; Susan Sontag, *On Photography* (New York: Farrar, Strauss and Giroux, 1973), p. 7.

58 John Grierson quoted in Guimond, *American Photography*, p. 6.

59 David W. Lewis, *The Art of Bromoil and Transfer* (North Bay: 1995), p. 15.

60 Ibid., p. 10.

61 John Grierson quoted in Guimond, *American Photography*, p. 6.

62 Patricia Pace, "Staging Childhood: Photographs of Child Labor," *The Lion and the Unicorn* 26 (2002), pp. 324–25; Alan Trachtenberg, ed. *Essays on Photography* (New Haven: Leete's Island Books, 1980), p. 109.

63 Trachtenberg, ed. *Essays on Photography*, pp. 110–11

64 Guimond, *American Photography*, p. 134.

65 Karin Becker Ohrn, *Dorothea Lange and the Documentary Tradition* (Baton Rouge: Louisiana State University Press, 1980), pp. 36–7.

66 Thomas Sugrue, *The Origins of the Urban Crisis: Race and Inequality in Post-war Detroit* (Princeton: Princeton University Press, 1997).

67 High, *Industrial Sunset*, p. 115.

68 Blackmar, "Modernist Ruins," pp. 336–7.

CHAPTER 1

INDUSTRIAL DEMOLITION AND THE MEANING OF ECONOMIC CHANGE

1 Iver Peterson, "Workers Lament Dodge Plant Destruction," *New York Times*, 17 January 1981, p. 8.

2 Ibid.

3 Quoted in Iver Peterson, *loc. cit.*

4 Jack Metzgar, "Blue-Collar Blues: The Demonization of Manufacturing," *New Labor Forum* (Spring-Summer 2002), p. 20.

5 Michel Foucault, *Discipline and Punish: The Birth of the Prison* (New York: Vintage, 1975), pp. 195–7.

6 Dudley, *End of the Line*, p. 59.

7 Ibid., pp. 175–6.

8 Zukin, *Landscapes of Power*, p. 3. For more on the spatial structures of economic production see: Anthony Giddens, "Time, Space and Regionalisation," in Derek Gregory and John Urry, eds. *Social Relations and Spatial Structures* (New York: St. Martin's Press, 1985). Giddens suggests that the process of regionalization involves the "zoning of time-space" vis-à-vis "routinised" social practices: "In most locales, the boundaries separating regions have physical or symbolic markers."

9 Jefferson Cowie, *Capital Moves: RCA's 70-Year Quest for Cheap Labor* (Ithaca: Cornell University Press, 1999), p. 185. Landscapes created for production are abandoned for the same reasons; periods of sudden, transformative economic change are marked by major spatial change as well. Doreen Massey, *Spatial Divisions of Labour: Social Structures and the Geography of Production* (London: Macmillan, 1984), p. 11. For more on the production of space in capitalism see Andrew Herod, "Workers, Space and Labor Geography," *International Labor and Working Class History* 64 (Fall 2003), pp. 112–38. William Wyckoff provides a fascinating local study: "Postindustrial Butte," *Geographical Review* 85, 4 (1995), pp. 478–96. For a critique of economic abstraction see Fred Block, *Postindustrial Possibilities: A Critique of Economic Discourse* (Berkeley: University of California Press, 1990).

10 Joseph Schumpeter, *Capitalism, Socialism and Democracy* (Toronto: Harper Torchbooks, 1975), pp. 82–3. Neil Smith calls uneven development the hallmark of capitalism in his *Uneven Development: Nature, Capital and the Production of Space* (Oxford: Basil Blackwell, 1984), p. ix. Landscapes of abandonment are usefully explored in Roger A. Salerno, *Landscapes of Abandonment: Capitalism,*

Modernity, and Estrangement (Albany: SUNY Press, 2003), p. 2.

11 Thomas J. Sugrue, *The Origins of the Urban Crisis: Race and Inequality in Postwar Detroit* (Princeton, N.J.: Princeton University Press, 1996), p. 5.

12 Elizabethport, New Jersey, was once known as a hard-working blue-collar neighbourhood. It is now considered an eyesore, a "crumbling, decaying place of the past." Katherine S. Newman, "Turning Your Backs On Tradition: Symbolic Analysis and Moral Critique in a Plant Shutdown," *Urban Anthropology* 14, 1–3 (1985), p. 146.

13 See Robert A. Beauregard, *Voices of Decline: The Postwar Fate of U.S. Cities* (Oxford: Blackwell, 1993), p. 6.

14 High, *Industrial Sunset*, especially ch. 1.

15 The Newfoundland cod moratorium of 1992 has received a great deal of scholarly attention in Canada, virtually all of it relevant to our discussion here. The best overview of the literature is provided by Sean Cadigan, "Whose Fish? Science, Ecosystems and Ethics in Fisheries Management Literature since 1992," *Acadiensis* 31, 1 (Autumn 2001), pp. 171–95. The post-moratorium politics of deindustrialization are examined by James Overton, " 'A Future of the Past'? Tourism Development, Outport Archaeology, and the Politics of Deindustrialization in Newfoundland and Labrador in the 1990s," *Urban History Review/Revue de l'histoire urbaine* 35, 2 (Spring 2007), pp. 60–74.

16 *The Boston Chronicle* 11, 6 (14 November 2002).

17 Dudley, *End of the Line*, p. 161.

18 Sally F. Moore and Barbara G. Myerhoff, eds., *Secular Ritual* (Amsterdam: Van Gorcum, 1977), p. 3.

19 Ibid., p. 16.

20 Ibid., p. 24.

21 Editorial, "To Grow Old Gracefully," *Globe and Mail*, 1 November 1977.

22 Martin O'Malley, "Bashing Buildings is Fun," *Globe and Mail*, 1 May 1972, p. A5.
23 Ibid.
24 Dick Beddoes, "Raising a Cry Against Razing," *Globe and Mail*, 16 January 1979, p. 8.
25 Herbert Gans quoted in Dolores Hayden, *The Power of Place: Urban Landscapes as Public History* (Cambridge, MA: MIT Press, 1996), p. 3.
26 Drawn to cheap rents in these transitional spaces, artists in many cities established studios and illicit apartments in lofts. Because these buildings were still zoned "industrial," Toronto artists were allowed to work, but not live, in them. Many did anyways. According to one journalist, "Illegals were often the only buffers standing between Toronto's best historic factories and the wrecker's ball. Toronto the Good just wasn't in the mood to permit sleeping and other naughtiness on the millions of square feet being kept free for non-existent factory work by non-existent workers." John Bentley Mays, "Good Move for Hogtown," *Globe and Mail*, 21 August 1996, p. C1.
27 Mike Wallace, "Industrial Museums and the History of Deindustrialization," *Public Historian* 9,1 (Winter 1987), p. 10. See also Lizabeth Cohen, "'What Kind of World Have We Lost?' Worker's Lives and Deindustrialization in the Museum," *American Quarterly* 41, 4 (1989), pp. 670–81.
28 Linkon and Russo, *Steeltown U.S.A.*
29 While the "Steel Heritage Task Force" sought to preserve part of the Homestead Works – site of the famous labour battle of 1892 – the group managed only to preserve the historic pump house. Virtually all the other mill buildings, including the blast furnaces, have come down. "Wrecker's Ball Hangs over Mills in Steel Valley," *Globe and Mail*, 9 February 1990, p. B2.

30 "A Rebirth in Bethlehem," Public Broadcasting Service, 8 August 2001. See also <www.pbs.org/newshour/bb/business/july-dec01/bethlehem_9-08.html >.
31 For an interesting discussion of the vision of adaptive reuse in Bethlehem, see the website created by "Save Our Steel!": <www.saveoursteel.org >.
32 Aries Keck, "Bethlehem, Pa., Gambles on Steel Mill Casino Plan," National Public Radio, 25 October 2005. See also <www.npr.org>.
33 David Climenhaga, "Greenspoon Firm Demolishes Ideas about Wrecking Business," *Globe and Mail*, 16 February 1987, p. B1.
34 Marcel Boudreau interviewed by Kristen O'Hare, 2004. The tape will be donated to the West Nipissing Public Library and will also be available at the Concordia Oral History Research Laboratory in Montreal.
35 Irwin Altman and Setha M. Low, eds., *Place Attachment* (New York: Plenum Press, 1992).
36 Doreen Massey and Pat Jess, eds., *A Place in the World? Places, Cultures and Globalization* (Oxford: Oxford University Press, 1995), pp. 2–3. One of the things we need to keep in mind is how class created and recreated the forms and meaning of community. Faue, "Community, Class and Comparison," p. 156.
37 Thomas Dunk, *It's A Working Man's Town: Male Working-Class Culture* (Montreal: McGill-Queen's University Press, 1991), Introduction.
38 Mike King, "After 83 Years, Vickers Blows its Stack," *Montreal Gazette*, January 1999, p. A5.
39 Dudley, *End of the Line*, p. xxiii. Historian Michael Frisch poses some key questions about industrial heritage as contested memorial terrain: "What is the role of memory and public memorializing in digesting changes so profound and traumatic? Even more,

what is the role of memory, memorializing, and history itself in shaping the present and future of communities and regions devastated by such change? What choices do they face, and what role, if any, should publicly enacted memory play in defining, much less making and managing these choices? Whose history should be remembered and memorialized, by whom, and to what end?" Michael Frisch, "De-, Re-, and Post-Industrialization: Industrial Heritage as Contested Memorial Terrain," *Journal of Folklore Research* 35, 3 (1998), p. 241.

40 Catherine Buckie, "Smokestack Demolition Party was a Blast for a while," *Montreal Gazette*, 18 April 1988, p. A3.

41 Ibid.

42 Ibid.

43 Dave Battagello, "Detroit's Seven Sisters Fall: Northeast Windsor Was Rocked by the Demolition of the Seven 100-metre Smokestacks that Have Marked the Detroit River Skyline for 81 Years," *Windsor Star* (12 August 1996), p. A5.

44 Dudley, *End of the Line*, p. xxv.

45 The official website of the Sydney Steel Company provides us with further evidence of how economic change is represented as orderly and inevitable. The site, for example, proclaimed that the mill's demolition was "on time" and "on budget." See Sydney Steel Company website: <www.sysco.ns.ca>.

46 Pat Connolly, "Game, Set and Match: Sysco is Gone, but Hope for Sydney Springs Eternal," *Halifax Daily News*, 1 September 2001, p. 2.

47 Ibid.

48 In their study of Port Alberni, British Columbia, Brian Egan and Susanne Klausen suggest that mill closings and job loss provided an opportunity to diversify the local economy, and to provide women with employment opportunities outside the home. See

their, "Female in a Forest Town: The Marginalization of Women in Port Alberni's Economy," *BC Studies* 118 (1998), pp. 5–40.

49 Alison Uncles, "End of an Era," *Kingston Whig Standard*, 23 July 1988, p. A1.

50 Ibid.

51 Frank Redican, "Wrecking Ball Blues," *Globe and Mail*, 21 March 1983, p. A7.

52 Christopher Hume, "Soya-nara to Waterfront's Silos: Victory Mills Demolition Underway," *Toronto Star*, 27 June 1995, p. C1.

53 Peter Cheney, "Stubborn Grain Silo Facing Final K.O.," *Toronto Star*, 10 February 1996, p. A4.

54 Ingrid Peritz, "Grain Elevator's Fate up in the Air," *Montreal Gazette*, 18 August 1996, p. A1.

55 Ibid.

56 Uncles, *loc. cit.*

57 Cheney, *loc. cit.*

58 In a paper presented to the annual meeting of the International Society of Explosive Engineers, Brent Blanchard, Operations Manager for Protec Documentation Services (a demolition company), noted the growing use of explosives since the 1960s. Television interest in the drama of explosive demolition encouraged its expanded use in the 1970s, as did interest from Hollywood in the 1980s. By then, implosions were drawing huge crowds. Brent Blanchard, "History of Structural Demolition in America," presented to the 28th Annual International Society for Explosive Engineers Conference in Las Vegas on 11 February 2000. See also <www.implosionworld.com>.

59 Cheney, *loc. cit.*

60 See <www.sysco.ns.ca>.

61 Pierre Bourdieu, "The Social Space and the Genesis of Groups," *Theory and Society* 14 (November 1985), pp. 723–44.

62 Richard V. Francaviglia, *Hard Places: Reading the Landscape of America's*

Historic Mining Districts (Iowa City: University of Iowa, 1991), p. 48.

CHAPTER 2
"TAKE ONLY PICTURES AND LEAVE ONLY FOOTPRINTS"

1   Peter Fritzsche, "Specters of History: On Nostalgia, Exile, and Modernity," *American Historical Review* (December 2001), p. 1588. For more on nostalgia see Kathleen Stewart, "Nostalgia – A Polemic," *Cultural Anthropology* 3, 3 (August 1988), pp. 227–41.

2   Fred Davis, *Yearning for Yesterday: A Sociology of Nostalgia* (New York: Free Press, 1979).

3   Fritzsche, "Specters of History," p. 1595.

4   Edensor, *Industrial Ruins*, p. 11.

5   Kathleen Stewart, *A Space On the Side of the Road: Cultural Poetics in an "Other" America* (Princeton: Princeton University Press, 1996), p. 95.

6   There is a growing international scholarship on industrial heritage tourism. See, for example, Diane Barthel, "Getting in Touch with History: The Role of Historic Preservation in Shaping Collective Memories," *Qualitative Sociology* 19, 3 (1996), pp. 345–64; James Green, *Taking History to Heart: The Power of the Past in Building Social Movements* (Amherst: University of Massachusetts, 2000); Gert-Jan Hospers, "Industrial Heritage Tourism and Regional Restructuring in the European Union," *European Planning Studies* 10, 3 (2002), pp. 397–404; Paul A. Shackel and Matthew Palus, "Remembering an Industrial Landscape," *International Journal of Historical Archaeology* 10, 1 (March 2006), pp. 49–71.

7   The ecomusuem movement is explored in a special issue of *Publics et Musées* 17–18 (janvier–juin 2000). See, in particular, Francois Mairess, "La belle histoire,

aux origines de la nouvelle muséologie," pp. 33–56. Another useful sources is Octave Debary, "Deindustrialization and Museumification: From Exhibited Memory to Forgotten History," *Sociology of Education* 69, 2 (April 1996), pp. 105–25.

8   J. Arwel Edwards and Joan Carles Llurdés i Coit, "Mines and Quarries: Industrial Heritage Tourism," *Annals of Tourism Research* 23, 2 (1996), p. 345.

9   Carolyn Strange, "Symbiotic Commemoration: The Stories of Kalaupapa," *History and Memory* 16, 1 (2004), pp. 86–117.

10 J. John Lennon and Malcolm Foley, *Dark Tourism: The Attraction of Death and Disaster* (London: Thomson Press, 2000), pp. 3–5; Kenneth E. Foote, *Shadowed Ground: America's Landscapes of Violence and Tragedy* (Austin, TX: University of Texas Press, 2001).

11 Roger A. Salerno, *Landscapes of Abandonment: Capitalism, Modernity, and Estrangement* (Albany: SUNY Press, 2003), see Introduction.

12 A zine is a cheaply made, self-published magazine with an intentionally amateurish formula, according to Stephen Duncombe in *Notes from Underground: Zines and the Politics of Alternative Politics of Alternative Culture* (New York: Verso, 1997). They are usually produced by an individual who is most likely a suburban, middle class youth. For Duncombe, zines had the ability to create a subculture, and not just communicate it.

13 Testimonial found at <www.collision-detection.net/mt/archives/2005/09/rip-ninjaliciou.html>. See also Darren Wershler-Henry, "Usufruct in the City," *Globe and Mail*, 31 December 2005, p. D11.

14 See the website of *Jinx Magazine: Worldwide Urban Adventure*: <www.jinxmagazine.com>. Published since 1997; online since 2001.

15 "Ninjalicious," *Wikipedia*: <http://en/wikipedia.org/wiki/Ninjalicious>. See

also "Ninjalicious, 1973–2005," *Toronto Eye Weekly*, 1 September 2005.

16   Carolyn Hughes, "Urban Explorers, Crawling and Climbing into the Past," *Washington Post*, 30 December 2001, p. F8.

17   Ninjalicious quoted in Bob Bates Jr. "Urban Explorers Dare to Investigate Seldom-Seen Pittsburgh Sites," *Pittsburgh Post-Gazette*, Sunday, 7 September 2003.

18   Edward W. Said, Orientalism (New York: Vintage, 1979); Patrick Brantlinger, "Victorians and Africans: The Genealogy of the Myth of the Dark Continent," *Critical Inquiry* 12, 1 (1985), pp. 166–203; and Patricia Seed, *Ceremonies of Possession in Europe's Conquest of the New World, 1492–1640* (New York: Cambridge University Press, 1995).

19   See, for example, Mary Louise Pratt, *Imperial Eyes: Travel Writing and Transculturation* (New York: Routledge, 1992). An interesting critique of aspects of the post-colonial literature is contained in Frederick Cooper, *Colonialism in Question: Theory, Knowledge, History* (Berkeley: University of California Press, 2005), especially the chapter on modernity.

20   On wilderness and the nineteenth century tourist gaze see Patricia Jasen, *Wild Things: Nature, Culture and Tourism in Ontario, 1790–1914* (Toronto: University of Toronto Press, 1995). The search for authenticity is usefully examined in Ian McKay, *The Quest for the Folk: Anti-Modernism and Cultural Selection in Twentieth-Century Nova Scotia* (Montreal: McGill-Queen's University Press, 1994).

21   Said, *Orientalism*, p. 20.

22   James Overton, *Making a World of Difference: Essays on Tourism, Culture and Development in Newfoundland* (St. John's: ISER, 1996).

23   The Urban Exploration Resource website, for example, contains over a thousand discussion threads and almost thirty thousand postings on its popular "forum." The postings are organized into a number of thematic categories, as well as regional ones. There are also trip logs.

24   Ninjaliciuos, Resources Section, posting dated 19 May 2004, <www.infiltration.com>.

25   Greil Marcus, *Lipstick Traces: A Secret History of the 20th Century* (Cambridge: Harvard University Press, 1990). Geographer David Pinder links the situationists to psycho-geography in his introduction to the special issue, "Arts of Urban Exploration," *Cultural Geographies* 121 (2005), pp.383–411. See also Doreen Massey, *For Space* (London: Sage, 2005).

26   Michel de Certeau asserts that the act of walking is a spatial acting-out that "affirms, suspects, tries out, transgresses, respects," and appropriates. See Michel de Certeau, *The Practice of Everyday Life* (Berkeley: University of California, 1984). According to Kevin Birth, "There is evidence of growing concern with issues of subjectivity, self, feeling, and emotion in cultural anthropology," with special reference to Raymond Williams' notion of "structures of feeling" or Frederic Jameson's "cognitive mapping." Kevin Birth, "The Immanent Past: Culture and Psyche at the Juncture of Memory and History," *ETHOS* 34, 2 (2006), p. 171.

27   For discussion of this theme, see Brian Wilson, "The Canadian Rave Scene and Five Theses on Youth Tesistance," *Canadian Journal of Sociology* 27, 3 (Summer 2002).

28   Nichole McGill, "The Taming of the Rave: Your Next Secret All-night Dance Party May Have a Corporate Sponsor," *The Ottawa Citizen*, 18 August 1997, p. B7.

29   Ariella Budick, "From Streets to Gallery: 'Graffiti' Goes Highbrow with a New

Show at the Brooklyn Museum," *Knight Ridder Tribune Business News*, 2 July 2006, wire feed. See also Nina Siegal, "From the Subways to the Streets," *New York Times*, 22 August 1999, p. CY1.

30 Budick, *loc. cit.*

31 Somini Sengupta, "Marks for the Underground: the Graffiti Esthetic Surfaces in the Arts," *New York Times*, 6 May 1999, p. B1.

32 Ibid.

33 Pat DiLillo opened "Phun Phactory" – a block-long, former factory in Long Island City, Queens – as a grand, graffiti canvass with space for seventy-one "pieces" of graffiti art on the walls.

34 The introduction of stainless steel "graffiti proof" cars in the mid-1980s was also significant.

35 See the discussion thread on Chapman's death on the Urban Exploration Resource website: <http://www.uer.ca>.

36 Cameron Gordon, "The Great Infiltrator," *This* 39, 4 (January/February 2006), p. 37.

37 Testimonial found at <www.collisiondetection.net/mt/archives/2005/09/rip-ninjalicious.html>.

38 A posting on Urban Exploration Resource, dated 8/24/2005.

39 A posting from a London, Ontario man on Urban Exploration Resource.

40 CBC Radio docudrama "Tunnel Runners," May 2006: <www.cbc.ca/showcase/schedule/may.html>. On his award-winning website "The Fabulous Ruins of Detroit," Lowell Boileau takes visitors on a visual tour of post-industrial Detroit: <http://detroityes.com>. In doing so, he explicitly compares the city's ruined factories, stores, and houses to the ancient ruins of Athens, Rome, and Africa. For him, the hulking ruins of Detroit are "larger and more extensive than those I found in my travels to Zimbabwe, El Tajin, Ephesus, Athens, or Rome." In 1998, several digital monuments to

lost industry were reviewed in Jason Chervokas and Tom Watson, "Digital Monuments of the Urban Past," *New York Times*, 1 March 1998.

41 Ninjalicious, *Access All Areas: A User's Guide to the Art of Urban Exploration* (Toronto: Infiltration, 2005). It is part tourist guidebook, and part "how to" manual.

42 Dave LeBlanc, "New DVD a Trespasser's Delight," *Globe and Mail*, 16 September 2005, p. G10.

43 This lesson was actually learned before I was of school age, while we lived beside the railroad yard in the Vickers Heights Road area.

44 This discussion thread can be found on the Urban Exploration Resource website: <http://www.uer.ca>.

45 Tim Edensor, "The Ghosts of Industrial Ruins: Ordering and Disordering Memory in Excessive Space," *Environment and Planning D: Society and Place* 23 (2005), p. 835.

46 Ninjalicious, statement in "theory" section of Infiltration website: <www.infiltration.org>.

47 Ibid.

48 Ibid.

49 "Ninjalicious, 1973–2005," *Toronto Eye Weekly*, 1 September 2005.

50 Urban Exploration Montreal, website: <http://uem.minimanga.com>.

51 Posting on Urban Exploration Resource website, dated 10/18/2005.

52 Ibid.

53 Posting on Urban Exploration Resource dated 6/19/2006.

54 Ibid.

55 Kelsey Lutz, quoted in Sam Knowlton, "Urban Intrigue: Denizens of the Concrete Jungle Explore Their Natural Habitat," *Lawrence Journal-World*, 22 July 2005.

56 Ibid.

57 The Urban Landscape (T.U.L.): <www.tul.ca>. This site features the

photographs of three Canadians, based in Ottawa and Montreal.

58 Website: *Jinx Magazine: Worldwide Urban Adventure*, <www.jinxmagazine.com>, published since 1997; online since 2001.

59 Ibid. The editors liked to associate themselves, and their movement, with explorer Sir Richard Frances Burton who was "one of the first westerners to penetrate the forbidden Muslim holy cities of Mecca and Medina." For more on this and on the scientific "empiricism" of urban exploration, see the chapter on "the Athenaeum" society in L.B. Deyo and David "Lefty" Leibowitz, *Invisible Frontier: Exploring the Tunnels, Ruins and Rooftops of Hidden New York* (New York: Three Rivers Press, 2003).

60 The relationship of working class children and youth to former industrial sites has yet to be studied. We simply do not know how class and distance shaped young people's views of these marginal spaces, and their relationship to them.

61 Jonathan Culler, "The Semiotics of Tourism," in *Framing the Sign: Criticism and its Institutions* (Oxford: Basil Blackwell, 1988), p. 156.

62 Jackson Lears, *No Place of Grace: Antimodernism and the Transformation of American Culture, 1880–1920* (New York: Pantheon, 1981), p. xiv.

63 Colin Campbell, *The Romantic Ethic and the Spirit of Modern Consumerism* (New York: Blackwell, 1987).

64 Jasen, *Wild Things*, p. 11.

65 John Urry, *The Tourist Gaze: Leisure and Travel in Contemporary Societies* (London: SAGE Publications, 1990), p. 20.

66 Malcolm Andrews, *The Search for the Picturesque: Landscape Aesthetics and Tourism in Britain, 1760–1800* (Palo Alto: Stanford University Press, 1989), p. vii.

67 Jasen, *Wild Things*, p. 9

68 David Nye, *American Technological Sublime* (Cambridge: MIT Press, 1994), p. 126. For more on the "rational factory" see Lindy Biggs, *The Rational Factory: Architecture, Technology and Work in America's Age of Mass Production* (Baltimore: Johns Hopkins University Press, 1996); on the industrial aesthetic see Dominic T. Alessio, "Capitalist Realist Art: Industrial Images of Hamilton, Ontario, 1884–1910," *Journal of Urban History* 18, 4 (1992), pp. 442–469; and, Sharon Zukin, *Landscapes of Power: From Detroit to Disney Land* (Berkeley: University of California Press, 1991).

69 The "image worlds" of industrial corporations such as General Electric, emphasized order, size, and managerial control.

70 The "Canada Works" narrative can be found in the "Journal" section of the Infiltration web site: <http://www.infiltration.org>.

71 Ibid.

72 The two exploration narratives can be found under "Canada Malt Plant" and "O'Keefe Brewery" on the Urban Exploration Montreal website: <http://uem.minimanga.com>.

73 Andrews, *The Search for the Picturesque*, p. 67.

74 Bill Scandlan interviewed by Steven High in February 1997. The interview recording is held at the McMaster University Archives, and at the Centre for Oral History and Digital Storytelling at Concordia University.

75 Ibid.

76 Urban Exploration London (Ontario): <http://uel/minimanga.com>.

77 Wraiths (Vancouver): <www.wraiths.org>.

78 Edensor, *Industrial Ruins*, p. 67.

79 Andrew Henderson's website "Forgotten Ohio" contains a number of visual tours of abandoned industrial buildings. See his tour of the Claycraft Brick Factory: <www.forgottenoh.com>.

80 Tim Edensor, "The Ghosts of Industrial Ruins," p. 837.
81 Ibid.
82 Edensor, "Specters of History", p. 829.
83 Tim Edensor, "The Ghosts of Industrial Ruins," p. 829.
84 Throckmorten, "The Canada Malting Plant," on Infiltration website: <www.infiltration.org>.
85 In making the case that memory is embodied and affective, Edensor leans heavily on Walter Benjamin's notion of "structures of feeling." Walter Benjamin, *Illuminations* (London: Verso, 1973), p. 8.
86 Edensor, "Specters of History," p. 846.
87 For more on how social space functions as symbolic space see Pierre Bourdieu, "Social Space and Symbolic Power," *Sociological Theory* 7, 1 (1989), pp. 20–1.
88 The group's festive parade of musicians playing scrap-iron instruments through the streets of New York City is viewed as a political act by David Pinder in "Arts of Urban Exploration," *Cultural Geographies* 121 (2005), pp. 383–411.
89 Participants sought to explore the cultural geography of the city by sensing, feeling and experiencing spaces differently. Several academic journals have also come and gone. See *Transgressions: A Journal of Urban Exploration* (1995–2001), and the *Journal of Psychogeography and Urban Research*.
90 Pinder, "Arts of Urban Exploration," p. 388.
91 Cultural geographers are not alone. Industrial archaeology emerged in the 1950s, at a time of public concern over vanishing industrial artifacts and buildings. The grassroots localism and preservationist impulse of the field of study was also heavily weighted towards artifact-based fieldwork. Industrial archaeology's popularity among enthusiasts may have contributed to its inability to fully establish itself in North American and European universities. Its politics were also suspect at a time when social history predominated. Albeit marginal to history and to archaeology, industrial archaeology has found a home in the growing number of industrial museums and heritage sites that have appeared in the wake of deindustrialization. See R.A.S. Hennessey, "Industrial Archaeology in Education," *The History Teacher* 9, 1 (November 1975); Barrie Trinder, "A New Course in Industrial Archaeology," *World Archaeology* 15, 2 (1983); and, Diane Barthel, "Getting in Touch with History: The Role of Historic Preservation in Shaping Collective Memories," *Qualitative Sociology* 19, 3 (1996).
92 Edensor, *Industrial Ruins*, p. 11.
93 Ibid., p. 7.
94 Ninjalicious, "Fisher Factory," journal on Infiltration web site, <www.infiltration.org>.
95 The *Toronto Star* review cited on the Infiltration website.
96 Edensor, *Industrial Ruins*, p. 165.
97 Urban Exploration Resource, posting dated 3/23/2006, <www.uer.ca>.
98 Kowalski, "How Can We Present our Photographs in a More Meaningful and Effective Manner?": <www.liminalcity.net/forum/>.
99 Urban Exploration Resource, posting by "Elizabeth," 14 May 2006, <www.uer.ca>. In early 2006, Kowalksi and Elizabeth launched their own online journal called "Liminal Cities: A Journal of Urban Exploration, Spatial Excavation, and Unceasing Transformation," <www.liminalcity.net>. While there has not been much activity yet, the journal's stated objective is to explore the "…margins of civilization, we walk and feel and breathe thresholds sandwiched between areas of control, niches of unvarnished and unregulated ambiguity, the places that have fallen out or never been built upon, the spaces with roles that can never be integrated into the public face of the econ-

omy." For its founders, "Liminal Cities" will be about "urban exploration, about seeing the built environment with different eyes, about what we find when we probe the boundaries of the urban." For his part, Kowalski hopes to encourage "more substantial and frequent storytelling about our experiences as explorers."

CHAPTER 3
FROM CRADLE
TO GRAVE

1 An earlier version of this chapter appeared as "Deindustrializing Youngstown: Memories of Resistance and Loss in the Decades Following 'Black Monday,'" *History Workshop Journal* 54 (2002), pp. 100–21. In revising this article for inclusion in *Corporate Wasteland*, I sought to engage with Sherry Lee Linkon and John Russo's *Steeltown USA: Work and Memory in Youngstown* (Lawrence: University of Kansas Press, 2002) which appeared soon after my article. In doing so, I draw from my review essay, "Capital and Community Reconsidered: The Politics and Meaning of Deindustrialization," *Labour/le Travail* 55 (Spring 2005), pp. 187–96.

2 Bluestone and Harrison, *Deindustrialization of America*, p. 252.

3 Staughton Lynd, "The Genesis of the Idea of a Community Right to Industrial Property in Youngstown and Pittsburgh, 1977–1987," *Journal of American History* 74, 3 (1987), pp. 926–58.

4 Daniel James, *Dona Maria's Story: Life History, Memory, and Political Identity* (Durham: Duke University Press, 2001), p. 186.

5 Ibid., p. 228.

6 For more on this, see Robert Bruno, *Steelworker Alley: How Class Works in Youngstown* (Ithaca: Cornell University Press, 1999). For another perspective,

see: Linkon and Russo, *Steeltown USA*, ch. 2.

7 Doreen Massey, "Places and their Pasts," p. 183.

8 Or, to borrow a phrase from Alon Confino, these can be viewed as "memory carriers." Alon Confino, "Collective Memory and Cultural History: Problems and Methods," *American Historical Review* (December 1997), p. 1395.

9 Film quoted in Charles J. Shindo, *Dust Bowl Migrants in the American Imagination* (Lawrence: University of Kansas Press, 1997), p. 162.

10 Dale Maharidge and Michael Williamson, *Journey to Nowhere: the Saga of the New Underclass*, Second Edition, with Introduction by Bruce Springsteen (New York, 1996), p. 8.

11 Ibid., p. 9.

12 Dale Maharidge quoted in an online article written by *Washington Post* staff writer Richard Harrington: "Steelworker's Song: Bruce Springsteen Gives Voice to a Story of America's New Homeless," 5 December 1995, see <www.luckytown.org/tgotj/y.txt>, Monday, March 12, 2001.

13 Maharidge and Williamson, *Journey to Nowhere*, p. 9.

14 Ibid., p. 191.

15 Historian Hayden White has written that a narrative is never neutral, because it involves choices. He also warned that narrative becomes a problem when "we wish to give to real events the form of a story." This is because a story is far more coherent than real life. See his *The Content of the Form: Narrative Discourse and Historical Representation* (Baltimore, MD: Johns Hopkins University Press, 1987), pp. 2–4.

16 Ibid., p. 28.

17 For a biographical account of the life and times of Bruce Springsteen, see Dave Marsh, *Glory Days: Bruce Springsteen in the 1980s* (New York: Pantheon, 1987),

and Jim Cullen, *Born in the USA: Bruce Springsteen and the American Tradition* (New York: Harper Collins, 1997).

18 Bruce Springsteen quoted in Bryan Garman, "The Ghost of History: Bruce Springsteen, Woody Guthrie and the Hurt Song," *Popular Music and Society* 20, 2 (1996), p. 108.

19 In a different context, historian William Westerman found that Central American refugees in the Sanctuary movement quickly learned that North American audiences wanted personal testimonials, not reasoned political arguments. William Westerman, "Central American Refugee Testimonies and Performed Life Histories in the Sanctuary Movement", in the *Oral History Reader*, ed. Robert Perks and Alistair Thomson, (London: Routledge, 1998), pp. 224–34.

20 Garman, "Ghost of History," p. 69.

21 Ibid., p. 75. Springsteen acquired a copy of Joe Klein's biography *Woody Guthrie: a Life* in November 1980, and soon began playing "This Land Is your Land" in his concerts. However, he chose not to sing the highly political verses of Guthrie's original version of the song.

22 Bruce Springsteen, "Introduction," in Maharidge and Williamson, *Journey to Nowhere*, p. 1.

23 "youngstown" by Bruce Springsteen, © 1995 Bruce Springsteen (ASCAP). Reprinted with permission.

24 Ibid.

25 For the local reaction to the song see the following articles that appeared in the *Youngstown Vindicator*: "Boss Wants to Perform in City," 6 December 1995; "Fifth Avenue Sellout: Springsteen Tickets Go Fast," 28 December 1995; "Concert Offers Valley Hope," 13 January 1996; "Glory Days Are Not Forgotten," 18 January 1996; "Singer's Own Experiences Aided in Getting Song's Tone Right," 1 February 1996.

26 Dale Peskin, "Area's Coalition Has Own Ballad," *Youngstown Vindicator*, 10 January 1978, p. A1.

27 Ibid. Tom Hunter's lyrics were printed in their entirety.

28 Bob Dyer, *Akron Beacon Journal*, 4 December 1995. Found on <www.luckytown.org/tgotj/y.txt>, 12 March 2001.

29 Jim Cullen, *Born in the USA*, p. 41; Maharidge quoted in Richard Harrington, "Steelworker's Song: Bruce Springsteen Gives Voice to a Story of America's New Homeless," 5 December 1995. See <www.luckytown.org/tgotj/y.txt>, 12 March 2001.

30 "Black Monday: Twenty Years Later," *Youngstown Vindicator*, 14 September 1997, p. 1.

31 George Walker, "Steel Missed, Hearth and Soul," *Youngstown Vindicator*, 14 September 1997, p.1.

32 "'Black Monday': One Year Later," *Youngstown Vindicator*, 18 September 1978.

33 Dale Peskin, "'Black Monday' Observance Held," *Youngstown Vindicator*, 19 September 1978, p. 1.

34 Ibid.

35 "'Black Monday' Two Years Later – Tax Loss Hurts, But Massive S & T Layoff Didn't Put Area on Skids," *Youngstown Vindicator*, 16 September 1979, p. A2.

36 "' Black Monday' Two Years Later – Part III: Groups to Attract New Industry Emerge; Some Fade Out," *Youngstown Vindicator*, 18 September 1979.

37 "District Mills Remain Dark," *Youngstown Vindicator*, 19 September 1982, p. 1.

38 "1977 Headlines' Recalled," *Youngstown Vindicator*, 19 September 1977, p. 2.

39 "Steel Workers Have Had Difficulty Finding Jobs Since 1977 Shutdown," *Youngstown Vindicator*, 20 September 1982, p. 1.

40 "CAC, Hunt Steel, Others Provide Hope for Valley," *Youngstown Vindicator*, 22 September 1982, p. 1.

41 Philip Bracey's interview with Mayor Philip Ritchey, 10 April 1981, Youngstown State University.

42 John Lis, "100 Gather to Remember Fateful Black Monday," *Youngstown Vindicator*, 20 September, 1987, p. 1.

43 Thomas Ott, "'Black Monday' Still a Painful Memory," *Youngstown Vindicator*, 19 September 1987, p. 1.

44 John Bodnar, *Remaking America: Public Memory, Commemoration, and Patriotism in the Twentieth Century* (Princeton, NJ, 1992), p. 15.

45 "Hopewell Group Makes Plans in Struthers – Will Begin Memorial," *Youngstown Vindicator*, 23 May 1976.

46 A case in point was the Struthers High School Art Club which proposed to paint a mural entitled "Cradle of Steel." Struthers High School Art Club, "Cradle of Steel: Commemorating Our Nation's Bicentennial," 1975, in Youngstown Public Library Vertical File: "Blast Furnaces."

47 Letter to the editor from Mrs. Marian Kutlesa, President, Struthers Historical Society, *Youngstown Vindicator*, 30 October 1979.

48 "Hopewell Memorial Message of a Year Ago Has Bitter Ring Today," *Youngstown Vindicator*, 25 September 1977, p. A2.

49 Editorial, "Segal's Steel Memorial," *Youngstown Vindicator*, 16 May 1980.

50 The two model steelworkers were reportedly chosen by the local union on the basis of their skill at work: the best first-worker and the best second-worker. Michael Braun, "City Dedicates Segal's Tribute to Steelmakers," *Youngstown Vindicator*, 15 May 1980.

51 Norman Leigh, "Monument to Steel Heritage May Get Respect at Museum". *Youngstown Vindicator*, 5 September 1988.

52 Dale Peskin, *Youngstown Vindicator*, 2 October 1979.

53 Louis Zora, quoted in Leigh, *loc. cit.*

54 The development of any such project necessarily involves "unstable alliances and sustained conflicts of vision, interest, and objectives": Michael Frisch, 'De-, Re-, and Post Industrialization: Industrial Heritage as Contested Memorial Terrain,' *Journal of Folklore Research* 35, 3 (1998), p. 243. While the abandoned mining landscapes of Butte, Montana and the picturesque mill towns of New England have been celebrated and preserved, this was not the case in Youngstown, Ohio. The wounds were too fresh. William Wyckoff, "Postindustrial Butte," *Geographical Review* 85, 4 (1995), p. 484; Mike Wallace, "Industrial Museums and the History of Deindustrialization," *Public Historian* 9, 1, (Winter 1987), p. 10; and his "Razor Ribbons, History Museums, and Civic Salvation," *Radical History Review* 57 (1993), pp. 234–5.

55 Dale Peskin, "Meshel, Society Envision Steel Museum," *Youngstown Vindicator*, 7 January 1979.

56 See, for example, George R. Reiss, "Meshel Proposes Brier Hill Plant Become National Steel Museum," *Youngstown Vindicator*, 10 July 1983, p. A-10; and "Blackwell Wants to Create Steel Museum," *Youngstown Vindicator*, 11 December 1985, p. 5. The building of the steel museum did not satisfy everyone. In 1992 the Jeannette Blast Furnace Preservation Association was formed by a group for whom the steel museum's displays would "never replace the real thing." See Mark C. Peyko and John Rose, "Time Runs Out for Jeannette," *Metro Eye*, October 1996, p. 7.

57 Norman Leigh, "Work Will Begin Soon on Wood St. Industry Museum," *Youngstown Vindicator*, 25 March 1988.

58 "Steel Industry Enshrined," *Progressive Architecture* 3: 90, pp. 84–7.

59 For local reaction to this article see Norman Leigh, "Steel Museum Debut Remains a Top Secret," *Youngstown*

NOTES **179**

Vindicator, 9 November 1989; and "Spotlight on Museum Illuminates Political Shortcomings in Ohio," *Youngstown/ Warren Business Journal Opinion*, November 1989.

60 "The (Empty) Steel Museum: A Stillborn Monument to a Dying Industry," *Newsweek*, 30 October 1989, p. 84.

61 Tim Roberts, "State Grant Will Help Industrial Museum Get Started," *Youngstown Vindicator*, 3 July 1983.

62 Nancy Christie, "May Groundbreaking for Industrial Museum," *Youngstown Business Journal*, mid-April, 1986, p. 6.

63 Karen Guy, "Dr. DeBlasio Heads Museum Project," *Youngstown Vindicator*, 18 March 1985.

64 Editorial, "The Industrial Museum's Importance," *Youngstown Vindicator*, 8 February 1986, p. 4.

65 Gary C. Ness, Director of the Ohio Historical Society, to staff, 11 January 1990. See Youngstown Historical Centre of Industry and Labor, Archives, Collection MSS0114, file: "Museum." Also see handwritten report, dated 11 January 1990.

66 Donna M. DeBlasio, "Oral History, Deindustrialization and the Museum Exhibit: 'By the Sweat of their Brow: Forging the Steel Valley,'" unpublished paper given to the American Oral History Association Meeting in Buffalo, New York, October 1998. For an excellent discussion of the trials and tribulations of a labour historian active in public history, see Craig Heron, "The Labour Historian and Public History," *Labour/Le Travail* 45 (Spring 2000), pp. 171–97.

67 Donna DeBlasio quoted in Norman Leigh, "People Giving Soul to Industrial Museum," *Youngstown Vindicator*, 14 September 1987.

68 Ibid.

69 Curtis Miner, Exhibition Review, "'By the Sweat of Their Brow: Forging the Steel Valley,' at the Youngstown Historical Center of Industry and Labor,"

Journal of American History, December 1993, p. 1,020.

70 Brian O'Donnell and Lizabeth Cohen, for example, have shown that visitors either emerge from these museums with an "optimistic view," or gain a "lament over the loss of a romanticized workers' community": Brian O'Donnell, "Memory and Hope: Four Local Museums in the Mill Towns of the Industrial Northeast," *Technology & Society* 37, 4 (October 1996), p. 817; and Lizabeth Cohen, "What Kind of World Have We Lost? Workers' Lives and Deindustrialization in the Museum," *American Quarterly* 41, 4 (1989), pp. 670–81.

71 Deindustrialization is also invoked at the Ecomusée in Montreal, Quebec. Here, the visitor is separated from a number of small photographs of people and abandoned homes by a waist-high, padlocked gate. Montreal's display of deindustrialization is also situated halfway through the horseshoe-shaped permanent exhibition. While the first half documents the world of the industrial worker, the second focuses, instead, on community redevelopment, and housing co-operatives. As a result, a much more hopeful political message is delivered in Montreal than in Youngstown.

72 Panel reproduced in Youngstown Historical Center of Industry and Labor, Archives, Collection MSS 0114, file: "Museum."

73 In what is surely the most extensive oral record of mill closings anywhere, fifty-five former steelworkers were interviewed in the early 1990s by the steel museum. Passages from five of these interviews made it into the exhibit. These five interviews were chosen on the premise that the story should include "an immigrant, a union activist, a woman, a manager, and an average steelworker." Nobody spoke on behalf of the Ecumenical Coalition. The steel

museum's emphasis on shop-floor perspectives recorded in the 1990s was in sharp contrast to an oral history project conducted by Youngstown State University ten years earlier, which focused on the failure of resistance.

74 During its first two years of operation, there were less than five thousand official visitors per annum. This figure had climbed to nearly 10,000 in 1995, and 15,000 in 1997. Chris Whitley, "Steel Museum Passes the Test of its Mettle," *Youngstown Vindicator*, 6 July 1997, A1, p. 4.

75 Bill Elder, "Valley's Glory Days Come Alive," *Youngstown Vindicator*, 27 December 1993.

76 Linkon and Russo, *Steeltown USA*, p. 129.

77 Ibid., p. 2.

78 Barry Wellman and Barry Leighton, "Networks, Neighborhoods and Communities: Approaches to the Study of the Community Problem," *Urban Affairs Quarterly* 14 (March 1979), pp. 363–90. See also Charles E. Connerly, "The Community Question: An Extension of Wellman and Leighton," *Urban Affairs Quarterly* 20, 4 (1985), pp. 537–56.

79 Robert N. Bellah, *Habits of the Heart: Individualism and Commitment in American Life* (Berkeley: University of California Press, 1985).

80 Ibid.

81 Christopher Lasch, "The Communitarian Critique of Liberalism," in Charles H. Reynolds and Ralph V. Norman, eds., *Community in America* (Berkeley: University of California Press, 1988), p. 177.

82 Miranda Joseph, *Against the Romance of Community* (Minneapolis: University of Minnesota Press, 2002), p. vii.

83 James Overton, " 'A Future in the Past': Tourism Development, Outport Archaeology, and the Politics of Deindustrialization in Newfoundland and Labrador in the 1990s," *Urban History Review* 35, 2 (Spring 1997), pp. 60–74.

84 Michael Frisch noticed that those interviewed by Studs Terkel in *Hard Times* recalled the 1930s as an individual or family experience. These memories, he surmised, effectively depoliticized the Depression. Was this a limited view of history, as Frisch claims, or were people bound to experience history as biography? In retreating to biography, have we deferred deeper political judgments? Michael Frisch, *A Shared Authority: Essays on the Craft and Meaning of Oral and Public History* (Albany: SUNY Press, 1990), p. 12.

CHAPTER 4
OUT OF PLACE

1 There have been a number of excellent studies that use oral sources to discover the meaning of deindustrialization. Among the best are: Milton Rogovin and Michael Frisch, *Portraits in Steel* (Ithaca: Cornell University Press, 1993); John Bodnar, "Power and Memory in Oral History: Workers and Managers at Studebaker," *Journal of American History* 75 (1989), pp. 1201–21; Thomas Dublin, *When the Mines Closed: Stories of Struggle in Hard Times* (Ithaca: Cornell University Press, 1998); Joy L. Hart and Tracy E. K'Meyer, "Worker Memory and Narrative: Personal Stories of Deindustrialization in Louisville, Kentucky," in Cowie and Heathcott, *Beyond the Ruins*, 284–304. See also Steve May and Laura Morrison, "Making Sense of Restructuring: Narrative of Accommodation among Downsized Workers," in the same volume, pp. 259–83. The best international example is Daniel James, *Dona Maria's Story* (Durham: Duke University Press, 2000). For a fascinating ethnographic approach, see Martha Norkunas, *Monuments and Memory: History and Representation in Lowell,*

Massachusetts (Washington: Smithsonian, 2002).

2 According to the 2001 census, 5978 people called Sturgeon Falls home. This represented a drop of 3 percent from 1996. The town had a strong French-speaking majority (4,140) and was overwhelmingly Roman Catholic (5,115).

3 The groundswell of local financial support for the mill – co-ordinated by the West Nipissing Economic Development Corporation (J.P. Charles, Denis Gauthier, Dan Olivier, Ron Beauchamp) – amounted to one million dollars in interest-free loans, locked in for five years. This story will be explored more fully in a future book.

4 Raymond Marcoux interviewed by Kristen O'Hare, 20 May 2004. The recordings of the Sturgeon Falls interviews are in the possession of the author. They will be donated to the Centre for Oral History and Digital Storytelling at Concordia University in Montreal, Quebec, and to the West Nipissing Public Library in Sturgeon Falls, Ontario, upon the completion of a second book project that will focus on the Sturgeon Falls story exclusively.

5 A life course interview is an open-ended interview that explores the entire life story of an interviewee.

6 Irwin Altman and Setha M. Low, eds., *Place Attachment* (New York: Plenum Press, 1992), p. 3.

7 Setha M. Low, "Symbolic Ties that Bind," in Altman and Low, *Place Attachment*, p. 167. Sociologist Pierre Bourdieu has shown that symbolic power "is the power to make things with words." Pierre Bourdieu, "Social Space and Symbolic Power," *Sociological Theory* 7, 1 (1989), pp. 20–3. See also Edward Said, *Culture and Imperialism* (New York: Alfred A. Knopf, 1993), p. xiii.

8 The town's white collar politicians celebrated the changes underway. "You know, the world is right: they're finally being punished for their non-education, and I can feel glad that I'm not like that," said one city councillor. Quoted in Dudley, *End of the Line*, p. 34.

9 As in Youngstown, without a unifying storyline, competing and separate communities of memory took hold: "While economic struggle was at the heart of deindustrialization, a parallel struggle emerged over representation itself." Linkon and Russo, *Steeltown USA*, p. 133.

10 Zukin, *Landscapes of Power*, pp. 28–9.

11 For a fascinating look at nostalgia and transformative change in the context of the French Revolution see Peter Fritzsche, "Specters of History: On Nostalgia, Exile, and Modernity," *American Historical Review* (December 2001), pp. 1587–1618.

12 Christopher Lasch, *The True and Only Heaven: Progress and Its Critics* (New York: W.W. Norton, 1991), p. 117.

13 Cowie and Heathcott, *Beyond the Ruins*, see the Introduction.

14 Ken Colquhoun interviewed by Steven High, June 2005.

15 "Lives 'Ripped Away' by Shutdown – Workers," *North Bay Nugget*, 30 November 2002.

16 Pierre Hardy interviewed by Kristen O'Hare. 12 December 2003. The follow-up interview was conducted by Steven High in June 2005.

17 Denis MacGregor interviewed by Kristen O'Hare, 17 June 2004.

18 Pierre Hardy interviewed by Kristen O'Hare, 12 December 2003. The follow-up interview was conducted by Steven High in June 2005.

19 Raymond Marcoux interviewed by Kristen O'Hare, 20 May 2004.

20 Among the documents that we have gathered, or copied, from people's basements, are copies of the mill newsletter, " The Insider." All of the documents

collected will be donated to the West Nipissing Public Library.

21 Marcel Boudreau interviewed by Kristen O'Hare, 1 December 2003.

22 He was commissioned to write a book on the history of Sturgeon Falls for the town's centenary in 1995. The book was a huge seller in the region; virtually every family has a copy. It presents a compelling narrative of the town's development. Wayne F. LeBelle, *Sturgeon Falls, 1895–1995* (Field, Ontario: WFL Communications, 1995). The history of the surrounding villages is explored in Wayne F. LeBelle, *West Nipissing Ouest* (Field, Ontario: WFL Communications, 1998).

23 Wayne LeBelle interviewed by Steven High, December 2005.

24 Wayne LeBelle interviewed by Kristen O'Hare, 6 September 2004. When Wayne LeBelle reviewed his quote, he said that in 2004, when the storm over the closure was still raging, he empathized strongly with the employees at the mill. In saying this, he was not demeaning of people who work for a living, but rather pointing out that in time, the mill became their economic trap. LeBelle observed that this same story is being replayed now in Smooth Rock Falls in northern Ontario.

25 Wayne LeBelle interviewed by Steven High, December 2005.

26 This story was repeated by several interviewees and is largely supported by newspaper coverage from the time. The incident did not get raised in my first interview with Cam Barrington. In the second interview, I raised the issue directly. Cam Barrington indicated that while the controversy did occur, he did not overtly threaten to "close the mill." Cam Barrington interviewed by Steven High, June 2005.

27 Ed Fortin interviewed by Kristen O'Hare, 5 August 2004.

28 Brian Egan and Suzanne Klaussen, "Female in a Forest Town: the Marginalization of Women in Port Alberni's Economy," *BC Studies* 118 (1998), p. 6.

29 Percy Allary interviewed by Kristen O'Hare, 9 June 2004. The follow-up interview was conducted by Steven High in June 2005.

30 Gender relations in Sturgeon Falls were strikingly similar to those described by anthropologist Thomas W. Dunk in Thunder Bay, Ontario. See his *It's A Working Man's Town: Male Working-Class Culture* (Montreal: McGill-Queen's University Press, 1991), especially ch. 1.

31 Randy Restoule interviewed by Kristen O'Hare, 5 August 2004.

32 Ruth Thompson interviewed by Kristen O'Hare, 22 June 2004.

33 The same situation held in forest-dependent localities in British Columbia. See Trevor J. Barnes and Roger Hayter, "Economic Restructuring, Local Development and Resource Towns: Forest Communities in Coastal British Columbia," *Canadian Journal of Regional Science* 17, 3 (Autumn 1994), p. 291.

34 Marc Côté interviewed by Kristen O'Hare, 30 January 2004.

35 Lawrence Pretty interviewed by Kristen O'Hare, 22 June 2004.

36 Marcel Boudreau interviewed by Steven High, June 2005. The initial interview was conducted by Kristen O'Hare, 1 December 2003.

37 Denis MacGregor interviewed by Kristen O'Hare, 17 June 2004.

38 Denis MacGregor interviewed by Kristen O'Hare, 17 June 2004.

39 Brandi Cramer, "Severance Packages, EI Running out for Former Weyerhaeuser Employees," *North Bay Nugget*, 22 January 2004, A2.

40 "Lives 'Ripped Away' by Shutdown – Workers," *North Bay Nugget*, 30 November 2002.

41 Dean Lisk, "Weyerhaeuser to Close in December," *Tribune*, 15 October 2002.

42 Anonymous interviewed by Kristen O'Hare, June 2004.

43 Pierre Hardy interviewed by Kristen O'Hare, 12 December 2003.

44 Dean Pigeau quoted in Dean Lisk and Susanne Gammon, "West Nipissing Marches," *The Tribune*, 10 December 2002.

45 Marcel Boudreau interviewed by Kristen O'Hare, 1 December 2003.

46 Pierre Hardy interviewed by Kristen O'Hare, 12 December 2003.

47 Pierre Hardy interviewed by Kristen O'Hare, 12 December 2003. This was raised again in the follow-up interview conducted by Steven High, June 2005.

48 Raymond Marcoux interviewed by Kristen O'Hare, 20 May 2004.

49 Marcel Boudreau interviewed by Kristen O'Hare, 1 December 2003.

50 The text of the speech is in the possession of Pierre Hardy, from 6 December 2002.

51 Phil Novak, "Mill Employees Punch Out for Good," *North Bay Nugget*, 6 December 2002.

52 It is significant that the news of another protest of some fifty people in September 2003, marking Weyerhaeuser's decision to demolish the mill, received the following headline: "Union Rallies outside Mill." The mill's connection to the community, explicitly stated in December 2002, had been cut. Dean Lisk, "Union Rallies outside Mill," *Tribune*, 9 September 2003.

53 Marcel Boudreau interviewed by Kristen O'Hare, 1 December 2003.

54 This comment hints at the shifting gender roles in mill families, as women often became the breadwinners in the wake of the closure. Marcel Boudreau interviewed by Kristen O'Hare, 1 December 2003.

55 Marcel Boudreau interviewed by Kristen O'Hare, 1 December 2003.

56 Ibid.

57 Ibid.

58 Pierre Hardy interviewed by Steven High, June 2005.

59 "Union More Determined than Ever" CEP Press Release, 29 November 2002, found in the records of Pierre Hardy.

60 Quoted in an article by Gord Young, "Former Weyerhaeuser Employees Want Province to Join Fight," *North Bay Nugget*, Friday February 7, 2003, p. 1.

61 "Weyerhaeuser Pulp and Paper Demolition," *Canada News Wire* (17 June 2004), p. 1.

62 Hubert Gervais interviewed by Steven High on multiple occasions, 2004–6.

63 Marcel Labbé interviewed by Steven High, June 2005.

64 In a second interview conducted months later, Marcel Labbé told us that he had been tipped off about the demolition of the stack by the guard at the gate, a local woman. It was a cold day and the town had not been notified beforehand. There were therefore not many people at the site. He took photographs of the demolition crew cutting the base of the stack – "like a tree" – and the rising dust after the stack hit the earth. He expressed disappointment that his camera was unable to record the falling stack itself.

65 Ruth Thompson interviewed by Kristen O'Hare, June 2004.

66 Pierre Hardy interviewed by Kristen O'Hare, 12 December 2003. Follow-up interview by Steven High, June 2005.

67 Randy Restoule interviewed by Kristen O'Hare, 5 August 2004.

68 Mike Lacroix interviewed by Steven High, December 2005.

69 The story was picked up by newspapers across the province. "Ministry Puts Brakes on Mill Demolition," *Sault Star*, 13 July 2004, B3; Maria

Calabrese, "Mill Demolition Will Go On: Air-Quality Monitors Focus of Concern," *Sudbury Star*, 15 July 2004, p. A2.

70 W.D. Lighthall, "Demolition of Former Mill Back on Track After Delay," *Daily Commercial News and Construction Record* 77, 144 (28 July 2004), p. 1.

71 Marc Côté interviewed by Kristen O'Hare, 30 January 2004.

72 Of course the mill's closing made a bad situation worse. It is estimated that 40 percent of the 140 mill workers were still unemployed in January 2004, two years after the mill's closure. The estimate comes from Mike Lacroix, a counsellor at the Action Centre, quoted in Cramer, *loc. cit.*

73 See, for example, the interviews with Raymond Marcoux and Lawrence Pretty.

74 J.P. Charles interviewed by Kristen O'Hare, 10 August 2004.

75 Anna Pickarski, "Loss of Mill Has Cost Town $1.4 Million," *Sudbury Star*, 20 July 2004, p. A2.

76 Brian Lafleche interviewed by Kristen O'Hare, 3 June 2004.

77 Gerry Stevens interviewed by Kristen O'Hare, 2 June 2004.

78 Brian Lafleche interviewed by Kristen O'Hare, 3 June 2004.

79 Ibid.

80 Wayne LeBelle interviewed by Kristen O'Hare, 6 September 2004.

81 Wayne LeBelle interviewed by Kristen O'Hare, August 2004.

82 Randy Restoule interviewed by Kristen O'Hare, 5 August 2004.

83 Mike Lacroix interviewed by Kristen O'Hare, 4 February 2004.

84 This point was emphasized by Wayne LeBelle in a private communication.

85 For more on the notion of community see: John Walsh and Steven High, "Rethinking the Concept of Community," *Histoire sociale/Social History* 17, 64 (November 1999), pp. 255–74

86 Bruce Colquhoun, "Mill Closure Will Affect Us All," *Tribune*, 22 October 2002.

87 This twin appeal mirrors what happened in the mining town of Britannia Beach, British Columbia. Katherine Rollwagen, "When Ghosts Hovered: Community and Crisis in a Company Town, Britannia Beach, British Columbia, 1957–1965," *Urban History Review* 35, 2 (Spring 2007), pp. 25–36.

88 Jane Hardy, "Weyerhaeuser's Not Fooling Anyone," *Tribune*, 10 December 2002.

89 Colquhoun, *loc. cit.*

90 Hardy, *loc.cit.*

91 Vera Charles, "Time for Action, Not Whining," *Tribune*, 17 December 2002.

92 Mike Parsons, "Weyerhaeuser Not So Bad," *Tribune*, 18 March 2003.

93 Ronald Beauchamp interviewed by Kristen O'Hare, 8 July 2004.

94 Dean Lisk, "CARC Releases Road Plan for West Nipissing," *Tribune*, 24 June 2003.

95 Wayne LeBelle interviewed by Steven High, December 2005.

96 Randy Restoule interviewed by Kristen O'Hare, 5 August 2004.

97 Hubert and Bruce are worker-historians who compiled the "Mill History" binder. This massive binder is a living memorial to the mill community. Hubert Gervais interviewed by Kristen O'Hare, 12 March 2004.

CHAPTER 6
DEINDUSTRIAL FRAGMENTS

1 John E. Sacco, "Slater Shutters Welland Mill, Lays Off 500," *American Metal Market*, 2 October 2003; John E. Sacco, "Summer of Discontent Wilts Two Mills," *American Metal Market*, 13 August 2003.

2 William Marentette, "Brewed in Windsor: The British American Brewery,
1882-1969," *Walkerville Times*, found at
<www.walkervilletimes.com/42/brewed-
windsor.html>.

3 I would like to thank Alan Mann, the local
historian in the Wallaceburg area, for his
invaluable assistance. See his *Gathering
at the Forks: The Story of Wallaceburg*
(Wallaceburg: Standard Press, 1984).

4 For a pictorial and storied approach
to the mine headframes of Northern
Ontario see Palu and Angus, *Industrial
Cathedrals*. For Angus, "These impos-
ing towers, each with their own unique
design, have become metaphors for both
an industry and a culture."

CHAPTER 7
KING COAL

1 Ronald L. Lewis, "Appalachian Restructuring in Historical Perspective: Coal,
Culture and Social Change in West Virginia," *Urban Studies* 30, 2 (1993), p. 299.
For a fascinating examination of race
and coal mining in the early twentieth
century see J.W. Trotter Jr. *Coal, Class,
and Color: Blacks in Southern West
Virginia, 1915–32* (Urbana: University of
Illinois Press, 1990).

2 *Matewan* (1987; 130 minutes; director:
John Sayles). For a behind-the-scenes
look at the making of the film, see John
Sayles, *Thinking in Pictures: The Making
of the Movie Matewan* (Boston: Hough-
ton Mifflin, 1987).

3 Lewis, "Appalachian Restructuring,"
p. 300.

4 Robert F. Munn, "The Development of
Model Towns in the Bituminous Coal
Fields," *West Virginia History* 40 (1979),
p. 246.

5 Merl E. Reed, "Some Additional Material
on the Coal Strike of 1943," *Labor History*
23,1 (Winter 1982), p. 92.

6 Richard Deverall's June 1943 memoran-
dum to Secretary of Interior Ickes, as
reproduced in Reed, pp. 94–101.

7 Ken Light and Melanie Light, *Coal
Hollow: Photographs and Oral Histor-
ies* (Berkeley: University of California
Press, 2006), p. 3.

8 Lewis, "Appalachian Restructuring,"
p. 305.

CHAPTER 8
**A VANISHING
LANDMARK**

1 Southwest Michigan First's website:
<www.southwestmichiganfirst.com>, 10
September 2004.

2 I would like to thank everyone in the
Department of History at Western
Michigan University for their generos-
ity during my visit to Kalamazoo in
February 2007. The walking tour of the
downtown area, and the automobile tour
of former industrial sites, provided me
with a much stronger grasp of the city.
I want especially to thank Nora Faires,
Kristin Szylvian, Michael Chiarappa,
Jose Brandao, Lynne Heasley, and How-
ard J. Dooley.

3 Ed Finnerty, "Falling to Rubble," *Kalamazoo Gazette*, 26 August 2004.

Index

abandonment, 42, 44, 47
Abitibi Pulp and Paper, 94–95
Agee, James, 13
Albertson, Dan J., 151
Algoma Steel (Sault Ste. Marie), 5
Allary, Percy, 98, 101
Allen Industries, 133, 139–42
Allied Paper (Kalamazoo), 150–54
Alperovitz, Gar, 65
Altman, Irwin, 32
"American Dream," 3
Anaconda (Montana), 8
Anastakis, Dimitry, 6
Armstrong Cork factory (Pittsburgh), 1–2
Atlas Steel, 131
Auto Pact (1965), 166n22
Avatar X, 44

Baldwin Felts Detective Agency, 145
Bamberger, Bill, 8
Barbeau, Jay, 107
Barrington, Cam, 97–98
Beauchamp, Ronald, 115–16, 182n3
Bellah, Robert N.: *Habits of the Heart*, 83
Bendix Automotive, 133, 137–38
Benjamin, Walter, 176n85
Benoit, Louis, 103
Bethlehem (Pennsylvania), 30–31
Bethlehem Steel Works, 30
Biggs, Lindy, 2
Black Monday, 65, 71, 73–78, 81–82
Blanchard, Brett, 37, 171n58
blue-collar workers, 3, 24–25, 93
Bluestone, Barry, 2, 84
Bodnar, John, 76
Boileau, Lowell, 9
Bombardier, 5
Boudreau, Marcel, 32, 95, 98–99, 101–5, 109–10

Bourdieu, Pierre, 39
Brassed Off, 167n40
Brier Hill mill (Youngstown), 69, 75, 79
British Columbia, 183n33
Britannia Beach (British Columbia), 185n87
Bryant Paper: *see* Allied Paper
bromoil process, 15
Budick, Ariella, 45
Buffalo (New York), 9
Bunge, Bill, 59
Butler Institute of American Art, 78

Calhoun, Craig, 12
Campbell, Colin, 51
Campbell Works (Youngstown), 65–66, 73–77
Canada: aerospace industry, 5; compared
    with United States, 4–8, 26–27, 133;
    equivalent to American Dream in,
    3; government intervention, 4–5;
    manufacturing, 24; medicare, 4; mining,
    146; nationalism, 4–5, 27, 133; pulp
    and paper mills, 5, 7; resource sector,
    6–7; Rust Belt, 26; trade unions, 4–5;
    unemployment, 4
Canada Dominion Sugar Company, 131, *132*
Canadair, 5
Canada Malting Plant (Toronto), 57
Canada Malt Plant (Montreal), 53–54
Canada Motor Lamp plant, 131, 136, *136–37*
Canada Steamship Line, 35
"Canada Works" (Hamilton), 52–53, 55, 58
Canadian Auto Workers, 5
Canadian Pulp and Paper Association, 7
Canadian Vickers (Montreal), 32
Cape Breton Island (Nova Scotia), 34–35, 38
capital, community vs., 84–85, 93
Carter, Jimmy, 65–66
CBC Radio, 46

Fisher Guide plant (Detroit), 60–61, *118*, 119–29
Flint (Michigan), 3
Ford, Henry, 2
forest industry, 98; *see also* pulp and paper industry
Fortin, Ed, 97
Foucault, Michel, 26
foundational myths, 66
Frechette, Paul, 33
"free market," 6
free trade, 7, 27, 92
Frisch, Michael, 9, 170n39
Fritzsche, Peter, 41
The Full Monty, 167n40

Gans, Herbert, 29
Garman, Bryan, 70
Gauthier, Denis, 182n3
gender, 96, 98, 107, 132
General Motors (GM), 119–29, 151, 166n20
geography, 26; cultural, 59–62, 176n91; imagined, 27, 32, 39, 43
Gervais, Hubert, 106, 117
ghost towns, 9
Giddens, Anthony, 169n8
Glen Rogers (West Virginia), *146–47*
Golden Horseshoe (Ontario), 26
graffiti art, 45–46
Grain Elevator No. 5 (Montreal), 36
grain terminal elevators, 35–37
Graves, Michael, 79
Great Britain, 45
Great Depression, 67, 73
Great Lakes Steel mill (Zug Island), 120, *121*
Greenspoon, Ira, 31
Grierson, John, 14, 15
Guimond, James, 3
Guthrie, Woody, 67–68; *Dust Bowl Ballads*, 67, 70; "Tom Joad," 67

Hamilton (Ontario), 37, 52–53, 55, 131, 133–35, 139–42
Hardy, Jane, 113–14
Hardy, Pierre, 95, 100–101, 103–6, 107, 109, 110
Harrison, Bennett, 2, 84

Hatfield, Sid, 145
Hayden, Delores, 2
Heathcott, Joseph: *Beyond the Ruins*, 2, 84, 94
Heaton, Daniel, 77
Heaton, James, 77
Henderson, Andrew, 44, 57; "Forgotten Ohio" website, 44
High, Steven: *Industrial Sunset*, 4, 26
Hinchey, Bill, 31
Hine, Lewis, 16
hinterland, geographies of 27
historic buildings, 28–31
"historic factories," 29
"historic industrial districts," 30
Homestead (Pennsylvania), 8, 30
Homestead Steel Works, 8
Hopewell Furnace (Youngstown), 77
Horne, Rosemary, 36
Houston (Texas), 69–70
Huard, Huguette, 36
Hudson's Department store (Detroit), 37
Hughes, Carolyn, 43
Hume, Christopher, 36
Hunter, Tom, 71–72; "Back to Work in Youngstown," 71–72

"I-75 Gypsies," 119, 128
iconography of dereliction, 62
identity, 32; place, 93, 94–99; sites of, 9
implosions, industrial, 37–39
Implosionworld, 37, 39, 47
individual rights, 61
industrial archaeology, 176n91
industrial demolition: *see* demolition
industrial dereliction, aesthetics of, 9
industrial heritage tourism, 17, 41–42
industrialism, transition from to post-industrialism, 24, 26–27, 39, 47, 77, 93
industrialization, 41
industrial landscapes: *see* landscape
industrial museums, 8, 9, 29, 30, 42, 67, 78–82
industrial ruins, 42, 44; materiality of, 58; mystification of, 60; narrating, 51–58; as points of transition, 57
industrial unions: *see* trade unions
industrial workplace, attachment to, 94
Infiltration magazine, 42–43

Infiltration website, 44, 46, 47
infrared film, 15
Inglis, 8
International Harvester, 132, 133–35

Jacobs, Jane, 45
James, Daniel, 66
Jameson, Frederic, 173n26
Jasen, Patricia, 52
Jeannette Blast Furnace (Youngstown), 29, 79
Jinx Magazine, 42–44, 50
job losses, 3–4, 25, 93–116
Johnson, Roosevelt, 23
Johnstown (Pennsylvania), 30
John Updike Company, 151
Joseph, Miranda, 84

Kalamazoo (Michigan), 150–54
Kelly, Eric, 37–38
Kenosha (Wisconsin), 8, 93
Kingston (Ontario), 35
Knobly, Peter, Jr., 77
Knowlton, Sam, 50
Koch, Edward, 46
"Kowalski": *see* Michael Cook

Labbé, Marcel, 106, 110
Labelle, Henri, 97
Lacroix, Mike, 92, 95, 99–101, 105–6, 110–11, 185n72
Lafleche, Brian, 108–9
Lafrance, Guy, 33
landscapes: of economic exclusion, 26–27; industrial, 2, 9, 15, 26, 44, 59, 62, 83, 121; moral, 2
Lange, Dorothea, 16
language, Sturgeon Falls and, 96–98
Lasch, Christopher, 84
Law and Order, 46
Lawrenson, Ed, 132–33, 137–38
Lebel, Rene, 103
LeBelle, Wayne, 96, 104, 109–10, 116, 185n84
LeBlanc, Dave, 47
Lewis, David, 13–16, 147, 151
libertarianism, 61
Light, Ken & Melanie: *Coal Hollow*, 147

"Liminal Cities," 176n99
Linkon, Sherry Lee, 12, 66, 82–85; *Steeltown USA*, 67, 82–85
Livingstone, John, 13, 132, 135
local, translocal and, 66
local culture, 12, 31, 67, 83
localism, 18, 84
locality, 39, 92; community and, 84
loss, nostalgia and, 41–42; resistance and, 66, 99–106; victimization and, 70, 81
Low, Setha M., 32
Lutz, Kelsey, 50
Lykes Corporation, 65, 72
Lynd, Staughton, 66

MacGregor, Denis, 95, 99
MacMillan Bloedel, 6, 92, 95, 106
Maharidge, Dale, 67–71, 73, 82; *Journey to Nowhere*, 67–69, 71, 73
Mahoning River Valley (Ohio), 65–86
Maple Leaf Mills (Toronto), 36
Marcoux, Raymond, 92, 95, 102, 185n73
Marcus, Greil, 45
Marshall, Joe, 69, 71
Massey, Doreen, 66, 93
Matewan (West Virginia), 145
McDowell County (West Virginia), 146
McLouth Steel (Trenton), 6, 120, 127
Mebane (North Carolina), 8
memory: community of, 83–84; meaning and, 66, 93–94; politics of, 65–86; sites of, 9, 14, 62, 67
Meshel, Harry, 79
Michigan Department of Natural Resources (MDNR), 152–53
"mine wars," 145
Miron quarry (Montreal), 32–33
Montreal (Quebec), 29, 32–33, 36
Moore, Michael, 3
Moore, Sally F., 27–28
Morrell, David: *Creepers*, 46
Morton, Don, 28
"museumification" of industrial landscapes, 9, 29
museums, industrial: *see* industrial museums
Myerhoff, Barbara G., 28

ruins, archaic and medieval, 41, 52; *see also* industrial ruins
Russo, John, 12, 66, 82–85; *Steeltown USA*, 67, 82–85
"Rust Belt," 8, 26–27, 62, 65, 71, 80

St. Clair (ship), 120
St. Lawrence Seaway, 35
Saskatchewan Wheat Pool, 9
Saunders, Jim, 24
Scandlan, Bill, 55
Schumpeter, Joseph, 7–8
Sears Merchandise Warehouse (Philadelphia), 37
Segal, George, 77–78
Senecal, Denis, 105
Sengupta, Somini, 45
"Seven Sisters" (Detroit), 33
severance pay, 4
Sheeler, Charles, 2
Sheet and Tube, 72, 75–77
"Shout Youngstown," 81
Situationism, 45, 59
slum clearance, 28
"smokestack nostalgia," 94
smokestacks, falling, 32–35
Solano, Gabriel, 60, 119–29
space, meaning and representation of, 43
spatial homogeneity, 48
Springsteen, Bruce, 65, 67, 70–73, 82; *the ghost of tom joad*, 70–71, 73; "the ghost of tom joad," 70, 73; "the new timer," 73; "youngstown," 67, 73
steel, cradle of, 67
Steel Heritage Task Force, 170n29
steel industry, 30–31, 65–86, 132
steel museum (Youngstown), 79–82
"steel valley," 65–66, 69, 74–75, 78, 80
Stein, Judith, 7
Steinbeck, John, 12, 67–68, 73; *The Grapes of Wrath*, 67–68, 85
Stelco (Hamilton), 37, 52–53, 55, 131–32
Stevens, Gerry, 109
Stewart, Kathleen, 41
storytelling, 32
Strange, Carolyn, 42

Sturgeon Falls (Ontario), 6, 32, *90–91*, 91–117
sublime, aesthetic category of, 41, 52; deindustrial, 8–13; technological, 36, 52
"Sun Belt," 26
Sysco (Sydney Steel), 34–35, 38

tar ponds, 34
Terkel, Studs, 14, 181n84
Thompson, Ruth, 98, 106
Thunder Bay (Ontario), 9–10, 30, 47
Toronto (Ohio), *ii, x,*
Toronto (Ontario), 5, 8, 28, 29, 35–36, 47, 57–58, 59
Toronto Historical Board, 36
Toronto Island Airport, 57
tourism, 30, 43; dark, 42; industrial heritage, 17, 41–42; romanticism and, 51–52; vs. travel, 51
"Toyshop" artist collective, 59
trade barriers, 7
trade liberalization, 92
trade unions, 4–5
travel narratives, 42, 43, 54
Trenton (Michigan), 6, 120, *127*
trespassing, urban exploration vs., 47–48, 50–51
Tribune (West Nipissing), 92, 104–5, 110–11, 113
True Temper, 132, 135
Truscon, 136

unemployment, 4
United Auto Workers, 133
United Mine Workers of America (UMW), 145
United Steelworkers, 4, 79
United States: compared with Canada, 4–8, 26–27, 133; Department of Housing and Urban Development, 65; Employee Stock Ownership Plan (ESOP), 6; Environmental Protection Agency (EPA), 152; manufacturing, 24; Rust Belt, 26–27
urban exploration (UE), 42–44; cultural geography and, 59–62; emergence of, 44–51; ethical code of, 49; narratives and, 51–58; politics of, 58–62; romanticism,

tourism, and, 51–52; trespassing vs., 47–48, 50–51; vandalism and, 48–49
Urban Exploration London, 56
Urban Exploration Montreal, 53–54
Urban Exploration Resource, 44, 173n23
Urban Explorers Network, 44
urbanization, 41
urban renewal, 28
U.S. Steel, 30, 66, 75, 146

vandalism, urban exploration and, 48–49
Vargo, James J., 76
Victory Mills (Toronto), 36
Vindicator (Youngstown), 74–76, 80

Wallaceburg (Ontario), 131, *132*
Weird U.S. travel guides, 46–47
Weisheimer, Rev. C. Edward, 74
Welland (Ontario), 131
Welland Tube, 131
Westerman, William, 178n19
West Nipissing Economic Development Corporation, 115, 182n3
West Virginia, coal mining in, *144–45*, 145–48
Weyerhaeuser, 6, 92–93, 95, 98, 99–100, 103, 105–6, 111, 113–14, 117
White, Hayden, 177n15
White Furniture (Mebane), 8
Wierton Steel (West Virginia), 6
wild/wilderness, 43, 56–57
Williams, Raymond, 173n26
Williamson, Michael, 67–71, 73, 82; *Journey to Nowhere*, 67–69, 71, 73
Windsor (Ontario), 6, 131, 133, 136–38
Wirth, Peter, 131, 136
workplace communities, attachment to, 94–116
"Wraiths" (Vancouver), 56, 61
wrecking ball, 28–31
Wyoming County (West Virginia), 146

Youngstown (Ohio), 29, 65–86, 92; commemoration of, 73–76; envisioning, 67–70; exhibiting, 78–82; memorializing, 76–78; singing about, 70–73
Youngstown Area Arts Council, 77

Youngstown Historical Center of Industry and Labor, 78
Youngstown State University, 75, 79, 82
youth culture, 44–46

Zona, Louis, 78
Zug Island (Michigan), 120–21
Zukin, Sharon, 2